The Museum Makers

THE STORY
OF THE ROYAL ONTARIO MUSEUM

The Museum Makers

THE STORY
OF THE ROYAL ONTARIO MUSEUM

Lovat Dickson

RÓM
ROYAL ONTARIO MUSEUM

Canadian Cataloguing in Publication Data

Dickson, Lovat, 1902–
   The museum makers

Includes bibliographical references and index.
ISBN 0-88854-326-3

1. Royal Ontario Museum—History. I. Royal
Ontario Museum. II. Title.

AM101.T6D52 1986   069.'09713'541   C86-094412-3

Jacket: *Homage to the First Principle*, Daoist wall-painting of the
Yuan dynasty, China (about A.D. 1325). Gift to the Far Eastern
collections from the Flavelle Foundation, in memory of Sir
Joseph Flavelle.

Design: Virginia Morin
Typesetting: Trigraph Inc.

Printed and bound in Canada at The Bryant Press

Contents

Preface

In the seventy-five years since its foundation the Royal Ontario Museum has attained international recognition for its collections and the scope of its world-wide field activity. With a vast renovation and expansion program in sight of completion, it seemed to the board of trustees an appropriate time to have the Museum's history written by someone other than a retired director or member of the staff. No conditions were imposed on the writer, who was given unrestricted access to the Museum's archives and to the curators and members of the staff, and allowed to form his own conclusions. After four years' immersion in the life of the Museum, the largest in Canada, and now ranked amongst the three largest in North America, I can testify that these conditions have been faithfully observed. While it is obvious that the book could not have been written without the unstinting and generous help of the curators, the arrangement has had the advantage of ensuring the accuracy of the facts while making, I hope, the reading easier for the general reader who wonders what goes on behind the galleries of a great museum.

The main documentary sources on which I have drawn, particularly for the early years, are the papers and journals of Sir Edmund Walker, held in the Thomas Fisher Rare Book Library of the University of Toronto; the Archives of the University of Toronto; and the Archives of the United Church of Canada at Victoria College, University of Toronto, which hold the quite extensive and revealing correspondence of Charles Currelly during his years in Egypt as an assistant to Flinders Petrie and a staff member of the Egypt Exploration Fund. I wish to record my gratitude to the members of the Walker family for permission to make unrestricted use of this source of material, given to me on behalf of the family by Professor C. Heidenreich of York University; and to Charles Currelly's surviving son and daughter, Judge John Currelly and Mrs Suzanne Hamilton, for similar permission for Charles Currelly's letters.

I have to thank the chairman of the Archives Committee of the Egypt

Exploration Society in London for permission to use Charles Currelly's letters to the Society in the period when he was an assistant to Flinders Petrie in Egypt. I want to thank also Dr Katharine Lochnan, curator of prints and drawings at the Art Gallery of Ontario, for permission to make use of her research notes and the fine introduction she wrote to the catalogue for a 1974 exhibition at the Art Gallery of Ontario, *Sir Edmund Walker: Print Collector.*

From these and other sources, during the four years spent in writing this book, has flowed an immense amount of material from which this history has been shaped. Here I want to acknowledge the unfailing help given me at every stage by John Campsie, head of Publication Services of the Museum, who worked with me chapter by chapter; and of Mary Terziano, who has copyedited the final version with skill. Barbara Ibronyi, editor, Publication Services, was responsible for the photographic research, and Barbarann Ruddell saw the several versions of the manuscript through the word processor. I owe a great deal to Dorothea Hecken, the now retired registrar of the Museum, who was assigned to me as a guide to this labyrinth, as it first appeared, and to what went on there. Her perceptive eye for what I wanted is reflected in the book, and her sharp comments are preserved in several phrases.

Finally to William Swinton, former director of the Royal Ontario Museum (1962–1966); to R. McCartney Samples, assistant director of the Museum at the time the form of the book was being discussed; to James Cruise, director of the Museum during the years when it was being written; to Richard Landon, librarian of the Thomas Fisher Rare Book Library, who guided me through my preliminary reading; and to Douglas Tushingham, retired chief archaeologist of the Museum, who spent many hours on my manuscript; and to the curators one and all, I offer my abiding thanks for seeing me through this rich experience.

Lovat Dickson
Toronto, Canada, 1982–1986

The Museum Makers

1

The Beginnings

On the west side of Queen's Park in Toronto, just south of Bloor Street, stands the great building that houses the Royal Ontario Museum. The long façade, built in 1931/1933 in a style loosely described as Romanesque, conceals both an older nucleus, now the west wing of the Museum, and two recent additions completed in 1982. One of these, on the south, is the new curatorial centre; the other, on the north, is a tier of gracefully receding, glass-fronted terrace galleries overlooking Bloor Street.

Bloor Street is one of Toronto's busiest thoroughfares both by day and by night. After dark, passers-by, as well as impatient motorists held up at the intersection, can see illuminated in the ground-level terrace gallery the tomb of a Chinese general of the late Ming dynasty, set at the end of its "spirit path". Just inside the first gateway, two stone camels, resting as from a journey, recline upon the ground. Beside them stand two large Yuan dynasty stone figures of officials, carved more than six hundred years ago in China.

Turning south on Queen's Park, one sees the long façade of the 1933 wing, broken at the centre by the massive main entrance. Above the entrance there is an arched opening of monumental proportions, in the tympanum of which is a seated female figure. On one side of the figure is carved a scene in which the buffalo and the totem pole are prominent, representative of the aboriginal condition of Canada; on the other side are the winged bull of Babylon and engines of construction intended to suggest the process of civilization. One is reminded of the façade of a medieval cathedral, with its carved faces of saints and goblins, of angels and griffins—a mixture of historical memories and ancient fables, preserved in our subconscious from early years when all of life was mysterious.

When and how did museums begin? Votive objects left at shrines; curiosities brought back from early voyages of discovery and dedicated to local gods as thank-offerings for a safe journey; animal and mineral curiosities sent back from his campaigns by Alexander the Great to his old tutor, Aristotle, to assist him in his scientific studies—such objects needed preservation and the need led eventually to the building of treasuries, which came in time to have the name *mouseion,* meaning a sanctuary dedicated to the Muses. The Romans, who inherited the tradition, translated this as *museum.*

Museums rose with empires, but did not fall with them. Hellenic science and culture had arisen in the 6th century B.C., following the founding of Greek city states along the shores of the Aegean. Rome carried her empire almost to the limits of the known world; her governors and proconsuls, soldiers and civil servants brought back to their villas and temples wondrous objects from every land and clime. At the height of her imperial power Rome was said to be full of museums.

But these were collections of paintings, statuary, and curiosities of natural history, devoid of any scholarly function. The great library at Alexandria is the nearest the ancient world came to the modern conception of a museum. Here, under the enlightened rule of the Ptolemies, had been assembled a library of classical literature that attracted scholars and men of science from all over the ancient world. The library engendered a university which became a renowned centre of research and teaching. The disorders that accompanied the fall of Rome, augmented by the sectarian contentions of the early centuries of Christianity, brought about the destruction of this great library.

For a thousand years the museum tradition lay dormant. During this period scholarship was preserved in the monasteries and abbeys where the monks, the only people who could write, copied manuscripts in their cells. When museums emerged again, it was not from a monastic source but from one that seemed at first to be in conflict with the tradition of the church. As Sir Basil Willey reminds us, however, in *Eighteenth Century Background,* the scientific discoveries of Copernicus, Kepler, and Galileo in the 16th and 17th centuries, which revealed Earth not as the centre of the universe but as a satellite moving with other planets in orderly procession around the sun, upset centuries of Christian dogma based on the biblical account of creation.

The astronomers, mathematicians, and philosophers who emerged in the 17th century—Descartes, Bacon, Newton, and the Fellows of the Royal Society—all believed in a divinely created universe; their discoveries simply proved that it worked by "rigidly determined laws of material causation". God as Creator appeared even greater than before, his universe the very pattern of order in which not only man but all nature had a part.

The freedom of intellect stimulated by the new scientific ideas found expression in a widespread spirit of inquiry. Men who had interests and professions of a non-scientific kind studied geology, palaeontology, and botany as hobbies. The famous collection donated to Oxford University by the antiquary Elias Ashmole became the foundation of the Ashmolean Museum. The equally famous collection left to the nation by Sir Hans Sloane, physician to George II, gave rise to the establishment of the British Museum. Besides antiquities and a fine library, the collection included plants, fossils, insects, and minerals, as well as zoological, anatomical, and pathological specimens.

In the English Midlands, where in the middle of the 18th century the Industrial Revolution was gathering force, the interest in practical science was making men's fortunes. Matthew Boulton had begun in Birmingham as a small manufacturer of buckles and toys. He had turned to the manufacture of scientific instruments, had prospered, and had built an ironworks near Birmingham, where in partnership with James Watt he produced steam engines. Josiah Wedgwood, who had been made wealthy by his potteries and was busy now developing porcelains, made use of the discoveries of men like James Watt, who invented the steam engine, and Joseph Priestley, who isolated oxygen. It was men like these that were to make England the leading industrial nation of the world. A central figure in all this activity was a busy Lichfield doctor, Erasmus Darwin, whose grandson Charles was to write *Origin of Species*.

Erasmus Darwin was the prime mover in the formation of the Lunar Society in Birmingham, a discussion group that met for dinner once a month on the night of the full moon. This arrangement allowed the dozen or more members five or six hours for their spirited discussions and enough light to see their way home. Museum curators are in some respects the modern equivalent of these early enthusiasts, whose lively correspondence and discussions at the Lunar Society were the forerunners of today's research papers and colloquia.

It was this blend of philosophical discussion and the excitement of invention that was to give the Industrial Revolution an intellectual quality that enabled it in the end to penetrate the ancient universities. In the 18th century, however, the universities were dominated still by theological interests; the study of mathematics and optics had been admitted, but the earth sciences were still for the most part unknown. It was not until the 19th century that instruction in the theory and practice of science, leading to science degrees, was given at Oxford and Cambridge.

A feeling of confidence and new-found intellectual freedom had enabled the philosophers to build on the scientific discoveries of the 16th and 17th centuries a nobler conception of life; the same feeling accompanied the practical application to manufacturing of the scientific discoveries of the 18th and early 19th centuries. This development had driven the rural population into the cities and had produced both museums and slums. But industrial power provided an unexpected benefit in compulsory education. This increased the demand for museums and libraries, both as sanctuaries of past ages where art recovered from ancient sites could be studied at first hand, and as repositories where the scientific study of man and his world was recorded and preserved.

The museum movement, which spread so rapidly through Europe in the early 19th century, was slow in reaching North America. The New World could not provide the great audiences available in the Old; nor did it have the time to stand and wonder. The first North American museum of natural history was established by Charles Willson Peale in Philadelphia in the aftermath of the American Revolution. It cast a brief shadow on Canadian museum history, for Charles Fothergill, a young ornithologist and painter who had emigrated from England to Canada in 1816, visited the museum and later made an unsuccessful effort to set up a similar one in Toronto. Peale was an artist, a naturalist, and an inventor; he was the first on this continent to use dioramas to display fauna against a natural background. For a time Peale's museum prospered and imitators sprang up. In the words of the historian of the museum, "Tawdry and specious museums appeared in almost every American city and town—cheap popular entertainment to attest what would one day become the cinema audience." But in the end Peale's museum failed.

Charles Fothergill was one of Upper Canada's early intellectuals. He was tireless in proposing new plans and expeditions. He managed to be elected to the Legislative Assembly of Upper Canada as the member for Durham County in 1825, and he remained a member until 1831. He did not endear himself to his fellow-members, for the Assembly was controlled by the Family Compact, of which Fothergill made himself a constant critic. He was well ahead of his time in recommending in 1825 that the British provinces of North America be united to create a federal state, a scheme dismissed as "visionary". His next proposal was that the governments of Upper and Lower Canada should join with the Hudson's Bay Company and several societies devoted to the study of literature, history, and natural science in a three-year scientific expedition to the

Pacific Coast to consider the possibilities of settlement there; he also proposed that he should be appointed zoologist to the expedition. This suggestion too fell on stony ground.

But Charles Fothergill left his impress on the history of museums in Canada. He died in 1840 in what his biographer, James L. Baillie, an early member of the ornithological department in the Royal Ontario Museum, described as "wretched circumstances", leaving behind the admirable watercolours he had made of birds, reptiles, and mammals, and several manuscripts, some of which were part of his great unpublished work entitled *Memoirs and Illustrations of the Natural History of the British Empire.* The first manuscript volumes were discovered almost a century after Fothergill's death and are now preserved in the Thomas Fisher Rare Book Library of the University of Toronto. Several other manuscripts subsequently turned up, and many of his drawings and watercolours have survived; in 1982 they were mounted in an impressive exhibition, with a fine catalogue, by the Thomas Fisher Rare Book Library. Fothergill's portrait hangs today in the Canadiana Department of the Royal Ontario Museum.

The first provincial museum in Ontario owed its origin to Egerton Ryerson, the chief superintendent of education for Upper Canada. A clause in the Public School Act of 1853 provided for a grant, "not to exceed £500 per annum", to be used by the chief superintendent "in the purchase from time to time of books, publications and objects suitable for a Canadian Library and Museum". The resulting collection was meant to serve as a tool for teachers-in-training at the Toronto Normal School, who would need to have at least a background knowledge of art. It was planned that the second floor of the recently completed Normal School building should be set aside for a museum to which the public could have access. In 1855/1856 Ryerson visited England and continental Europe; he far overspent the paltry sum at his disposal, but he brought back a bountiful harvest: 250 copies of famous paintings, a collection of engravings, and scores of casts of statues and busts of famous figures. The public flocked to see the Normal School Museum, fulfilling Ryerson's purpose of popular education, but the display received adverse comment from more sophisticated visitors.

The next significant contribution to the evolution of Ontario museums was that of David Boyle, a Scot, who in 1856 at the age of fourteen had emigrated to Canada with his family. Between 1860 and 1864 he completed his secondary school education at the Elora Grammar School and obtained a teaching certificate from the Wellington County Board of Education, while earning his livelihood as a blacksmith. The year 1871 saw him back in Elora as principal of the Elora Public School, a position he was to hold for a decade. During that time he ardently pursued his interest in natural history, geology, and past Indian occupations of Ontario. Boyle's field work was to lead eventually to his annual *Archaeological Report*, published as an appendix to the report of the Ontario Department of Education, and to international recognition as an archaeologist and ethnologist.

After moving to Toronto, Boyle donated his personal archaeological collection to the Canadian Institute (now the Royal Canadian Institute), and in 1884 he was appointed curator of the institute's museum. He soon became fully absorbed in his new career as a museum curator, archaeologist, and ethnologist, particularly after the Ontario Department of Education made its first archaeological grant to the Canadian Institute in 1887, in the amount of one thousand dollars.

In 1896 a third floor was added to the Toronto Normal School to be used for an archaeological museum. Boyle was appointed curator, and the now quite valuable collection of the Canadian Institute was removed to the new museum. Boyle's knowledge of and genuine interest in archaeology did a good deal for the standing of the museum, which continued under the direction of the minister of education. But the department provided little money for acquisitions and paid Boyle an exiguous salary, only partially making up for its parsimony by appointing Boyle superintendent of the entire museum in 1901 and a few years later exalting its name to Ontario Provincial Museum.

The colleges of the University of Toronto had held themselves aloof from these activities and interests. When the scientific thrust of the middle years of the 19th century invaded a curriculum principally devoted to philosophy and history, they began to assemble collections, primarily for teaching purposes. Some excellent men had joined the faculties. Professor William Hincks, who had been professor of natural history at Queen's College in Cork, had been appointed to the chair of natural history established in University College in 1853, defeating for the post T. H. Huxley, whose application was supported by Charles Darwin and the president of the Royal Society. Seven years later Huxley was to become Darwin's champion when *Origin of Species* was published. Hincks meanwhile had become the driving force to establish a biological museum in Toronto.

In the same year Daniel Wilson from Edinburgh was appointed professor of history and English literature at University College; he had a strong interest in archaeology. Among those who initiated scientific courses in University College was Professor Edward Chapman, whose field was the earth sciences and who established the collection that was destroyed by fire in 1890. The "spirit of scientific curiosity" was there, but the collections and the student body were both small, and the half-dozen denominational colleges had not yet federated.

Men with scientific interests found their outlet in the Canadian Institute, which had been founded in 1849 by "a few architects, land surveyors, and civil engineers". The institute soon extended the sphere of its membership and was described in its charter, granted in November 1851, as "a Society for the encouragement and general advancement of the Physical Sciences, the Arts and Manufactures". In his recent book, *Science, God, and Nature in Victorian Canada,* Professor Carl Berger of the University of Toronto, setting out with his customary skill the history of the scientific movement in Canada, noted, "One of the most distinctive features of natural history was the association of the study of nature with aesthetic appreciation and religious feelings." He went on to say, "The implanting and growth of science in Victorian Canada was one strand in a complex fabric of transplanted British civilization overseas." His account shows that collecting natural history specimens was then the engrossing hobby not only of young amateur naturalists but also of prominent businessmen.

In the 1850s University College professors like Daniel Wilson, John Cherriman, and Edward Chapman, all of British origin, joined the Canadian Institute. At one point forty-eight members of the institute, representing nearly one-third of its membership, had university affiliations. Weekly meetings were held, at which papers were read and discussed. Attendance at these meetings rose and fell, but the institute remained an influential assembly, and it was through its agency that the Royal Ontario Museum was first advocated. Byron Edmund Walker, general manager of the Canadian Bank of Commerce in Toronto, who combined a passionate interest in science with a growing reputation in North American financial circles, made "Canadian Surveys and Museums and the Need of Increased Expenditure Thereon" the subject of his presidential address to the Canadian Institute in 1899.

2

The Founders

Byron Edmund Walker was appointed to the board of trustees of the University of Toronto in 1892. As general manager of Canada's largest bank, he held a prominent place in the professional life of the growing city. His appointment as a trustee was recognition of him as a public figure, and his appointment to the senate of the University in the following year indicated an active interest in University affairs. The board of trustees managed the University's property, but the senate made academic policy.

The University of Toronto was passing through a critical time. It had originally been a group of denominational colleges and was not yet a fully unified institution. Although the University Federation Act had been proclaimed in 1887, there had been stiff opposition to it. Chancellor Nathanael Burwash of Victoria College had championed the proposal, and University College had supported it; but there had been some notable holdouts, cherishing with evangelical fervour the rights and privileges granted them in their charters.

It was obvious that federation was not only necessary but inevitable if the group of colleges was ever to become a national university. In the 1890s the increasing interest in science created the need for expensive laboratory equipment to supplement the inadequate teaching collections of the colleges; this need had to be supplied if the University was not to see its students going to the United States to complete their training. And the Ontario government recognized the inefficiency and wastefulness of dealing with multiple budgets instead of one.

Edmund Walker did not look the sort of man who could reconcile, by tact and understanding alone, the differences existing amongst so many disputants. Tall, thin, and rather remote in manner, he might be expected,

by the exercise of his banking skills, to help to bring order into the
financial affairs of the University, where muddles had accumulated under
a president with limited powers and an almost non-existent administration. But these skills did not promise any capacity for solving the
problems of a university uncertain about which way it wanted to go.

The appearance in this case was to prove deceptive. In a little more than
ten years Walker had won the support of the professors. He had played an
important conciliatory role in the process by which the remaining
colleges were brought into federation, and in 1904 Trinity College, in its
last independent convocation, granted him an honorary doctorate for his
services. But Walker's principal contribution had been to persuade the
Ontario government to set up a Royal Commission to examine the future
of the University following federation.

Like many successful businessmen of the 19th century, Edmund Walker
came of a farming family. The Walkers had been settled for some
generations on a farm near Caledonia in Upper Canada, where Edmund
was born in 1848. His father was a thoughtful, unambitious man, far more
interested in palaeontology, which had early in his life become a hobby,
than in his work on the family farm, which he disliked. "At home,"
Edmund remembered later, " . . . we talked about flowers, music, fossils,
science, a new poem or novel—nothing very learned or difficult."

When Edmund was still a small boy, his father and mother moved to
Hamilton, where his mother's family, the Murtons, were in business.
Here, at the age of four, he had his first schooling. He was a thin,
undersized boy, delicate in health. At the age of twelve, when he was
preparing for Normal School, the path that traditionally led clever rural
boys away from the drudgery of farming, he was taken out of school for a
while on the advice of the family doctor, "to run about and get some meat
on his bones". He never went back. He was put to work in his uncle's
banking exchange office in Hamilton, and in 1868, at the age of twenty,
he entered the service of the Canadian Bank of Commerce, which had
been founded only the year before.

Edmund had made up for his lost years of schooling by intense study
and endless hours of reading. Such close application to study might have
turned him into a prig, but some saving grace protected him from self-
satisfaction. The interest in palaeontology he shared with his father
broadened his view, and he found himself eagerly following the debate
about Charles Darwin's theory of natural selection as the key to the
evolutionary process that had produced man. This had aroused heated
discussion in Canada during the years when he had been in his uncle's
office and his first years in the bank. Evidence drawn from the variations

of plant and animal life seemed to support the case for natural selection. But not entirely, for Darwin claimed that the fossil record was incomplete and fragmentary, and unreliable as evidence.

Out of all this close study emerged the withdrawn young man, sharply intelligent, determined to get on, leading a double life as banker by day and earnest scholar at night. Within a year his manager wrote of him in his staff report to head office:

> Though Mr Walker is nominally discount clerk, he willingly performs a variety of duties when necessary. He is an invaluable officer, competent in every respect to discharge *all* the duties of Bank Accounting. He has a cool clear head and is as sharp as a needle. Unfortunately, however, he is in weak health at present, caused in some measure by constant night work, occasioned by his willingness to cover the incompetence of others.

At the age of twenty-four Walker was sent to New York as the junior agent in the bank's office. He was there for two years. It was during this period that he had his first contact with the city's great museums, which began for him to take the place of books as the means of study. He was brought back to Canada and spent several years in the management of senior branches before again being posted to New York in 1881, this time as joint agent. He was there for a further five years before returning to Toronto in 1886.

The bank had been going through a difficult period in the previous four years. Its assets had shrunk by almost twenty per cent, and the reserve had been depleted to meet bad debts. In 1886 there was a change in the top structure of the organization, and Walker was given the key position of general manager. He began immediately to reorganize and retrench, with such effect that between 1896 and 1906 the Canadian Bank of Commerce more than tripled its assets and transformed itself from a provincial Ontario bank to a national financial institution.

In 1874 Walker had married Mary Alexander, whose brother William John Alexander became a professor of English at University College in 1889. Mary Walker shared her husband's interests and he relaxed in her company. Family life humanized him, smoothing some of the sharper edges of his character. On his return to Toronto in 1886, his wife's connections brought him into close contact with the University's professors, so that when he was appointed a trustee in 1892, and in the next year a member of the senate, he found himself far more at ease in academic company than most successful businessmen holding these offices.

~~

The Royal Commission to inquire into the affairs of the University of Toronto was set up in October 1905. Of the commissioners appointed, four were from the scholarly world: Goldwin Smith, who had been regius professor of modern history at Oxford, but had settled in Toronto; Sir William Meredith, chancellor of the University of Toronto; the Reverend H. J. Cody, a member of the faculty of Wycliffe College; and the Reverend D. Bruce Macdonald, principal of St Andrew's College, a leading boys' private school in Toronto. Two members, Joseph Flavelle and Edmund Walker, were from the business world, and the secretary, A. H. U. Colquhoun, was a journalist. Goldwin Smith was invited to be chairman of the commission, an obvious choice since he had been active at Oxford in university reform and had participated in the Royal Commission set up to examine that university. But he declined, and Joseph Flavelle was appointed chairman.

Walker and Flavelle were unquestionably the dynamic figures in this distinguished body, which met frequently during the winter of 1905/1906 in Goldwin Smith's home, The Grange. The commission's report, presented in April 1906, showed the hand of Walker throughout. There is little doubt that its noble and at times eloquent language was his, a conviction sustained after reading some hundreds of his letters in the Thomas Fisher Rare Book Library of the University of Toronto. Here is revealed the intricacy of the plan for a museum that Walker had been nurturing ever since his years in the bank's service in New York, when much of his leisure time had been spent in the splendid museums in that city. The University of Toronto's prime need of a museum had been the subject of only one among a dozen recommendations in the Royal Commission's report, but it was one expressed with great firmness regarding the necessity for immediate action. "Every year's delay," the report proclaimed, "is a misfortune, not only to the education of the students of the University of Toronto, but to the education and material welfare of the people of Ontario generally." The report recommended that "a site be selected in the University grounds adjacent to a public thoroughfare" and that a museum be built as early as possible.

Among the report's most important recommendations for restoring discipline in the University and making federation work was the replacement of the board of trustees by a board of governors. This body was to be responsible not only for the management of the University's money and properties but also for all appointments to and dismissals from the faculty, a function which up to that time had been exercised by the Ontario minister of education. Academic matters were to remain the concern of the senate of the University. The board of governors would have sole power to appoint the president of the University, who would be given much more authority and would be answerable to the board.

The commission had done its work with dispatch, and the Ontario government was equally prompt. Within a month Premier James Whitney had introduced the necessary legislation to give effect to all the commission's recommendations. The bill was given assent on 14 May and the University Act 1906 came into effect on 15 June.

While the recommendations had been chiefly concerned with the management and administration necessary for a federated university, what was proposed was a masterpiece of shared responsibility between the Ontario government, obligated to provide its citizens with education, and the University of Toronto, committed to maintaining standards. For the discharge of this responsibility a museum was recognized as a necessary institution in an age of scientific education, but its costs were to be borne and its privileges shared by all citizens. What Walker was aiming at was a museum that would be comparable with those he had haunted in New York.

Walker was not a dreamer; he was a practical man of affairs. In setting about his plan he was aware that Toronto was not New York; the Canadian temper, and particularly the Ontarian, was wary of high-falutin plans. That temper was a distinctive blend, compounded of ties to England, distrust of the United States, caution where the expenditure of money was concerned, and Victorian reserve tinged with the Methodist flavour of some of the province's most successful businessmen. But there was also another element that contributed to the tenor of Ontario society: the tradition of sophistication and wit inherited with wealth and learning and the broad Church of England background which the Establishment, known as the Family Compact, had nourished from early days. Their descendants were particularly conscious, from frequent visits to New York, of the relative backwardness of their city and were anxious to bring it up to date.

～～

The creation of the Royal Ontario Museum was not, of course, all one man's work, but the controlling hand that was to bring the several forces—some of them hostile to the proposal, others suspicious of an alliance of public and university interests, still others too keen and impatient—to the moment when both the main parties to the contract were committed to the idea was unquestionably Walker's. During this process he was to be greatly helped, and not infrequently harassed, by a young man called Charles Trick Currelly, who had been a friend of his eldest son, Edmund, at Harbord Collegiate, where Chancellor Burwash's son Ned had also been a student.

In the summer of 1902 Burwash made a hasty visit to England; on his return he reported to Walker that to his great surprise he had run across Currelly, who had been taken on as an assistant by the famous archaeologist Flinders Petrie and would be going out to Egypt that winter to excavate with Petrie. Then Walker's son had a letter from Currelly, written from Petrie's camp in Upper Egypt, telling of the antiquities that could be purchased at rock-bottom prices at the excavation sites. Walker had been an ardent collector ever since his years in New York. There is no evidence that he knew of Currelly other than as a friend of his son's, but the mention of Petrie's name in the letter gave him an excuse to write to the young man himself on 9 September 1902.

> I had the pleasure of meeting Flinders Petrie at the British Association in Bristol. I should certainly like to invest a little money in Egyptian antiquities, especially in glass, mosaic beads and scarabs. I hope you will let me know of your movements so that I may remit a small sum of money for this purpose.

Walker was not thinking here of the museum-to-be, although that was never far from his mind, but of his own collection. The Royal Commission's report was still some three years away. Chancellor Burwash, too, was excited at discovering the connection Currelly had made, since this offered a prospect of enriching the museum Victoria College was then planning. Thus began the strange relationship between Edmund Walker and Charles Currelly that was to determine fundamentally the character of what was to become the Royal Ontario Museum.

Charles Currelly's family were Methodists of the upper rank. He was the only son of parents whose ancestors on both sides had come from Devon in the 1830s and had settled in the neighbourhood of Port Hope. They had been educated and had prospered. One of Currelly's cousins, John Treble, married the only daughter of Hart Almerrin Massey, a son of the founder of what was to become the Massey Manufacturing Company and later the Massey-Harris Company. His mother's cousin, John Hoskin, was chairman of the board of trustees (later the board of governors) of the University of Toronto for many years. Money was never a worry in this circle. The Currellys were not rich, but they were comfortable and had the right connections.

Charles Currelly's mother was Mary Treble. She and a sister were greatly attached to one another, and when the sister married John Trick the two couples moved to the pretty little village of Exeter in Huron County, where they shared adjoining houses. Here Charles Trick Currelly was born on 11 January 1876, and as the only child in either household he became the object of the constant affection of both families. He does not seem to have had playmates: he writes about himself in early childhood as a solitary boy watching men at work. He spent much of his time lying in a hammock reading, and his son believes that it was in this way that he developed his fantastic memory for facts and his reading speed.

But his life was shaping him for what he was to become. Ancient history fascinated him, especially the Old Testament, whole chapters of which he could repeat from memory in dramatic tones that varied with each character. Carefully guarded by his "four parents", he found his inclination to make friends, which was natural to his open, affectionate nature, subdued to the necessity of getting on in the world.

When Charles was nine years old, his parents moved to Toronto; but they did not like the city and soon returned to Exeter, where they engaged a private tutor who taught him Latin. A few years later, when it was time for him to begin high school, they made another attempt at Toronto, entering him at Harbord Collegiate, where Ned Burwash, the son of the chancellor of Victoria College, became his closest friend.

In due course Currelly entered Victoria College, from which he graduated in 1898. Professor James Mavor, an unpredictable man who found amusement from time to time in disturbing Victoria's theological solemnity, had had an influence on the impressionable young man. By the time of his graduation Currelly had persuaded himself that he was a socialist, and he planned to spend two years in Europe getting to know how the poor lived. But Chancellor Burwash urged instead that before beginning his postgraduate work Currelly should go out to northern Manitoba for two years as a missionary-in-training. Settlers were pouring in to take up new land and there was urgent need of religious services to christen, marry, and bury them. The prospect of becoming a missionary, ever in the saddle, moving from community to community, offered a considerably less dazzling prospect than Europe, but obediently, and to please his mother, Currelly went.

Currelly records his experiences in the second chapter of *I Brought the Ages Home,* an autobiographical account of the very different life that was to follow the abandonment of his plans to become a minister of the church. The deprivations of the solitary life and the bitter cold of the winters were not as hard to endure as the stark mental simplicity of his parishioners, whose unquestioning acceptance of the biblical story of creation was more than a young graduate in the natural sciences could bear. His attempts to enlighten them about the relationship between myth and historical fact were not successful, and his missionary calls and services in primitive farmhouses did not always leave peace behind.

Nor did Currelly's outlook pass unnoticed at Methodist headquarters in Winnipeg. Starting back to Toronto at the end of his term in the field, he received a telegram to say that his progress towards ordination could not be approved. This prohibition was very soon followed by reinstatement. Currelly entered the theological department at Victoria College, where he remained for two years, but before settling down he decided to fulfil his ambition to spend some time in Europe.

In the spring of 1902 he went to Europe by cattle-boat—the traditional means of transport for students—proposing to work for two years in France and England as a wood-carver. He took with him a letter from Professor Mavor to Prince Peter Kropotkin, the Russian anarchist who was then living in London, and also an introduction to another of Mavor's numerous friends, the keeper of coins and medals at the British Museum, who would be able to identify some Roman coins Currelly had acquired for his collection.

Mavor's friend at the British Museum had retired, but H. A. Grueber, the assistant keeper, agreed to examine the coins. While he was doing this, a little shawabty figure, an object always associated with Egyptian funerary furnishings, fell on the table. Currelly had bought it at one of the many little antiquity shops that crowd the streets around the museum and had wrapped it in his handkerchief for safety. Grueber picked it up and asked him almost casually if he was interested in Egypt. "Enormously," was Currelly's immediate response.

Grueber suggested that Currelly should go along to University College to see Flinders Petrie, who was in town for the day, and to expedite matters he took out one of his visiting cards and wrote an introduction on it. Grueber went on to explain that Petrie was attached to the Egypt Exploration Fund as an archaeologist. He did not explain the origin of the Fund or its purpose—how it had been founded in 1882 under the presidency of Sir Erasmus Wilson, president of the Royal College of Surgeons, who had a great interest in Egyptian antiquities. Wilson is remembered now as having paid the cost, amounting to ten thousand pounds, of transporting Cleopatra's Needle from Egypt to its present position on the Embankment in London.

The moving spirit behind the establishment of the Egypt Exploration Fund, however, had been an intrepid woman author and traveller, Amelia B. Edwards. She had been appalled during her travels in Egypt by the wanton destruction of antiquities that she observed everywhere; both she and Sir Erasmus Wilson were convinced that the only remedy lay in scientific excavation. The Fund was founded with that purpose in view, and it began to send expeditions to Egypt under either Professor Henri Édouard Naville, a world-famous Swiss archaeologist, or Professor Flinders Petrie, the most famous English one.

The Fund was supported by interested private subscribers and by various museums around the world, who were entitled to a share of the finds in proportion to the amount of their subscriptions; the season's finds were exhibited each year in London. Grueber was honorary treasurer of the Fund, a fact he had not revealed to Currelly when he sent him to talk to Flinders Petrie. The interview with Petrie was brief. Currelly describes it in *I Brought the Ages Home.*

> I do not know the record time on foot between the British Museum and University College, Gower Street, but whatever it is, I hold it. I went up a crazy little stair into the Edwards Library, which was fitted up for the books that Amelia Edwards, the novelist, had left them, but was mainly a museum for teaching Egyptian archaeology. At the end of the library I saw a man, very handsome, who looked like the portrait of some of the Babylonian kings. His snapping black eyes seemed to be as full of fun as they could be. I presented my card and nervously stated my case. The first questions were: "Can you draw?" "Yes." "Well enough for illustrations?" "Yes." "Could you make a survey?" "Yes." After some more talk, Petrie said: "If you will come on the eighteenth of June for a few weeks, we will know each other better."

Petrie was by this time forty-nine and at the high point of his career. For ten years he had been professor of Egyptology in University College, London, the holder of the chair established by Amelia Edwards's will. The annual exhibition was usually held in the Edwards Library, which, under Petrie's direction, had become a unique centre for the teaching of all branches of Egyptology. The *Dictionary of National Biography* records that directly or indirectly every field worker of the next generation was to be a disciple of Petrie.

Soon after the exhibition opened, Currelly was added to the staff of the Egypt Exploration Fund as Petrie's assistant. Petrie, as we know from his autobiography, usually had four or five of these young assistants. Some of them had had a year or two of experience and were working for an archaeological degree at one of the big universities. They were given room and board for the season and a small salary, which varied with their experience and their ability to take responsibility and to work on their own. Currelly said that his beginning salary was $260 a season; later it was increased to $400 a season.

Currelly's position was unique. Petrie took him to live at his home in Forest Hill, a suburb of London, while they were waiting to sail for Egypt. Here in the evenings Petrie would reminisce about his archaeological experiences and show Currelly how a worker in the field often had to make his own tools from whatever relics of the past were lying about, in order to deal with particular problems in the excavation of precious objects. Petrie even engaged a packer from Shoolbred's, a department store, to teach Currelly how to pack precious objects for shipment, and he persuaded his friend Flaxman Spurrell, a noted anthropologist, to give Currelly lessons in prehistory.

To all this Currelly responded, his sharp intelligence and retentive memory absorbing everything that he heard. The help he received also says something for Currelly's charm, for all these qualities would have been necessary to win the affection and support of so many distinguished men, of whom Petrie was to be only the first. They were to include Holman Hunt, the famous painter and the co-founder of the Pre-Raphaelite brotherhood, whose homes in London and the country were to provide Currelly with continuous and extended hospitality; and Robert (later Sir Robert) Mond, a successful chemist with a keen interest in Egyptology, who, in addition to constant hospitality and good advice, was to provide cheques from time to time to cover Currelly's purchases.

Currelly experienced his first excitement in the field when under Petrie's observant eye he laid out his first trenches. After a month of training on the cemetery at the site of the ancient city of Abydos, he was dispatched with some workmen to finish on his own a tomb that Petrie had started to work on in the previous season. This was the great tomb, or cenotaph, of King Senwosret III, and nearby Currelly made the exciting discovery of the cenotaph and temple of King Ahmose I.

At the excavation site at Abydos workmen would offer objects they claimed to have found, and every morning dealers would bring their antiquities and offer them for sale at prices well below the market in London and New York. Currelly's letters home were an endearing mixture of anecdotes of adventure and rapturous descriptions of wondrous objects available for ridiculous prices, if they could be acquired at the point of discovery and not when agents landed them at auction rooms in London and New York. And the letters were aimed in the right direction. When he wrote young Edmund Walker about his work with Flinders Petrie and the objects so plentifully available, he was possibly not greatly surprised to receive a reply from Edmund's father. The "small sum" Walker remitted through his bank in London was fifty pounds.

Currelly at first was not sure of his judgement, and he bought cautiously. But by the beginning of the 1903/1904 season his confidence had grown, as his letter to Walker indicates.

> Last year when I first came out I was afraid to trust myself to buy much unless Professor Petrie was by as the forgeries number about ten to one of the material on the market. . . . This year I have not expended all the money. Prices are something awful and I have been waiting to get a few things somewhere in reason. Managed to get a few things and am having them sent direct by registered post.

He lists the articles and the prices he had paid for them, totalling £15.16s: two cornelian necklaces, one garnet necklace, two scarabs, one Roman terracotta head ("the kind of thing the Roman provincial delighted in"—no doubt a phrase picked up from Petrie), a good silver tetradrachma of Alexander the Great ("I think this is the coin Ruskin lectured on"), a Byzantine gold piece.

Currelly continued to work under Petrie at Ehnasya near the Fayum, in Lower Egypt, and in Sinai until August 1905, when Petrie left the Egypt Exploration Fund. By this time Currelly had so increased his skill and reputation that Petrie had invited him to contribute chapters to the Abydos, Ehnasya, and Sinai reports, as well as to supply a number of drawings for the first two. Currelly's name appears on the title pages of these volumes. It was a triumph for a young archaeologist to be associated with this great teacher.

Currelly did not follow Petrie when the latter broke with the Egypt Exploration Fund. This seeming ingratitude to the man who had taught him everything he knew, who had taken him into his home and treated him as a favourite pupil, has to be considered in the light of what Currelly had become by that time. He was now much more a collector than an archaeologist. In the beginning the latent collector's instinct had been prompted by a desire to show off. He had only his allowance from his father and his annual salary of $260 a year from the Egypt Exploration Fund. Edmund Walker's interest in acquiring objects must have suggested to him that others might share the same interest. Following the Royal Commission's report, when pressure for a university museum began to mount and Victoria College decided to turn over its own collection to the University of Toronto, Currelly saw that he might become the authorized collector for the University, with a salary and an acquisition fund, and might operate on a much wider scale.

3

Laying the Foundations

In the autumn of 1905 Currelly had sailed for home to see his family. Chancellor Burwash had given a reception for him in Toronto, at which Currelly had aroused the interest of some of the professors present. One of them encouraged him to call on Edmund Walker, who was leaving soon to visit England. The account of Currelly's meeting with Walker given in *I Brought the Ages Home* makes it plain that he worked on Walker to good advantage. Walker was excited by Currelly's description of the treasures that were still available to a keen buyer with a knowledge of prices, a sufficient acquisition fund, and authority to buy, and he promised to bring up at the next meeting of the board of trustees of the University the possibility of Currelly's being appointed official collector for the University, with a limited acquisition allowance.

Currelly was back in Egypt when the outcome was relayed to him by Walker in a letter of 3 February 1906. The University had appointed him official collector, with a salary of five hundred dollars a year and an acquisition fund of the same amount. There was not much that could be bought with five hundred dollars, and Currelly continued to press for better terms and a more generous allowance.

It had been the promise implicit in these developments that had prompted Currelly's decision to remain with the Egypt Exploration Fund. He had joined Édouard Naville and H. R. Hall at Naville's excavation at Deir el-Bahri, on a huge mound on the south side of the Great Temple, where Dynasty XI remains had been found in an earlier excavation in 1897—among them one of the finest wooden coffins with all its paraphernalia, discovered at the foot of the Hathor shrine. At Deir el-Bahri Currelly seems to have been given a position of some authority and responsibility.

But he was still not content. He was now complaining that the title of collector was a commercial one, and so had to be kept quiet in London as it would "unclass" him at once. He wanted an academic appointment. Walker responded that with the successor to the retiring president of the University of Toronto, James Loudon, not yet named, nothing more could be done for the moment. As to an academic appointment, that was outside his powers.

During the winter of 1906/1907 a light-hearted Toronto party— including Edmund Osler, Mr and Mrs H. D. Warren, and Charles Cockshutt—had appeared from the river, mounted on camels. The mock-serious purpose of their mission to Egypt had been to find a better tobacco than the one being used in Toronto for the York Club's handmade Egyptian cigarettes. No doubt Edmund Walker had suggested the call on Currelly. If so, it was a suggestion that bore fruit: members of this party were to become the Museum's most generous early benefactors.

They found Currelly engaged in making a cast of a portion of the wall-reliefs of Queen Hatshepsut on the expedition to Punt. The owner of the *New York Sun,* a guest of John Pierpont Morgan on his *dahabiyah* (houseboat), had commissioned Currelly to make the cast for the Metropolitan Museum of Art in New York for a fee of one thousand dollars and a gift to the Egypt Exploration Fund of five thousand dollars. Currelly, his nose for possible benefactors now sharply perceptive, explained to the Toronto visitors that he was taking the opportunity to make a duplicate for the Toronto museum but hadn't the means to colour it, which would amount to fifteen hundred dollars. "I think we could attend to this between us, Osler, couldn't we?" Warren asked drily. It was agreed that they could, and after being shown over the excavations at the temple the party returned to their *dahabiyah.*

By now Currelly was becoming known as a keen buyer, and other museums—the Royal Scottish Museum in Edinburgh and the Fitzwilliam in Cambridge, both subscribers to the Egypt Exploration Fund—had commissioned him to collect for them. Through Petrie he had met Sir William Ridgeway, professor of archaeology at Cambridge, and had frequently been asked to stay with him. This famous scholar was another of the older men who felt drawn to befriend Currelly. Such important connections helped Currelly to impress the University authorities in Toronto with his growing reputation.

Already, however, there were signs that Currelly's activities as a collector were causing some unease among those for whom he worked. In a particularly agitated letter to the Egypt Exploration Fund, the secretary of the Royal Scottish Museum had written on 19 April 1906:

I have received a letter today from Mr Currelly dated simply Cairo 9:4:06 in which he tells me that he has bought for us a number of things in Egypt & asking me to have a considerable sum paid, at once, into the Canadian Bank of Commerce. Most unfortunately although I wrote to him some time ago he has kept us quite in the dark as to his doings or wants until now. . . . Mr Currelly gives absolutely no details as to the sort of things he has got & without even the names of the objects for which the money is wanted the department could not be asked to provide it.

Currelly renewed his endeavours with the people in Toronto. The Metropolitan Museum of Art, under the forceful presidency of John Pierpont Morgan, had decided to withdraw from the Egypt Exploration Fund, to which it had long been a major subscriber, and to set up in Egypt an exploration fund of its own. Currelly wrote Walker that he had been offered the directorship of it. This was only slightly an exaggeration. Morgan had interviewed him ("a splendid fellow" was how Currelly, familiar now with famous men, described him), and had offered him a position as local representative for the Metropolitan, with some seniority. Meanwhile Currelly had been supporting his own case in Toronto by sending back large shipments of purchases which he had made on the University's behalf, with a value quite beyond the extent of the small acquisition fund of five hundred dollars a year that he had been authorized, on 3 February 1906, to spend. These tactics, especially the report of the John Pierpont Morgan offer, had persuaded the board of governors of the University of Toronto to give Currelly the title of Curator of Oriental Archaeology, with a salary of one thousand dollars a year and an acquisition fund of fifteen hundred.

For Currelly a time of decision was now approaching. "This has been the last campaign, and there will be no more at Deir el-Bahari," Naville had written in his preface to the account of the 1906/1907 season's work. Currelly had been left by Naville to clear up the site. He wrote to Miss Paterson of the Egypt Exploration Fund on 17 April 1907, enclosing a certificate, probably from the Egyptian authorities, to say that the site was "left in a clean and orderly condition". He went on:

No doubt you have seen Sir John [Sir John Evans, president of the Egypt Exploration Fund]. When he was here I told him that it would be necessary for me to resign from the work of the Fund and no doubt he has mentioned the matter to Mr Grueber. If he has not brought it up before the committee will you please do so. As you know I intended to leave Egypt last year and it was only the financial conditions that caused me to remain. However I am bound to return to Toronto by the arrangement I made with my chief there when I was at home before. I explained to Sir John however that if for any reason the Fund felt that they were being left in a way that caused them undue inconvenience I would lay the matter before the University authorities and that I thought they would release me for another year or that if the work of the Fund went on that I might be obtained as a stop gap by an application to the University authorities. This will be all the more important to you as every man I know of is taken up in the enormous Nubian scheme by which the Egyptian Government tries to dig Nubia before the dam is built. As they offer £400 per annum for five years it is naturally a thing to be desired.

I think Sir John's request that a special meeting be called as soon as I arrive in England will be better than letters to put things in shape.

At this point in his career Currelly was trying to keep several balls in the air at the same time. Paramount in his calculations was the creation of the museum in Toronto with himself in charge of it. At the same time he did not want to relinquish any of the links that connected him to the archaeological discoveries still being made in Egypt. And his position on the staff of the Egypt Exploration Fund gave him official status. If he had been reluctant to abandon the rich field of artifacts continually available in Luxor when Petrie left, he was still more reluctant now that he had secured a curatorial post with a reasonable salary and acquisition fund. Hence, in April 1907, his circuitous method of conveying his intention to resign through Sir John Evans, his hint that he might remain as a stop-gap, his conclusion that all had better be left until his return to England— a suggestion attributed to Sir John Evans but possibly springing from Currelly's own anxiety not to burn any bridges until the museum was being built.

By the beginning of July Currelly had made up his mind to return to Toronto for a few months, and on 8 July he sent in his resignation. He spent the summer with the Holman Hunts in England, from whose house he wrote to his old friend Professor Mavor.

I feel I cannot drive workmen any longer—too hard on the nerves, and too little in it. I hope to return to Canada for about three months. Not ill, but seriously used up. I would like to return to England to devote myself completely to the study necessary for the museum work.

It was in Currelly's nature to spring back from utter exhaustion to a renewed burst of activity. In *I Brought the Ages Home* he writes of his visit to Canada in 1907.

I returned to Toronto in 1907 about five thousand dollars in debt, and was extremely relieved when the money was arranged for. . . . As soon as I arrived there was talk of an exhibition. . . . The packing cases were brought together from different university buildings. They were emptied, and covered with paper, and made into tables for the exhibition. When it was opened [at Wycliffe College] it ran for a month, all day and in the evening, and I did what I could to talk to either small or large groups to spread information and develop interest.

Inspired by this display of interest and by the possibility of a grant of five thousand dollars from the Ontario government for acquisitions, which Walker had told him was under consideration, Currelly returned to Cairo. He spent the winter of 1907/1908 with G. D. Hornblower, who was an inspector for the Department of the Interior and an amateur archaeologist and had lived in Cairo for many years. Currelly and Hornblower had become friends when Currelly was leading his men from Sinai to the Nile valley across the Sinai desert. His way had been blocked at one point by hostile tribesmen, and he had sent for the police to move them. Hornblower had been the official responsible for the area, and it was in this way that the two men met. Currelly described his friendship with Hornblower as "one of the most fortunate things that happened to me in my relationship to the museum". The dealers were all friends of Hornblower's and anxious to please him.

With Hornblower often accompanying him or making the way smooth for him if he went alone, Currelly had a profitable winter. He did not have much to spend, and prices were booming as supplies dried up, but he managed to obtain a few Persian carpets reasonably, and also some examples of Persian potteries from Rayy and Sultanabad which were trickling into Cairo and causing great excitement. He was also able to procure some Greek Island embroideries through a dealer who without Hornblower's introduction would never have bothered to talk to a man who had so little to spend and took such pleasure in the bargaining process. As it was, the dealer, for Hornblower's sake, gave the embroideries to Currelly at prices that had obtained thirty years before.

That winter was memorable for a find that Hornblower had made shortly before Currelly's arrival and had kept for him. This was two Chinese ceramic pieces which a Cairo watchmaker had bought during a visit to China and had put in his shop window on his return. They seemed to be duplicates of two Han dynasty pieces obtained for the South Kensington Museum by Stephen Bushell, one of which appeared in his work *Chinese Art*. "Bushell had suggested that probably more would be found," Currelly writes in *I Brought the Ages Home,* "but it seemed to me too wonderful to be true that the next two that I saw should come to Toronto, as Hornblower, with his usual generosity, turned them over to me." In March 1908 Currelly wrote to Walker.

> I have not written as I thought you probably were about half dead with the financial difficulties. . . .
>
> I have just had a letter from Salomon Reinach of the Louvre who advised me to work my hardest—as the crisis has brought out a good many things that never would have been seen otherwise. This is particularly so of Cairo where speculation was mad. I hope that the plans have gone through and that the building will start soon. It means everything to us. Our people will give us money as soon as we have a building. *I do so hope the Government* will send the $5000 that was spoken of. I can get three times its value just now.

Walker answered on 16 April 1908 that the Ontario government had made the grant of five thousand dollars for acquisitions, and quoted the provincial treasurer as saying, "The amount will doubtless be repeated for two further years." Walker added, "I think we have to thank E. B. Osler for pressing this matter . . . it was his influence that brought about success." He could not, Walker explained in the same letter, offer much comfort regarding the museum building. So many members of the faculty had to be consulted, and this entailed delay. "The real difficulty," Walker went on, "is that we are erecting two or three very important University buildings and they are so pressing that the Museum suffers somewhat in consequence."

On 13 May 1908 Currelly wrote from Cairo, very upset by a letter he had had from Professor Mavor saying that the museum building was to consist of "a few grand halls like the New York museum and stacks or some kind of thing for the remainder". Currelly's letter reflects his anxiety.

> I do so hope no change will be made in Darling's plans [Darling and Pearson were the architects appointed by the University]. . . .
>
> The plans Darling had when I left were as *nearly perfect* as they can be. . . . If I can get into the workshops as Darling promised . . . in October we could be open by the next October or perhaps for the British Association when they come out for the Winnipeg meeting and that would mean a good deal for us. I am terribly afraid of a set back. . . .
>
> I hope to hear that a start has been made and that the men are at work on the foundations. If ever so little can be built at once, just half of what was spoken of, it is a start. . . . Please excuse me for worrying you with letters but it means so much to me.

Patiently the busy banker dealt with this fretful man who had become essential to his intricate scheme for associating the University of Toronto and the Province of Ontario in joint responsibility for building and maintaining a museum. Hardly a note of impatience escaped Walker. "It means so much to me," Currelly kept crying, his whole future, he felt, depending on Walker. Walker was aware how much the powerful financial and political support necessary for fulfilling his hopes had been stimulated by the energy, luck, and skill with which the younger man was assembling the artifacts and treasures that would make a great museum.

~~~

In the spring of 1908 Currelly and Hornblower went to Spain to visit museums; then they parted, and Currelly went on to London. He spent much time at the beginning of the summer at the British and the South Kensington museums, preparing himself for the post of curator which he hoped to occupy in Toronto as soon as the building was up. At the same time he sought the acquaintance of London dealers, though finding himself in these historic surroundings among long-established museums and dealers of great experience, he was cautious about adding to his debts.

But it was not in Currelly's nature to retain an air of modest submission among experts for long. He had been a regular guest at the home of Dr Allen Sturge, who had been Queen Victoria's physician and was a well-known collector of antiquities. The two men had met at the Egypt Exploration Fund exhibition in 1905, and Sturge had invited Currelly to his home in Suffolk to see his collection of prehistoric bronze implements and weapons and his huge collection of patinated flints. It was no doubt through Sturge's influence that Currelly was invited to read a paper on the patination of flints to one of the sections of the British Association meeting in Dublin in the summer of 1908. In Currelly's own words, he was "severely hammered by all and sundry of the older pre-historians". But he was undismayed and inwardly cheered by dinners with kindly professors who, having savaged him for his pretentiousness, gave him much good advice. The conference was even more fruitful in enabling him to meet one of his hosts in Dublin, Dr C. G. Seligman, a famous anthropologist and a professor at the University of London, who invited Currelly to call on him when he returned to London.

Then Currelly went north to Ballymena to see the Knowles collection of prehistoric material, about which Robert Mond had told him. Knowles allowed him to go through his collection and pick out what he wanted from the Stone Age material. Currelly then started what he called "a good old-time bargaining" session for the price. On his return to London he went to stay with Robert Mond in the country and told him of his experience with Knowles and what he had picked out. "Have you any money to pay for them?" asked Mond; and when Currelly said no, Mond went immediately to his writing table and wrote out a cheque for the amount.

~~

Everyone was dazzled by Currelly, and letters like the following, written on 8 December 1908 before he left London for a Christmas visit to Toronto, no doubt were read by more than Walker, to whom it was addressed.

> I am in very good mood today. I have rarely had such a run of luck in my life. On Friday I went hunting as usual and ended up at a very high-priced porcelain place. The man had an Imperial yellow vase wonderfully decorated in colour glaze. It was about five feet high. I started to talk about it and the merchant, Sparks, one of the best-known and most honest dealers in London, told me about the vase. It was [one of a pair] made about 1680 for the palace, looted, and Sparks bought the pair for £100. Last week a man wanted one and refused both so Sparks charged him £125 for one. I offered him £25 for the other. . . . I got the vase.
>
> Yesterday Seligman . . . took me to a friend of his, a big wholesale modern porcelain dealer, as this man occasionally obtains fine old pieces, but will not sell privately. Seligman explained that I was a friend and would keep quiet about things, so we were shown around. I asked if he ever obtained any old Sung dynasty pieces. . . . To my surprise he said that their agent had just obtained the results of the excavation of a great tomb, and that it had just been unpacked. We went to the packing room and there was stuff that made me dance. I cannot express my feelings when I saw what he had. I am in with the biggest collectors and writers now. . . . This man had the most precious things and for a few pounds each. I could hardly hold myself. Things that I never dreamed that we could have were there at the prices of modern porcelain and also they were in very good condition for the most part. I am looking forward eagerly to the time when you will see them.

The vase to which the letter refers is not in the Royal Ontario Museum collections, but it was letters such as this that excited the donors in Toronto and made Currelly now an indispensable factor in pushing on the plans for the museum.

Walker had succeeded to the presidency of the Canadian Bank of Commerce in 1907. The following year had been one of financial crisis for Canada, and he had been under great strain. Concurrently he had had to give close attention to University of Toronto affairs, which included the establishment of the Royal Ontario Museum.

Currelly's return to Toronto just after Christmas 1908 proved opportune. What he had accumulated in the previous two years had been fantastic. It was a museum of archaeology; all it required was a building. The exhibition Currelly put on at the end of January 1909, and through February, was sensational both in the scope of the collection it revealed and in the individual artifacts, many of them as striking and unusual as those to be seen in the great museums of London and New York.

The moment had come for Walker to marshal all his forces and get the Ontario government to advance the necessary funds to build the museum. The premier and some of his cabinet had been induced to visit the exhibition and had gone away impressed. The exhibition had also played its part in activating a campaign by the professors of the University. A letter addressed to Walker, dated 22 February 1909 and signed by William Arthur Parks, professor of geology, writing on behalf also of the other professors of geology and mineralogy, announced that the matter of the new museum had become desperately urgent, as their collections had grown to the point of absolute congestion. This important letter bears the mark of having been prompted by Walker, since the draft, as well as a copy of the finished letter, is among his papers.

At this point Walker wrote to the chairman of the board of governors of the University of Toronto, asking the board to give its approval to the policy of building the first section of the museum, provided suitable arrangements could be made, and to appoint a committee to interview the government. He enclosed plans for a building ninety metres in length and three storeys high from ground level. The plan of the building was based on several years' study of a number of museums throughout the world and provided for a building as nearly perfect as could be made. Walker enclosed estimates of cost totalling $400 000, including the cost of display cases, and outlined his proposal that the Ontario government and the University should each provide half of the capital and half of the cost of maintenance. To stress the urgency of the matter, he asked the board's approval of the action he proposed taking, simply on the strength of his letter. The board agreed. It appointed a committee that included John Hoskin, chairman of the board of governors, Edmund Osler, and Walker himself.

Currelly had known of the impending meeting between the committee and the government, and he received Walker's account of it soon after his return to England. The Conservative premier, now Sir James Whit-

ney, had had misgivings about his ability to persuade the legislature to put
up half the total cost of the building over a four-year period, as well as half
the annual maintenance costs. Osler had put an end to the tremulous
twitterings with "That's all right, Whitney; you give it to us, and if there's
any objection from the House I'll pay it out of my own pocket." Since
Osler was chairman of the Conservative caucus, the implication was
plain. Whitney agreed to introduce the bill setting up the Royal Ontario
Museum and meanwhile to authorize the advance of the payments so that
construction could be started without waiting for the formality of the
bill's passage.

Rarely does Walker reveal his emotions, but the relief of knowing that
what he had been planning for so many years was at last to be realized is
recognizable in a letter he wrote to Chancellor Burwash of Victoria
College on 13 May.

> This morning I received from the Premier the concurrence of the Govern-
> ment in our general plan for the Museum, and direct consent to join the
> University in immediately building the foundation. . . . I recall the morn-
> ing when you consented to the material collected down to that time by
> Currelly, and other material collected by friends of, and owned by, Victoria
> passing into such a general museum, and I may say that the encouragement
> received at that time had a very great influence upon the writer in persisting
> in what has been a long and wearisome struggle.

With this great goal achieved, Walker could now afford the time to
take an extended holiday. With his wife and three of their children he
arrived in London in the middle of July. The Walkers' visit, as it happened, came at a rather inconvenient time for Currelly, for he was in the
midst of wedding plans. He had fallen in love the year before with a
handsome and serene young woman he had met at a dinner at the Lyceum
Club. Mary Newton was a graduate of Bedford College and was working
in the Civil Service. There had been no chance of their marriage for some
time after their meeting, for Currelly's debts were higher than ever and he
had no assurance at that point that the museum for which he was buying
so assiduously would ever be built. When he had learnt from Walker that
the building was to be started and that the University of Toronto and the
Province of Ontario between them were to guarantee him a grant for
acquisitions for three years and for the first time to pay his expenses, his
future had seemed assured, even if his debts remained to be met. With this
news had come also the news of the Walkers' intended visit to England.

The Walkers spent much of their time in Britain touring England and

Scotland by car, visiting museums and art galleries and cathedrals, and staying at great houses. They returned to London at intervals for sittings for a portrait of Walker which the bank had commissioned from Sir John Lavery, a well-known portrait painter, and for bank meetings and the entertainment offered by the bankers of London to so distinguished a visitor. Walker's journal, which contains contributions by Mary Walker and the family, mentions the frequent days spent with Currelly visiting dealers—especially S. M. Franck and Company where, through Currelly, Walker was now on the best of terms with the senior partner, J. Spiers. Walker and Currelly were fascinated, as all London was in 1909, by the talk of an exhibition of early Chinese ceramics that was to come to the Burlington Fine Arts Club the following year.

The Walkers returned to London from the country especially for Currelly's wedding on 4 August. The occasion is noted in Walker's journal as taking place in the afternoon; the entry is followed by "Evening engaged in packing for our motor trip." Walker's frequent absences gave Currelly time to take his wife on a round of museums and the dealers he regularly visited, and Mary Currelly began to have an inkling of what she was in for. Her husband was a whirlwind of activity but a delightful companion. She shared his joy over his increased acquisition fund.

The Walkers sailed from Cherbourg on 5 November after a month's tour of the Continent, and the Currellys were free at last to finish their honeymoon with a tour of the museums of Europe. It was while they were on their journey that Currelly received a letter which Walker had written him on 6 December, almost immediately after his return to Toronto. It was to confirm what Walker had told him earlier was the intention: the Ontario government and the University of Toronto had combined to give him a grant of ten thousand dollars a year for acquisitions, guaranteed for three years, and to pay his travelling expenses. In addition, Edmund Osler had covenanted to subscribe ten thousand dollars in 1909 and the same sum in succeeding years until the total reached fifty thousand dollars. Z. A. Lash, another member of the board of governors of the University, had covenanted to pay five thousand in three yearly instalments. These undertakings, given following Walker's return to Toronto, no doubt were prompted by his favourable report of Currelly's activities in London. In conveying this good news to Currelly, the cautious banker warned, "I think, however, it will be well not to expend the entire amount of the two instalments, because there will be a feeling that you are pushing things a little too rapidly."

The Currellys continued their honeymoon, visiting French, German, Austrian, and Italian museums before crossing to Africa. In Cairo they were joined by Professor Pelham Edgar of the University of Toronto and Mrs Edgar; M. Langmuir, a manufacturer in Toronto, and his wife and daughter; and the daughter's friend, a Miss Scott. A *dahabiyah* was hired and they made a journey up the Nile, stopping at places of interest like Luxor for a visit to the Valleys of the Kings and Queens.

Miss Scott kept a diary which has now found its way into the archives of the Royal Ontario Museum. She and her friend found the journey exciting, as well they might with such an experienced guide and so good a raconteur. Dining on deck in the moonlight, while watching the monuments of past ages rising against the night sky, was an experience ideal for recording in the diary of a leisurely journey. Pelham Edgar and Currelly were old friends, and the conversation must have been good. But Currelly wrote to Walker that he was finding the voyage in these circumstances "unhappy". The unaccustomed inactivity, the lack of stress and striving, were abhorrent to his active nature; even the chatter about mutual friends in Toronto got on his nerves. He was eager to get going again. And so the party broke up beyond Luxor. The Currellys returned to Alexandria by rail and continued their honeymoon through Palestine and Syria and Turkey, buying extensively, as Currelly's letters to Walker show, and laying the foundation of the Museum's West Asian collection.

Currelly still had moments of anxiety, chiefly over the rising total of his debts, not all of which he had disclosed to Walker. But he had other patrons now. Robert Mond was endlessly generous. Sigmund Samuel, a wealthy Canadian through whom Currelly had met Mond, was to become more and more involved in plans for the Toronto museum and soon his benefactions were to cover nearly every aspect of Currelly's collections.

Mrs H. D. Warren, another generous supporter, had been a member of the party mounted on camels that had appeared at the Deir el-Bahri site in 1906/1907. Currelly had not missed the opportunity on that occasion to enlist a contribution for the coloration of the cast of the wall-reliefs which he was making for the museum-to-be in Toronto. That had been the beginning of many years' benefactions and dedicated service by Mrs Warren to the Royal Ontario Museum.

When the Currellys returned to England in 1910 to prepare the final shipments arising from their tour before sailing to Canada, they went immediately to stay a few days with Holman Hunt in the country. This famous old artist, now well past the days of his greatest fame, had been endlessly kind and hospitable to Currelly, many of whose letters were written from one or other of his houses. Hunt seems to have treated Currelly as a son. The artist had done some of his greatest paintings in

Egypt and Palestine, and perhaps this neophyte's enthusiasm reminded him of the deep emotions those ancient lands and their monuments had aroused in him.

On the night the Currellys left to return to London, Holman Hunt was taken seriously ill. A few days later he was brought back to his London house, where he died. Both his sons had posts abroad, and Mrs Hunt turned to Currelly to make the funeral arrangements. And so it fell to this young Canadian to carry the urn containing Holman Hunt's ashes up the steps of St Paul's and into the nave before an immense congregation, and to place it on the bier.

Currelly records this without any pride or other emotion. There could be no doubt of his deep affection for Holman Hunt, or of his gratitude to Flinders Petrie. But it was not in his nature to display these private feelings or to relax for a single moment the tension he had been under for the last few years. Matrimony, the death of an old friend—these were natural events. But the discovery of a unique collection of more than a hundred pieces of old lace, put together to show the evolutionary history of lace, was a miracle about which at this time he wrote to Walker at length. Currelly's problem, of course, was lack of funds to purchase the lace. As often happened, Mrs H. D. Warren came to the rescue several months later.

Then Currelly fell ill. It was nervous prostration, the effect of years of stress, culminating now in worry about the load of his debts. He had to take to his bed, and for six weeks he was incapable of doing anything, even of writing a letter. Nursed by his wife, he recovered; but he was always to feel from now on that there was a limit to the strain he could bear. There were to be several recurrences of the illness, and always from the same cause.

The changed financial circumstances—from the five hundred dollars a year salary and five hundred for acquisitions of four years before to the collected covenants of 1909—reflect the confidence in Currelly's judgement and the enthusiasm in backing him now shared by all in Toronto. His slightest wish was given consideration, and even a refusal to accede to some request of his, however outrageous, was always softened by a further contribution. In September 1910, before sailing for home, he had written Walker of the need he would have of a trained assistant and had asked for authority to bring with him an Arab boy who had served under him. This was Aûd, son of Mudakhil who comes into Currelly's memoir as the most intelligent chieftain in the Sinai peninsula. On one occasion Aûd acted as messenger and emissary for Currelly, and he seems to have attached himself to Currelly thereafter. Currelly's letter demanded an answer by cable. Walker—Sir Edmund Walker, as he now was, following George V's first honours list—used by this time to Currelly's urgent messages, wrote a three-page letter on 14 October saying that nothing as yet had been done regarding the organization of the management of the museum.

>   This being the case I am not in a position to discuss the appointment of assistants, etc., just yet. Indeed we need someone like yourself, possessing expert knowledge, who could be of assistance in planning a system of management.
>   I cannot therefore have the Arab boy regularly employed without provoking discussion regarding many other things. . . . I am willing to guarantee personally, to the extent of his wages for six months at the rate mentioned by you, that he will be employed.

Aûd came, and Currelly took him into his home to live with him and Mrs Currelly. A Toronto winter must have been a strange experience for an Arab boy. Since no further mention is made of him, he must have returned to Egypt when the six months were up.

The Currellys sailed for home, where they arrived on Christmas Day. Impatient to see what progress had been made with the building, Currelly was no sooner in the house that he had rented on Webster Avenue, close to the Museum, than he was out of it and on his way to the site. Work on the building had been started, following the plan that Currelly and Walker had evolved together with the architects, and the first section of the Museum had started to rise.

In March 1911, after two months of fretting delays, Currelly moved into the basement, which was temporarily covered while the work of building the Museum went on. There he was happily busy, unpacking his cases and spreading out the harvest of five years' collecting, and seeing it all again for the first time. The walls crept up around him and, like an animal in its burrow, he was happy. Indeed, all the noise and dust, the continual banging, and the odour of building materials and damp cement assured him of progress.

4

The Opening

Sequestering himself with his numerous cases in the still damp basement, with the temporary roof covered by tar-paper and the cold modified by five old furnaces with exhaust pipes sticking through the windows, Currelly set about unpacking his treasures. In this task he had the help of a young Scot, Alexander Gillan, who had come to Canada to visit his brother and had found work as a carpenter at University College. Gillan soon became so interested in the Museum, and so attached to Currelly, that he sent to Scotland for his fiancée and settled down to work with Currelly for the rest of his life.

The shipments that Currelly had been sending back from his earliest days in Egypt, which had provided material for the two exhibitions in 1907 and 1909, together with those that had been steadily accumulating since he became a full-time collector for the University of Toronto, were stored in colleges and other premises all over Toronto. Some of the most valuable items were in the vaults of the Canadian Bank of Commerce and in Long Garth, Sir Edmund Walker's home on St George Street. As late as 1912, when the upper floors of the Museum were being completed, Walker was writing Currelly to remind him of eighty-five items at Long Garth, ranging from a suit of Japanese armour and specimens of pavement from a house in Pompeii to Chinese and Persian rugs. "All this material," Walker reminded him, "has accumulated on my hands during the last few years because I seemed to be the only person representing your side of the Museum in your absence."

Setting all this out now with the aid of pine boards and trestles, Currelly was so impressed that he wrote an article entitled "The New Museum" for the March 1911 number of the *University of Toronto Monthly*. This article, appearing a year before the act formally establishing the

33

Royal Ontario Museum, produced the first of many crises in which Sir Edmund Walker had to act as a patient and methodical mediator between the professors who had been thinking of the museum ever since 1905 as *theirs,* and Currelly who had been thinking of it all the time as *his.* The professors, having given up their several plans for their own museums, had offered to undertake a large part of the duties of curatorship without extra remuneration if a general museum were built. They were understandably upset by the assumption in the article that the sole attraction of the "New Museum" would be Currelly's collections. Walker smoothed the ruffled feathers.

~~

Parliamentary bills can take longer than buildings to complete. After the momentous meeting with Premier Sir James Whitney in 1909, the Museum had no longer been a matter for doubt. The site was quickly chosen: two lots at the northeast corner of the University of Toronto's property, where Bloor Street meets Queen's Park. The building was to go up on the western section of this space, allowing for future expansion eastwards towards Queen's Park. There were outcries from some who believed that this was too far from the centre of the city, but Sir Edmund Walker was firm. Toronto would grow northwards; it would not be long before Bloor Street would be the centre of the city.

The plans for the building prepared by Darling and Pearson, the architects chosen by the University, called for the construction of an H-shaped structure, with three storeys above ground and one below, and with an entrance facing Bloor Street. In *I Brought the Ages Home,* Currelly recalls finding himself seated in a railway carriage with Sir Aston Webb, the noted architect, when returning from a Royal Academy outing to Windsor Castle. Webb was just then completing the addition to the Victoria and Albert Museum, and Currelly told him of the museum building that would soon be going up in Toronto. On being asked what he thought was the best design for a new museum, Webb pulled from his pocket an envelope on which he sketched what he had concluded would be the perfect form of museum if someone were starting a new one. It was an H-shaped structure, which would provide the greatest light and ventilation. Currelly records that he sent this sketch and the measurements to Sir Edmund Walker, who turned them over to Darling and Pearson.

There is no documentary evidence to support this account, but the H-plan was the design adopted by the architects. It had the advantage of allowing for building by stages as funds became available. What was being constructed between 1910 and 1912 was to be the west upright of the H-plan. The completion of the design, which had to wait until 1931/1933, is clearly shown in the hand-lettered, illuminated address, handsomely bound in inlaid and tooled leather, which was presented to the governor general, the Duke of Connaught, by Sir Edmund Walker at the official opening in 1914.

The estimated cost of construction of the 1910/1912 building was $400 000. The Ontario government had undertaken to pay half this sum in four annual instalments of $50 000. Pending the passing of the act that would bring the Museum into being, a "committee of five" was constituted on 19 May 1911, three members being nominated by the lieutenant governor in council and two by the University of Toronto, with powers to spend the money as though the act had already been passed. The University's nominees were the chancellor and Sir Edmund Walker; the Crown's, two ministers and Edmund Osler.

On 26 February 1912, Bill 138 establishing the Royal Ontario Museum was introduced to the Ontario Legislature. It had its second reading on 18 March, its third on 27 March, and received royal assent on 16 April 1912. In outline the bill followed with almost complete fidelity the high purpose expressed in the 1906 Royal Commission's report, "to provide a home for culture and science under the same academical roof, uniting them as far as possible, yet leaving each in its own way untrammelled by the union".

The act vested control of the Royal Ontario Museum in a board of trustees of ten members, representing in almost equal proportions the partnership of the University of Toronto and the Province of Ontario. It gave powers to the board to make by-laws, rules, and regulations for carrying out the purpose for which the Museum was being established, and went on to state that each of the departments of the Museum might "be designated the Royal Ontario Museum of [its particular discipline] . . . and that the person having the supervision of a department be called the Director of it". It is unclear how the attribute "royal" became attached to the museums. It first appears in the wording of Bill 138 in 1912, two years before the Duke of Connaught opened the Museum, and seems to have had no other sanction than that of parliamentary use.

At its meeting on 12 November 1912, the new board of trustees of the Museum promptly enacted its second by-law, establishing the Royal Ontario Museum of Archaeology and appointing Charles Trick Currelly its director. By-law no. 3, enacted on 3 April 1913, brought into being the Royal Ontario Museum of Geology (Professor Arthur Philemon Coleman, director), of Mineralogy (Professor Thomas Leonard Walker, director), and of Palaeontology (Professor William Arthur Parks, director). In October of that year the board's fourth by-law created the Royal Ontario Museum of Natural History (Professor Benjamin Arthur Bensley, director); a few months later the name was changed to Royal Ontario Museum of Zoology.

~~~

Already by December 1911 the roof of the building had been completed, and in the spring of 1912, when temporary lighting was connected, the movement of the collections towards their allotted spaces had begun. The allocation of space had caused some animosities. Currelly's archaeological collection, by far the largest, was to have the first and second floors; the third floor was to be shared by mineralogy, palaeontology, and zoology; geology, perhaps appropriately, was to have two-thirds of the floor below ground, the remaining one-third being reserved for storage space.

Again Sir Edmund Walker, the first chairman of the board of trustees, had to soothe painful rivalries. In the end the order of arrangement was accepted, cases for display were ordered, and all through 1913 preparations were under way. Walker's practical way of dealing with the possibility of friction had been to form the directors into a committee under the chairmanship of Professor Coleman, the oldest as well as the most distinguished of their number. Coleman, professor of geology in the University of Toronto, was president of the Royal Society of Canada and a fellow of the Royal Society of England. In 1914 he became president-elect of the Geological Society of America, the first Canadian to be so honoured. With his unquestioned authority and kindly manner, he could be relied on to suppress Currelly's occasional outbursts prompted by the conviction that he was the only museum man among them, and his collection the one the public would come to see.

Tact was not one of Currelly's finer points, and it was perhaps to avoid further outbursts that, at the suggestion of the president of the University, he was sent out in the spring of 1913 on a lecture tour. This took him through the southwestern United States, where he met Dr Edgar Lee Hewett, the founder of a school for the study of southwestern archaeology. A firm and lasting friendship was established between the two men and it was through Hewett that Currelly was later able to purchase for the Museum part of an important collection of southwestern Casas Grandes pottery.

Returning up the Pacific coast in 1913, Currelly's attention was caught by the cedar-bark garments of the West Coast Indians and by their intricate basketwork and pottery. In British Columbia he met the Canadian ethnologist Marius Barbeau, who had just returned from Oxford University and had joined the museum of the Geological Survey of Canada. It was through Barbeau that Currelly later acquired three of the four giant totem poles that were to become a feature of the new wing of the Royal Ontario Museum erected in 1931/1933. They are still to be seen just beyond the Rotunda in the two stairwells encircled by the main staircases to the upper floors.

Currelly returned imbued with the idea of starting an ethnological display. He knew that the Smithsonian Institution had dioramas in which life-size plaster figures were used in habitat groups depicting the activities of various peoples. In 1916 he wrote the Smithsonian asking for information. Sir Edmund Walker then approached the Canadian National Exhibition for funds to build similar habitat groups for the galleries of the Royal Ontario Museum of Archaeology. Currelly made a trip to Washington to arrange with the Smithsonian to supervise the work and to engage the sculptor Ulric S. J. Dunbar to create a group of plaster figures representing the Mohawk Indians who had followed Joseph Brant into Canada. When the shipment finally reached Toronto in five wooden crates, all the figures except one, a woman grinding corn, were smashed. The sculptor offered to come to Toronto to repair them, and the diorama was finally completed in August 1917 and exhibited at the Canadian National Exhibition, which eventually funded full-scale dioramas of several other Indian groups.

~~

At last, on 14 January 1914, the committee of directors of the Royal Ontario Museum met to discuss a date for the opening, with Sir Edmund Walker present as chairman of the board of trustees. March 19 was chosen, provided that the date was suitable both to Sir Edmund Osler, the most powerful man in the consortium responsible for the Museum (he had been knighted in 1912), and to the governor general of Canada, the Duke of Connaught, who was to be invited to perform the opening ceremony. Colonel Farquhar, military secretary to the governor general, found the date not quite convenient and asked for alternatives. But years of toil were not to be obstructed. The date had been chosen because precisely then everything would be in readiness. Sir Edmund Walker gently urged; the Duke of Connaught agreed.

Fifteen hundred invitations were sent out for the several events that were to mark the day. Some were for an inspection of the Museum at eleven o'clock, ending up with the arrival of the governor general at noon; others for a luncheon at the York Club to honour the governor general and to enable him to meet leading citizens; yet others were for the official opening at three o'clock, after which the public would be admitted to view the Museum for themselves. There was also to be a dinner in the evening at the York Club for the benefactors and those who might be expected to follow their example; and finally, at eight o'clock, a grand reception for invited citizens, who were to listen to addresses from distinguished directors of American museums.

Everyone agreed that the building was impressive. It broke away completely from the prevailing Toronto fashion of solid brownstone, the mark of a prospering city, exemplified in the handsome residences of the wealthy that faced it across Bloor Street. It stood out in contrast with the Gothic flourishes of McMaster University, its nearest neighbour, then situated on Bloor Street immediately to the west. In a day when drabness of colour and mediocrity of design were the normal characteristics of Canadian building, a critic records the Museum as "a remarkably successful essay in modernized Byzantine, with not a little of the Romanesque flavour and more than a suggestion of Northern Italian, its façades of buff-coloured brick and terracotta striking a new note in the architecture of the City". How far this daring essay in modernity was due to Sir Aston Webb we shall never know.

Part of the pleasure the building aroused was derived from its position, bounded on the west side by Philosopher's Walk, the winding pathway between grassy banks leading down to the heart of the University, and on the east by an area that stretched to broad tree-lined Queen's Park and was reserved for future additions to the Museum. With its unique colouring and its isolation from other buildings, the new museum had about it the air of a temple, the imposing proportions, the broad stone steps leading up to the entrance, and the tall windows between stone piers all combining to give this impression.

From the day of the opening the Museum was off to a flying start. Perhaps it had helped that the visiting speakers had emphasized geology—the science of the earth—as the basic science and with oratorical flights had enlivened what might have been at that evening hour a hard subject. Palaeontology too was recognized by references to rocks in which "lie buried the remains of the unending lines of our ancestry from the hoary beginnings of earth history; from them we have drawn our physical frame, its organs and their functions.... And so this Museum becomes a veritable Temple of the Muses."

Within a few days of the opening Currelly was reporting to Sir Edmund Walker: "Gifts have been coming in with a rapidity that is simply amazing.... Men from all over the Province have been coming to see me to say that this was what they have been waiting for all their lives, and that they are anxious to assist in any way that is possible. There has been frequently asked the question—if it were possible in any way to place a valuation upon the Collections." Currelly was the only director to list the value of the gifts in his museum. For the science directors the task was clearly impossible.

A few days later Walker wrote to the Honourable W. H. Hearst, minister of lands, forests, and mines, and the senior of the two ministers who were members *ex officio* of the board of trustees of the Museum. He listed the donors and set the value of their gifts at $564 850. At the same time he quoted the turnstile record of visitors in the few days since the Museum had opened as 7345.

The small staff by this time had grown to about twenty. They were underpaid and worked long hours without overtime or supper money. They became skilled technicians, devoted to the Museum and to their respective directors. The atmosphere was that of a family, and the sense of community broke down the stiffness and jealousy that had existed up to the time of the opening. The Royal Ontario Museum, the dream of so many over so many years, was at last established and from that hour began to assume a character and vitality of its own.

But within six months the outbreak of World War I threatened the Museum's continued existence. Almost immediately attendance figures fell. A national coal crisis in 1916 raised the threat of the closing of public buildings at a time when families could not get enough fuel to heat their homes. Men with special qualifications were called away to war work, and in some of the science museums their absence imposed an extra burden on the directors, who had departmental responsibilities in an already short-staffed university.

The finances of the Museum were in a state of crisis. On the night Great Britain declared war, Sir Edmund Walker had been summoned to Ottawa from his summer place on Lake Simcoe for consultations with an anxious government. In compliance with the general mood of austerity, the trustees of the Museum issued a stern directive to the committee of directors: there were to be no further acquisitions unless the money to pay for them was already in hand, or they were offered as exchanges by other institutions.

The Museum survived without closing. Attendance figures picked up as Toronto became a leave centre for troops. The collections grew by gifts, donations, and exchanges, and by the spring of 1918 field work began again.

5

The Age of Innocence

What saved the Museum in its early days of financial stringency was the benefactors. Sir Edmund Walker had led the way, not only in backing Charles Currelly but also in the gifts he continually contributed to all the museums, though chiefly to the Royal Ontario Museum of Archaeology where his own special interests as a collector lay. He had carried with him several other members of the board of governors of the University, notably Edmund Osler, Joseph Flavelle, and Z. A. Lash, wealthier men than him, who could well afford the guarantees which together had provided Currelly with an acquisition fund of almost thirty thousand dollars a year during his last two years in Europe.

One of the most consistently generous of all the early benefactors was Mrs H. D. Warren. On her husband's death in 1909 Mrs Warren had assumed his position as chairman of the board of directors of the Dominion Rubber Company, which his family had controlled. Under her direction, and helped by the nascent automobile revolution, the company had greatly increased its profits, and she had added to what must have been a considerable fortune. She was the only woman appointed to the first board of trustees of the Royal Ontario Museum and she took her responsibilities seriously. Intelligent, charming, witty as well as pretty, she seems to have enjoyed her activities and to have derived pleasure from the unending series of gifts she made to the Museum. She and Robert Mond and Sigmund Samuel formed a protective ring around Currelly, often saving him at the last moment from the consequences of some expensive purchase he had not been authorized to make. "Do you want me to go to gaol?" asked Currelly dramatically on one occasion when Mrs Warren questioned the purchase of some article which the Museum "simply had to have". The answer, as always in the end, was a cheque.

As one looks back to those early days of the Museum's history, the social and academic stratifications, which would arouse resentment today, seem innocent and endearing. The descent from the wealthy members of the board of trustees to the hard-working, less than affluent professor/directors was precipitous enough; but the further descent from there to the underpaid technicians was as steep as Lucifer's fall from heaven. It was the way the world went then. The generosity of the donors was as important to the life of the Museum as the inspired work of the directors, who were themselves helpless without the skill of the preparators, artists, cabinetmakers, and technicians.

The Reuben Wells Leonard bequest was a notable example of this generosity. Colonel Reuben Wells Leonard had graduated with honours in engineering from the Royal Military College, Kingston, in 1883. He had served as a staff officer in charge of transport during the North West Rebellion of 1885, and on returning to civil life had become involved in the first development of hydroelectric power at Niagara Falls. He had gone on to make a fortune in mining and then had retired from business at the beginning of World War I to devote his life and his large fortune to a variety of philanthropic causes. As a governor of the University of Toronto, he was aware of the difficulties of the fledgling Museum, and he was one of the early members of the "Ten Friends of the Arts", a group of people, including Mrs Warren, who committed themselves to pay five hundred dollars each annually into an acquisition fund for Currelly's museum.

Leonard died in 1930. His will provided that one-sixth of his estate should constitute a trust fund, the income from which was to be shared among the five component museums of the Royal Ontario Museum in proportions approved by his wife and by the president of the Toronto General Trusts Corporation, of which he had been a director. The trust provided funding for a number of research programs and field expeditions and archaeological excavations, which otherwise would have been beyond the Museum's means. It was also used to acquire for the Royal Ontario Museum of Mineralogy a small collection of gems with colourful names, including a fine faceted chrysoberyl, a chrysoberyl cat's-eye, a large freeform Australian opal, and two large Brazilian amethysts. But owing perhaps to the force of Currelly's representations, fifty per cent of the income went to the Royal Ontario Museum of Archaeology, including five thousand dollars for the long-overdue task of cataloguing the archaeological collection.

The collections had all grown, even during the war, and growth had been particularly rapid in the early years of the 1920s. Thanks largely to the diligent work and extensive surveys of the Geological Survey of Canada and the Ontario Bureau of Mines (now the Ontario Geological Survey), invaluable evidence had been provided of the great age of Canada's geological history. By charting those areas in which minerals might be found, these surveys had led the mining companies to their rich discoveries, and notably to the spectacular gold and silver discoveries in northern Ontario.

Geology and mineralogy, although separate departments, had been closely related in the University of Toronto, sharing quarters in the Mining Building. When the collections were moved to the new museum, their separation was more visible, geology being housed in the basement, while mineralogy shared the top floor with palaeontology and zoology. But there could have been little to differentiate the geology and mineralogy galleries to the uninstructed eye of the Museum visitor, since both collections dealt with earth sciences, and included, among other specimens, displays of precious metals.

What gave the mineralogical collection special interest was that the opening of the Royal Ontario Museum of Mineralogy had coincided with the development of the silver mines at Cobalt and with the gold discoveries at Kirkland Lake and in the Porcupine district of Ontario. Large quantities of minerals were turned over by the mining companies, and the gem collection also benefited from gifts from the mining corporations and from magnates like Colonel Reuben Wells Leonard for the purchase of gemstones. These gemstones from Brazil, Sri Lanka, Australia, Mexico, and Colombia added to the attraction of the gallery, but few could have foreseen the growth of the mineralogical collection, which was eventually to become one of the largest in the world.

Zoology had found an eager audience waiting for it when it came out from behind the walls of the University. Toronto was a paradise for nature lovers. The small city was situated on rising land between two rivers, with heavily treed ravines, relics of the glacial age, running down to Lake Ontario, and its outskirts offered a perfect haven for wildlife. In Victorian times, before the city became thoroughly industrialized, it was not much of a walk to the Don River in the east, or the Humber in the west, where mammals and birds of great variety crossed the paths of the walkers or swooped over their heads.

A natural history collection, mounted by some enthusiast in the family, had been a feature of Victorian homes in Ontario. The specimens in the Museum were prepared and mounted by trained technicians. The technicians in the natural history sections of the Museum, who were expert naturalists and masters of casting, modelling, painting, and taxidermy, founded the Toronto Naturalists' Club (later the Brodie Club), which was limited to thirty members. Rules were rigorous and attendance was compulsory, and yet there was a waiting list for membership, which was dearly prized. The meetings were held in the laboratory of the Royal Ontario Museum of Zoology, after the Museum had closed for the day. The technicians demonstrated laboratory techniques, and under their instruction amateurs became knowledgeable specialists.

~~~

Professor W. A. Parks had been impatiently awaiting the end of World War I to resume his field work in the dinosaur graveyard along the Badlands in the Red Deer River valley of Alberta. He was able to mount his first expedition in the last year of the war, and thereafter year by year to continue the astounding discoveries of new species that were to make the Royal Ontario Museum's dinosaur collection among the greatest in North America.

Dinosaur bones and other fossils had been found by members of the Geological Survey of Canada as early as 1884 in the valley of the Red Deer River. Twenty-six years later, in 1910, Barnum Brown of the American Museum of Natural History began what was to be a six-year field program along the Red Deer. These expeditions unearthed and removed a series of remarkable skulls and skeletons, using the techniques that Brown and other American professional collectors had developed. In 1914 the University of Toronto had sent a prospecting party into western Canada under Professor Maclean of the Department of Geology to look for fossil vertebrates. Before this, the Geological Survey of Canada had invited Charles H. Sternberg, a professional fossil-hunter since 1870, to join its service, and he and his three sons moved to Drumheller in the Red Deer River valley in 1912. Levi Sternberg, the youngest son, came to the Museum in 1919, and when Professor Parks mounted his expedition that year, Levi was assigned to be its guide and preparator.

The Sternbergs were a family of specialists; they did not have university degrees, but this made no difference to their professional competence. Charles H. Sternberg, who with his son Levi had left the Geological Survey in 1916, was familiar with the techniques which had been developed by Barnum Brown and was an expert in removing skeletons. Levi, who had worked with his father, had inherited these skills. In the Royal Ontario Museum of Palaeontology, where Parks did his graduate teaching and his laboratory work, Levi was only the technician, to be treated as such, but in the field he spoke with the voice of authority.

The Badlands in Alberta extend about forty kilometres along the Red

Deer River and five to six kilometres back from the gorge. The earth here is a mixture of sandstone and shale. Some of the former was quite hard to dig, always requiring a pick or a hammer and chisel, and sometimes even dynamite. Prospecting involved walking and climbing all over the Badlands in search of bone fragments uncovered by erosion. A fragment might be the tail bone of a dinosaur, with the rest of the great frame buried under a tonne or more of earth. The first task was to remove enough of the overburden to determine if there was a skeleton. This required digging down to within thirty centimetres of the skeleton's frame with large tools, and then working with small tools to trace the outline of the skeleton. When the outline was traced, a trench was dug around it and it was studied for natural cracks or other places where the entire skeleton could be subdivided into blocks of manageable size. These were trenched and undercut as much as possible and then covered with wet paper and finally with layers of burlap and plaster. Once the plaster was cured, in a day or so, the block was further undercut so that it could be turned over. The excess rock and part of the first plaster were then removed and the other side was wrapped in plaster and burlap. The blocks were crated for transportation. The crated specimens could weigh over a tonne and had to be raised with block and tackle; a horse-drawn wagon was then run underneath to receive the load for transport to the nearest station for shipment to Toronto. Sometimes, in the early days, a rough road had to be dug to the spot.

Levi's field experience under his father, along with his youth and strength, was a great asset to Professor Parks, who in fact knew less than Levi did about the technique of removing these vast skeletons from the earth and rock in which they lay buried. From 1920 to 1931 it was left to Levi to lead the annual expeditions. He seemed to have an intuition for what lay under the earth from which some ancient bone protruded. When the 1932 expedition ended, there were placed in the new dinosaur gallery ten complete skeletons and between fifteen and twenty partial skeletons and heads, about half of which represented either new genera or new species of already recorded genera. Dr Gordon Edmund, now curator in the Department of Vertebrate Palaeontology, took part in the last Royal Ontario Museum expedition to the Badlands in 1954, along with Levi Sternberg and Ralph Hornell.

Professor Parks was to say on more than one occasion, "Too bad Levi didn't go to college—he could have been head of the department after me." This was said not in a condescending way, but with real regret.

Late on a day in 1918, when the Museum was on the point of closing, a visitor asked for Currelly, who was busy at the time showing the president of the University of Manitoba over the Museum. The visitor left his card. Twenty minutes later Currelly, reading on it the name of George Crofts, realized with a shock whom he had turned away.

George Crofts was a prosperous fur merchant with a large factory in Tientsin (Tianjin), whose business had been established in China for many years. Chinese antiquities had been his hobby, not his main activity, but he had been appointed the agent in China for S. M. Franck and Company, the largest importers into Britain of the valuable Chinese antiquities then coming on the market. Franck's had been anxious that the source of their unique Chinese antiquities should not be known to their rivals, but Currelly's curiosity had extracted the name from Dr Seligman.

It was through Crofts that Franck's had acquired a Luohan figure which Mrs Warren had bought for the Museum, and it had been Robert Mond's suggestion that a coloured postcard should be made of it to give publicity to the Museum's collections. It was the sight of one of these cards at the news-stand of the King Edward Hotel that had brought George Crofts, passing through Toronto on his way back to China from a London visit, to call at the Museum to see what other Chinese antiquities it had.

Currelly lost no time in pursuing his visitor, only to find that he was out. Mrs Crofts offered him tea, and Currelly, all his acquisitive instincts aroused, waited until Crofts came in. Currelly, with his utter honesty, told Crofts that the Museum hadn't a farthing to spend. Crofts replied that he wasn't interested in selling; he had merely been curious to see the Chinese antiquities in a museum that could boast in its collection the rare Luohan figure which he had sold to Franck's.

Thus began a friendship which Currelly says in his memoirs brought to the Museum $10 million worth of Chinese treasures that could have been sold to another museum at many times what the Royal Ontario Museum paid for them. It was to be more than a friendship, at least on Crofts's part; for him it became an emotional attachment to Currelly as a person. The Museum in the end became so much Crofts's project that he often used his own personal funds to pay for collections that he thought the Museum should have but could not conveniently afford at the time. His way of expressing himself was often flamboyant and frequently confused. When embarrassed by emotion he would slip into impersonal locutions; "I" would become "we", and "we" would dissolve into "Mr Crofts". He explained to Currelly, "In matters of this kind I endeavour always to be impersonal, and therefore in a sense I like to efface myself and judge the work on behalf of the Museum as if same were coming from another person than myself." About one particular shipment which had cost more than the estimate he had given Currelly, he wrote on 17 July 1919:

> We believe the collection to be wonderfully cheap for the reason we have made no charge for time, commission or work entailed generally ... therefore we can candidly confess that if the whole had been sent to London, it could easily have been invoiced for the full amount, with additions for commission, etc. . . . Mr Crofts feels rather selfconscious in regard to the whole business. . . . because he has planned many additions to the Collection and is rather afraid he has sent you too many Potteries of a similar nature.

In the end the honours were equal, if not by conventional measures of value at least in what they represented to each man. There is a letter from Currelly to the president of the University of Toronto, reminding him insistently of the value of all that Crofts had done for the University and the Museum and urging that an honorary degree be conferred on him. The degree of Doctor of Laws was conferred on Crofts at convocation in 1922. Crofts was greatly honoured and wrote to Currelly:

> It is not easy for me to express my thanks and full appreciation because I feel you are responsible for this honour by your work on my behalf, or otherwise the recognition would not be possible. I can only state that I appreciate [it] to the utmost, and that the Collection and Museum generally receive the fruits from this recognition in a measure as unexpected as the honour was to me.

Currelly himself purchased the cap and gown for the convocation as a token of his own affection for Crofts.

George Crofts died in 1925, leaving hardly enough money to pay for his funeral and provide a small legacy for his wife. The fall in world prices for fur, aggravated by a dock strike in London which delayed for some weeks a large shipment he had sent, had ruined him. The factory he had built in Tientsin had to be closed down and the large staff dismissed. He had been ill, and when he returned to London cancer was diagnosed.

Some time before his death he sent the Royal Ontario Museum two little Wei statuettes and two terracotta figures of the Ming dynasty. Perhaps he knew the extent of his losses, for he wrote to Currelly that he was not invoicing the Museum for the figures, nor did he want them labelled as part of the George Crofts Collection. "I am keeping the group," Crofts said, "as a bit of insurance for my wife, who has had such a hard time."

When Currelly knew how little his friend had been able to leave, he wrote to Mrs Crofts:

> I have no power to speak, but only to recommend, but if you will empower me, I will make this recommendation to the Board of Trustees of the Museum, that they pay to you the sum of $6000 (United States dollars) for the Wei objects and the two Ming pieces. If I could make the sum $25 000 I should have done so, because our debt to Mr Crofts is one that we cannot estimate.

~~~

About the same time that Currelly and Crofts first met in the King Edward Hotel, a new phenomenon presented itself to the committee of directors of the Museum, causing some alarm, and at first active opposition. Currelly reported having been approached by a Miss Margaret MacLean, who asked if she might be taken on as a guide to the Museum. Margaret MacLean had spent several years in Japan, where her father had been appointed commercial agent by the federal government of Prime Minister Wilfrid Laurier. She and her father had arrived in Japan in the middle of the Russo-Japanese conflict, and she had joined the Volunteer Nurses Association of the Japanese Red Cross. In 1906, when the Russo-Japanese War was over, she had visited China, where her father was later appointed commercial counsellor attached to the legation.

Miss MacLean's experiences of travel in China resulted in a book, *Chinese Ladies at Home.* Her travels by rickshaw, by river barge, and on one occasion by a wheelbarrow that also supported a ninety-kilogram missionary, showed what an intrepid woman she was. Following her father's death in 1908, she made two round-the-world journeys and then returned to settle in Toronto, just as the Royal Ontario Museum was opening. It might have been the news of her exploits that alarmed the directors, instantly protective of their own fiefs.

Miss MacLean had visited the Museum frequently and had made herself familiar with every part of it. She possessed just the qualifications needed for a guide, a post which the directors had discussed as part of their plans for publicity to bolster the falling attendance. But they had done nothing about it at the time, and the bold proposal by a woman that she should undertake the task produced on this occasion a tight-lipped resolution for the minutes, reading "Letter read from Miss MacLean. . . . Lengthy discussion as to the employment of guides followed. Resolution passed governing this matter." The decision, conveyed by Currelly to Margaret MacLean, was that there was no such position. And that was supposed to be that.

But Miss MacLean was not easily put off, and Currelly agreed that she might study in the Museum. She began her own course of studies, reading up on North American Indians, Palaeolithic and Neolithic times, Rome, Greece, Egypt, China, and Japan. Currelly, seeing her labouring away day after day, and fearing she might have misunderstood him, reaffirmed that there was no possibility of a staff appointment. Even if a guide were appointed, the position would be an unofficial one, and unpaid. Miss MacLean said she understood, but she began anyway to guide a growing number of visitors, especially those with children. It was then agreed that she might be authorized to organize outside parties and lecture to them for a small fee, on the understanding that she was not on the staff and might not conduct them around any of the science museums without the permission of that museum's director. Miss MacLean, unperturbed by official discouragement, prepared her own brochures and sent them to schools and clubs. In that first winter of freelance work she lectured to more than six hundred people.

The publicity problem was solved. This was the way to improve the attendance. By the beginning of 1919 Miss MacLean was hired by the board of trustees of the Museum to lecture three days a week and was put on salary, and on 22 February 1919 all the Toronto newspapers carried the story under headings such as "Woman Guide for the Museum". The story confirmed that Miss MacLean would be the Museum's official guide and that organizations and schools could arrange for special lectures during the week.

On Saturday afternoons at two-thirty there was now to be a study hour for children, and at three-thirty a lecture for adults. Miss MacLean had battled her way into the Museum and was to become one of its characters. At first the science directors refused her access to their museums; but by the year's end, after she had lectured to more adults and children, the barriers were taken down and she was free to enter, with her train of followers, all the component museums.

At some point very early on Margaret MacLean met George Crofts. Probably Currelly introduced them because of her Chinese experiences. They started a correspondence, confined to a few lengthy letters on his part and answers from her, which he acknowledged but which are now missing. The precise teacher and lecturer must have corrected Crofts's imprecise description of some of the objects he had acquired for the Museum, sending him sketches of them and noting the points in his attribution that she disputed—as, for example, the angel figure in a particular Tibetan painting, a common enough feature in temple paint-ings but in this instance quite distinct from the angels appearing in most

Tibetan paintings and frescos reaching the West. Miss MacLean sent Crofts a pencil sketch showing the differences and explaining that the two paintings he had shipped to the Museum pertained only to Lamaism as practised in Tibet. These and many other examples show her scholarship, which Crofts came to admire and respect, as his letter to her of 27 March 1923 indicates.

> Your letters like yourself are intensely interesting, because they contain a mass of information clearly illustrating the great ability which you possess in connection with the work in the Museum. It affords me great pleasure to congratulate you on your good taste and executive ability. I have not mentioned this before, but I had the pleasure of listening, unknown to your goodself, to two of your lectures, and was really surprised at the depth of your knowledge and the clearness of your explanations. I rather envied you the faculty and the fullness of your expressions which conveyed so much in a very few words to your silent listeners. Thanks muchly for the pleasure.

A year later Margaret MacLean was forced through illness to give up her work for the Museum, and in 1925 she died.

These two remarkable figures, Margaret MacLean and George Crofts, connect through Currelly and typify the accidental encounters that so frequently in Currelly's life led to developments in the museum that had become his life. They had begun with that first visit to the British Museum and his subsequent meeting with Flinders Petrie. If it had not been for that, although the Toronto museum would still have been created, it would have been an entirely different institution. Out of Margaret MacLean's persistence was to develop the educational activity of the Royal Ontario Museum. Immediately on her death her successor was appointed. If it had not been for the emergence of George Crofts as the source from which so much was to be added to the Museum's already notable Chinese collection, the Royal Ontario Museum would not today have a Chinese collection which in many respects, and for particular periods in China's long civilized history, is without equal in the Western world.

~~~

An air of innocence and joy hangs over those early years of the Museum's history. It was considered an honour to be associated with the Museum. The pay was minuscule, even non-existent in those many cases where the bracketed word "unpaid" appears after a name in the registry. The directors, of course, gave their services. There were as yet no curators. The directors were "keepers" of their collections, preferring the British term to the American "curator", which was not to come into general use until the sheer range of the collections required closer supervision of the various parts.

The Museum staff included draftsmen, who painted the wooden labels, three carpenters of such skill that they might better have been called cabinetmakers, and four preparators, who combined the work of present-day conservators and preparators. Accessions were recorded by simple entry. Books for the library of each museum were catalogued. Photographs, made by an outside firm, were listed and cross-indexed with catalogue numbers.

In the Royal Ontario Museum of Archaeology there was a quarter-hour of relaxation in the afternoon at three-thirty, ordained by Currelly for his small staff, when there was a daily tea in that part of the basement not occupied by the Royal Ontario Museum of Geology or used for storage. Currelly had a special chair and would sit there, on one recorded occasion loudly slurping his tea from the saucer; when someone appeared shocked he went into the history of cups and saucers to explain the origin of the saucer. Once the anecdotal vein was tapped by tea and company, he always found something to talk about.

Currelly kept a bed in a room next to his office in the Museum, and sometimes in the summer he slept there, when Mrs Currelly closed the house in Wychwood Park and she and the family went to their farm at Welcome. Guards would find him in the night wandering around the galleries in his nightshirt. It was as though he could not bear to part from the museum which had come utterly to absorb his life. During the day he would emerge from his office and wander through the building, lost in thought and frequently whistling meditatively "Beautiful Dreamer" or "Songs My Mother Taught Me". He was becoming impressed as a legendary figure on the minds of all the workers, who would remember, long after they had left the Museum's service, the approaching sound of the crêpe-soled shoes he habitually wore, the distant strain of the whistle that accompanied his brooding thought, and then the looming appearance of the sturdy figure, dressed always in tweeds. Outside the Museum, looking even larger than life, he would wear the bulky cape he had had designed for himself as a winter coat, topped by a tweed hat of the same material as the suit. Fresh outfits were bought, when required, during visits to London.

〜〜

The work of the Museum was always behindhand. Acquisitions came in faster than the small staff could cope with them. Assistants attached to the

University professors were expected to deal with some of the professors' university work. Elvira Hamel, who joined the Museum staff in 1913 as a girl of eighteen direct from school, recalls her duties. Her work was mostly in palaeontology and geology, and later on in mineralogy; it included cataloguing, cleaning fossils, chipping rocks, and preparing specimens for exhibition in the galleries. She was expected to spend some time in the Mining Building of the University, looking after the teaching sets in palaeontology and geology.

When T. M. (Terry) Shortt, a young artist aged twenty-two from Winnipeg, was invited to join the Museum in 1930 as an assistant, he came thinking he would be employed in illustrating zoological reports; he found himself "involved in taxidermy, sign writing, moulding and casting, carpentry, wall painting and even sweeping floors". But he found too that there was an opportunity to participate in field work and to study animals. In one of the many books he was to write recording his experiences in the field from the Arctic Ocean to the Galápagos Islands, from India to Central Africa, he remembers in a nostalgic passage the homecoming at the end of every journey and the excitement of finding what new acquisitions there had been in his absence, and he recalls the voices of Currelly and Parks and other pioneers introducing him to them.

L. L. Snyder, T. B. Kurata, E. B. S. (Shelley) Logier, J. L. Baillie, and Levi Sternberg were others in those early days who joined the Museum as assistants. When Shelley Logier came to the Royal Ontario Museum of Zoology in 1915 at the age of twenty-two, his appointment was marked "without pay". Only at the end of a year was his status raised to that of "artist". Logier had always drawn well as a boy. A lodger in his family's home had been a friend both of Tom Thomson and of Arthur Lismer of the Group of Seven, and these artists encouraged the boy's talent in recording nature and all living things. Logier took part in field work in various regions of Canada, becoming a pioneer in Canadian herpetology. His published work on snakes, which with amphibians became his specialty, was extensive.

Lester Snyder had been one of the founding members of the Toronto Naturalists' Club, which met in the Museum. The club was unique in having no officers; and though membership was limited, it was open to all who were interested in natural history. The Museum collections could be used for study. Space being at a premium, preparation for an evening meeting was left to the last moment of the day. The laboratory was swept and cleaned, and tables and chairs were arranged.

Sometimes at a weekend the members of the club would go to a shack they had built themselves in the woods near Pottageville, close to the old radial line that ran from the city limits. Those who could not find beds in the shack slept out under the stars. The outings were immensely popular. Though membership in the Toronto Naturalists' Club had to be limited because of the shortage of space in the Museum, on these outdoor excursions visitors were welcome.

But while life for the young assistants in the natural science museums had its lighter and more relaxed moments, serious and important work was being accomplished. These men were responsible for the first main stage in the history of scientific research in the Museum, when studies of individual regions were carried out jointly by workers in the separate fields of interest—mammalogy, ichthyology, herpetology, entomology, ornithology, and palaeontology—to determine the extent of the different faunas and to provide knowledge of the basic biology of individual animal species.

Dr Edwin Crossman, a curator in the Department of Ichthyology and Herpetology, calls this the "inventory stage". Once the researchers had completed their findings they moved into the second stage—that of synthesizing their findings with those from other areas. The resulting publications gave the detailed distribution across Ontario, and eventually across Canada, of the various species.

The third stage consisted of more interpretive studies of Ontario's and Canada's animals. In some cases the work was carried on by these same men, but in the late 1940s and the 1950s it was undertaken by curators with postgraduate degrees—back from the war or out of the universities—who wanted to do research and teach in a museum context. Many of the men without advanced degrees did acquire the status of scholars in the eyes of their academic colleagues and some, like Snyder, Logier, and Baillie, were eventually given curatorial title.

And so the function of natural history museums was moving inexorably towards the addition to field work of the microscope and the laboratory. This is what Dr Crossman's analysis shows. It is the view, too, of Susan Sheets-Pyenson, the historian of the Peter Redpath Museum at McGill University in Montreal, who discerned the same trend to a future that offered greater inducements to the geneticist in the laboratory than to the ornithologist or the mammalogist in the field. This movement was to mark a transition in the Museum's history that was inevitable if the Museum was to continue to grow, but it was not to be achieved without some private distress. Distress was inherent in a situation in which scientific scholarship was given recognition at two different levels, the criterion being, at least to some extent, the possession or lack of formal qualifications. On one level were those with full academic qualifications;

on a different, lower level were those whose work was of a scholarly calibre, but whose lack of a postgraduate degree impeded their advancement in the curatorial ranks.

The science collections all bore the marks of scholarly attention and purpose, evident in the carefully typed labels attached to every exhibit giving the date and locality of the object's discovery, exciting evidence of the evolutionary development of the different species. Even the precise arrangement of the exhibits in their uniform cases set back in alcoves or filling the middle aisle reflected the view the scientific directors had of their function in the Museum: a continuing line of scholars dedicated to a discipline.

And, in a category unique and all his own, there was Charles Currelly. The professors' primary aim was to serve the scholar and student; Currelly's was to educate the public. His vision was of a museum of the material arts of man from the beginning to an undefined present. But he knew how important scholarship was to archaeology and anthropology, which were new disciplines in the Museum's early days. He appointed scholars like Dr Cornelia Harcum and gradually built up a qualified curatorial staff. When Dr Homer Thompson, world-renowned classical archaeologist, was appointed head of the newly established Department of Archaeology of the University of Toronto, he was simultaneously named associate director of the Royal Ontario Museum of Archaeology and keeper of its classical collections. When T. F. McIlwraith was appointed lecturer in anthropology at the University in 1925, he was also made keeper of the Museum's ethnological collections.

Currelly's collection was uniquely his own. He had seized on everything that came his way, from relics of the Stone Age to porcelain from the finest period of China's long civilization, from Venetian glass, European pottery and ceramics, velvets and laces to arms and armour and English furniture.

Currelly had matched his dreams against the achievements of the British and European museums that had spent more than 150 years in adding to the outstanding collections they had inherited. He had displayed great daring and had been lucky, for frequently he had not had the money to pay for what he had bought. His infectious enthusiasm for what he was doing had impressed older people. He was not egotistical; but so firm was his conviction that a particular artifact or treasure was essential to the Royal Ontario Museum of Archaeology, and so intense his single-minded pursuit of it, that even dealers weakened in their resolve to get the price they had asked for some desired object. Experience in Egypt had sharpened Currelly's bargaining powers.

And so when the Royal Ontario Museum of Archaeology was opened to the public, the variety and interest of its collection were impressive. The objects extended from the Stone Age, through the early civilizations of Babylonia and Egypt, to Etruscan bronzes and Greek statuary, including a superb Venus of the lst century B.C. The native art of the New World was represented in small ivory Eskimo carvings, and the life of the North American Indian in the paintings of Edmund Morris and Paul Kane.

All the colour and historical richness of the archaeological museum contrasted strongly with the displays in the science museums; yet the disparity between the two types of collection would not have been immediately apparent to the majority of visitors in the early years. Both were part of what a great museum was expected to provide—knowledge. Professor Carl Berger, in *Science, God, and Nature in Victorian Canada,* has observed acutely that the attitude of the Canadian public to the world of science duplicated the blend of vigorous localism and continuing participation in the imperial system displayed in Canadian political and social life. Antiquities and art of other ages were to be admired; but geology, mineralogy, palaeontology, and zoology displayed the rock and metal, the buried life of glacial and interglacial periods, and the living nature of the Canadian homeland.

6

The End of the Beginning

Although he was almost seventy-one at the time of the armistice in 1918, Sir Edmund Walker seemed still as vigorous as he had been some thirty years earlier when he became general manager of the Canadian Bank of Commerce. As soon as the end of the war was in sight, he had pressed the Ontario government to add the long-promised second wing to the Royal Ontario Museum. The existing building had become so unbearably crowded that there was scarcely room to pass in the aisles, and new acquisitions and gifts were piling up in storerooms elsewhere in the city. The premier of Ontario, at Walker's invitation, had visited the Museum at the end of 1918 to see for himself the condition it was in. He had gone away impressed and had invited Walker to submit plans and estimates for the new wing.

These plans had been discussed by the trustees and directors of the Museum, and architects had already been instructed. The approved plan did not differ in any detail from the H-shaped structure of the original design. It would complete this design by providing a parallel wing on the eastern side facing Queen's Park, with a connecting building linking the two wings. A new main entrance to the building would face Queen's Park. The cost was estimated to be $1 million.

Before a decision had been reached, Walker set out on 15 March 1919 on an extended visit to the Orient in the bank's interest. Lady Walker had had heart trouble and was advised not to travel, and so he took his eldest daughter, Dorothy, with him. They went first to Japan and then on to Korea, and thence to China, passing through Mukden (Shenyang) and Peking (Beijing) before taking a train south to Hankow (Hankou). Here they boarded a steamer and sailed down the Yangtze River (Chang Jiang) to Shanghai. On deck Walker read Marco Polo, making a largely vain attempt to identify the historic places Polo mentions from their modern Chinese names. This visit to the Orient left a lasting impression on him. From his journal it is plain that he spent as much time in visiting museums and collections of Chinese paintings as in meeting British, American, and Canadian banking and government officials, all of them eager to entertain him at their clubs.

Sir Edmund Walker had been one of the first collectors in North America to become interested in Japanese prints; this interest went back to his early days as the bank's agent in New York, a period that coincided with the first movement of Japanese print collecting in North America, to which it had spread from Paris. He had made a close study of the development of Japanese prints from the 17th to the 19th century and had amassed one of the largest private collections in North America. His journey to Japan in 1919 provided an opportunity to enrich a collection that was already important. After his death most of his collection of Japanese prints came to the Royal Ontario Museum, where, as the Sir Edmund Walker Collection, it remains the single outstanding component of the Japanese collection of the Far Eastern Department.

Just as through Currelly we see a side of Sir Edmund Walker not visible in the public figure of the successful banker and administrator, so through another Canadian, Henry P. Rossiter, we are enabled to see, even more clearly, the genuineness and depth of Walker's feelings for works of art, as they showed themselves in his activities as a collector of prints. Walker had secured the appointment of Rossiter to the position of curator of prints and drawings at the National Gallery of Canada, a position which Walker himself had been instrumental in creating by the simple expedient of going directly to the prime minister of Canada, Sir Robert Borden. Rossiter had not been long in Ottawa, however, before the Museum of Fine Arts, Boston, where he had worked before taking up his appointment at the National Gallery, invited him to return as acting curator of prints and drawings. The post provided not merely a higher salary, but also travel opportunities and funds for the acquisition of prints beyond anything that the National Gallery could afford. The chance was too good to miss, and Rossiter accepted the offer, with Walker's full approval.

Rossiter visited Europe to study prints in the British Museum and famous collections in Paris, Madrid, Berlin, and Dresden. His visits to London sometimes coincided with Sir Edmund Walker's, and they often lunched and dined together and haunted the print galleries around Museum Street. On his many visits to Toronto to see his family, Rossiter was a familiar guest at Long Garth and at Broadeaves, Walker's house on Lake Simcoe.

There emerges from Rossiter's memories of Walker the scholar depicted in a photograph where he is caught turning from examining an etching on an easel in his library. This is a figure altogether different from the composed and dignified man of affairs who looks out from the oil portraits by Sir John Lavery, Sir E. Wyly Grier, and others.

Rossiter's memories supplement the impression revealed in Currelly's letters and in his memoir. But Rossiter's memories are even more finely drawn, as though his expertise in judging the fine lines of engravings enabled him to appreciate qualities of mind and feelings which were concealed from others by Walker's habitual reserve. Rossiter called Walker the greatest humanist Canada had produced, and his salty comments on the official Canadian attitude to art in his time made his praise of this one man all the more emphatic. The fact that no life of Sir Edmund Walker has been written except an account of his successful career as a banker, which spares only some dozen pages for his contribution to the artistic life of Canada, lends colour to Rossiter's view of Canada, as far as culture was concerned, as "the world's largest, bleakest and most arid dust-bowl".

Sir Edmund Walker returned from his long visit to the Orient to find that the Ontario government had come to no decision on the new wing for the Royal Ontario Museum, and he mounted a fresh assault. But growing unemployment as Canada reverted to a peacetime economy made it impossible for the government to approve an expenditure of public funds on the necessary scale. Walker must have been bitterly disappointed by this decision, but he kept his own counsel. In 1921 he went on an extended visit with other officials of the bank to South American countries where the bank was considering establishing branches.

In July 1923 Sir Edmund Walker suffered a heavy blow with the sudden death of his wife. She had been his close companion for almost fifty years, from the days when they had started life together in Hamilton six years after he had joined the bank as a junior clerk. He was now seventy-five, but he was back at work within two days of the funeral, determined as he had been at the start of his working life to carry on. In October he was appointed chancellor of the University of Toronto in succession to Sir William Meredith.

In November of the same year Charles Currelly asked for leave for a few months in order to seek treatment for his nerves from a specialist in England and to assist the Royal Ontario Museum of Archaeology's agent in Europe and Britain, Thomas Sutton, with bidding at auction sales. He wrote to Walker from London on 3 March 1924 to say that he had been in

Torquay for a month undergoing treatment, and that he was now recovered and was starting his search for acquisitions for the Museum. Walker replied that he would be in London at the end of March and would join Currelly there. The hunt was on again, and he must have been the more eager now to get away and join Currelly in a renewal of the discoveries they had made together in London in the old days.

Just before sailing Walker accompanied the Mendelssohn Choir, of which he was honorary president, to a performance in New York. He returned with a heavy cold, which in a day or two turned to pneumonia. On 27 March 1924, the day he was to sail, he died.

Sir Edmund Walker seems now, sixty years after his death, a late Victorian figure, and it is true that more than half his life was spent in the Victorian era as he struggled upwards from boyhood on an Ontario farm to prominence as a successful banker and an intellectual. Along the way he had acquired the gravity of manner and appearance that went in those times with banking and great learning. But he was no dilettante interesting himself in art and science as pastimes, and the staid appearance could be deceptive, concealing the passion of his search for beautiful things and for knowledge. As a boy he had been a collector of fossils, and through all his ill-paid years as a bank clerk and junior manager he added to his palaeontological collection, making himself so much a master of the subject that he could impress a room full of professors with his learning. When he handed over his palaeontological collection to Trinity College in 1904, it was so complete and so much the envy of great institutions that the secretary of the Smithsonian Institution in Washington later wrote to thank him for having placed it "where it will be of permanent service to all interested in geology and palaeontology".

Every interior photograph of Long Garth shows the walls crowded with paintings, majolica ware, and other articles of beauty. But no prints were on display in the halls or the drawing room or dining room. These were kept in Walker's study in a series of drawers behind three panelled doors. The etchings were in a separate cabinet reaching from floor to ceiling, with glass doors which opened like leaves of a book. Walker spent many happy hours studying every detail of his etchings. Rossiter repeats a story that Walker's detailed study of the art of engraving dated from a time when, as a young boy in his uncle's exchange office, he had allowed a counterfeit bill to get by his usual close scrutiny.

Sir Edmund Walker was never a rich man. Although highly paid by the bank—his salary is recorded as having been fifty thousand dollars a year—he had a large family of his own, and he also supported some of his Murton relatives of his mother's generation. Throughout his life all that he could spare was spent on his collections and in supporting, to the extent that he was able, the museum that he had helped to bring into being and the other institutions with which he was involved—the National Gallery of Canada, the Art Museum of Toronto (now the Art Gallery of Ontario), and the Champlain Society, to name a few. He enjoyed bargaining as much as Currelly did; and what he did not keep he gave to museums and galleries. Having persuaded Goldwin Smith, renowned controversialist and scholar, who had married the widow of Harry Boulton, the owner of The Grange, to give Toronto's grandest house to the Art Museum of Toronto, he himself bought and donated the land surrounding it so that the city should not have to appropriate property for further expansion of the art gallery. "Father gave and gave," recorded his daughter, Mrs Dorothy Webb, many years later in writing to Dr Katharine Lochnan, then the assistant curator of the Department of Prints and Etchings at the Art Gallery of Ontario, on the occasion of an exhibition in Walker's honour. "His was a life of giving, but he never spoke of anything he gave, whether time, effort, money, or objects."

When Sir Edmund Walker died, the Royal Ontario Museum was firmly established, so that neither the long years of the Depression nor the coming to power in Ontario of Mitchell F. Hepburn's government dedicated to radical reform—the expression of the impatient and angry politics of the Depression—could threaten its existence. Budgets were cut, and the already low salaries of the staff were further reduced, but the Museum survived. There were too many powerful financial men in Toronto now committed to its survival, including James B. O'Brian, who had been vice-chairman of the board of trustees ever since the opening, and who had succeeded Sir Edmund Walker as chairman. O'Brian was to remain chairman until 1942, by which time everything would have changed—the Museum, Toronto, and the world. When peace came again after World War II, the Museum would have to adjust itself to a new world altogether; this would not be done without some stresses and strains as the basic differences of aim between a university museum and a public museum became exposed.

7

Education in the Museum

The committee of directors of the Royal Ontario Museum had only grudgingly given way in 1919 to Margaret MacLean's importunings to be appointed a guide to the collections. While eventually expressing their approval of the general principle of having a common guide for all five component museums, they informed the trustees that she must first satisfy each director of her competence to act as a guide to his collection; the director's approval had then to be sent to the board of trustees before her appointment was confirmed. Through this very narrow aperture, education came to the Museum.

It is amusing to compare that early resolution with the one passed by the committee some five years later when illness compelled Margaret MacLean's retirement. On this occasion a notice was dispatched to the board of trustees recording the directors' pleasure at learning that the board had appointed as her successor Miss Dorothy Haines (later Hoover), who had worked with Margaret MacLean for five years as her assistant. They ventured the hope that in the very near future the board might be in a position to appoint an additional guide to conduct classes through the natural history museums.

It comes as a shock to be reminded that ten years after the original conception of five independent museums housed in one building, now so greatly crowded that it was almost impossible to tell where one museum ended and another began, each was still a separate bailiwick in which the director was lord of his domain. Above them reigned the sovereign body, the board of trustees, charged with the management of the museums. Below them were the technicians, the cataloguers and assistants, the preparators and craftsmen, some attached to a particular museum, others at the service of all.

So long as Sir Edmund Walker and his successor, James B. O'Brian, held the post of chairman of the board of trustees, the directors, for all their undisputed power within their own museums, neither individually nor collectively had any executive authority on the wider scene. O'Brian, like Walker, also held the chairmanship of the University of Toronto's board of governors. Both men exercised a paternalistic authority and won consent for decisions that maintained a balance between the Museum's interests and those of the University.

It was the maintenance of this balance, along with his own infinite tact, that enabled Walker to manage the directors of the museums, who otherwise might have chafed at the restrictions of their role. Only occasionally did his patience burst its restraint, when Currelly had to be suppressed, or the professors reminded that museums did not exist to serve graduates and undergraduates only; the public, including small children, had an interest too.

When, after three years, Dorothy Haines was forced by ill health to resign, her place was taken by a woman of a very different character. The directors were advised that Miss Ruth Home had been appointed museum lecturer and guide in succession to Dorothy Haines. It was announced that she would give lectures in the Royal Ontario Museum of Archaeology, and upon request would conduct parties wanting a general tour of the Museum. O'Brian hoped that sufficient funds would be available for a lecturer for the natural history museums next year.

What had seemed an intrusion on the directors' territorial rights less that ten years before had become the solution to the problem of attendance. Children had found in the Museum a place where their boundless imagination could play. It had been Margaret MacLean's idea to have lectures, which were really story-hours, for children unaccompanied by adults an hour earlier than the Saturday afternoon lectures to adults. Ruth Home expanded this into the Saturday Morning Club for children. For twenty-six years after her departure, this creative and imaginative program, which still today touches the lives of hundreds of children, was to be guided by an artist and sculptress, Eugenia Berlin.

The idea of classes in the Museum caught on, and in 1928 the Toronto Board of Education appointed a fully qualified teacher, Miss Lilian Payne, to conduct four classes a day for Toronto schoolchildren. She was to continue to do so with skill and devotion for twenty-one years. A decade later the Museum appointed its first qualified teacher, Miss Ella Martin, whose special province until her retirement in 1971 was secondary and adult education.

~~

In 1934 the board of trustees formed a permanent subcommittee to be called the Education Committee and to have jurisdiction over all public instruction in the Museum. The subcommittee's powers were to extend over both Ruth Home and Lilian Payne.

But even this august body was not proof against Ruth Home's determination to have a say in educational policy. The alarm had already been sounded by Currelly. At a meeting of the committee of directors in December 1933, Currelly, with his characteristically deceptive air of innocence, had raised the question whether Miss Home should be charged a fee for the use of the lecture room between five and six o'clock in the afternoon for a course she was giving in interior decoration. He had gone on to "call attention to the fact" that there appeared to be no understanding as to the relation between the instructions given Miss Home (given by whom? was the question left quivering in the air) and the supervision necessary by the individual directors (a reminder of their authority in their own museums and an unspoken rebuke to the trustees for disregarding it). Miss Helen Reynar, the secretary to the committee of directors, who was also secretary to the board of trustees, disclosed that Miss Home had been given permission to give her course by the board; and further that she had been authorized by the board's secretary to open an account at the Canadian Bank of Commerce in the name of the Royal Ontario Museum Department of Public Instruction for the purpose of receiving all fees from those enrolling for the course and of meeting all expenses connected with it.

A strongly worded resolution was forwarded by the directors to the board aimed at regulating Ruth Home's activities; even if these were not under the control of the directors, it declared, they should at all times be within their knowledge. The directors also regretted the setting up of a separate Department of Public Instruction. The board approved the terms of the resolution but saw no good reason to abandon the title of Department of Public Instruction, which was to endure until 1946 when the department was incorporated in the new Division of Extension.

Ruth Home was to remain with the Museum for seventeen years, during which time she effected dramatic changes. She was brilliant but, for that very reason, impatient with the slowness of some of the men in charge of the museums to grasp her innovative ideas. Dr Loris Russell, at that time assistant director of vertebrate palaeontology, liked her, finding her full of brilliant ideas. But Dr. J. R. Dymond, director of the Royal Ontario Museum of Zoology, felt that she involved the directors in her schemes without consulting them. The chairman of the board of trustees was very keen about education as part of the Museum's function, and Ruth

Home took to approaching the board directly when she wanted approval for some new venture, instead of going through the committee of directors, as protocol and discipline demanded.

Nobody could deny Ruth Home's brilliance and competence. One of her ideas was to persuade the Canadian National Railways to put on special cars to bring school classes from the country to the Museum. They came from as far away as North Bay, the children sitting up all night, when necessary. Sometimes as many as five hundred children would descend on the Museum. Dorothy Burnhan (then Macdonald), a former curator of the textile collections, remembers standing before an easel and sketching costumes through the ages for school classes, the sketches disappearing as fast as she drew them.

Another of Ruth Home's ideas was to have the artist Sylvia Hahn commissioned to paint murals of the Vikings as a background to the Saturday Morning Club's activities. Currelly took up the idea of murals for the Armour Court, on some of whose walls Sylvia Hahn depicted knights in suits of armour, with their squires, engaged in a joust. A box of noble spectators of the tourney showed unmistakable likenesses of Currelly and some of the keepers and preparators of the Museum.

Education was simultaneously entertainment and a search for knowledge. So successful was the Saturday Morning Club that the numbers had to be limited to four hundred. Its popularity had no doubt been the reason for setting up the powerful Education Committee, for some kind of buffer was necessary between the directors and this disrespectful but invaluable initiator. It is a tribute to Ruth Home's forceful nature that the Education Committee weakened in its initial determination to be exclusive and in 1936 passed a resolution that she be admitted to their meetings when her work was discussed. Then, to preserve the dignity of the committee of directors, its chairman was asked to be an *ex officio* member. By this time the committee of directors had been enlarged to admit assistant directors, and additional directors were appointed to the Education Committee on an annual basis.

As a result of these adjustments, all went well as long as O'Brian remained chairman of the board. He was Ruth Home's champion, and that kept criticism muted. His death in 1942 altered the situation, and Ruth Home grew unhappy. In 1946 the board of trustees decided to form a Division of Extension to include all educational matters and extension services of the Museum; Edwin C. Cross, who had been a curator of mammalogy, was appointed to head the new department. Ruth Home found it intolerable to have a man brought in over her head and resigned, transferring her unquestioned talent to the Ontario College of Art.

Cross had had a long and distinguished career with the University of Toronto. He had been appointed acting curator of mammals in the Royal Ontario Museum of Zoology in 1936, when he was also an executive aide in the University's Department of Biology. In the Museum he was largely concerned with organizing the mammalogical work and collections. In World War II, although over age, he had joined the Royal Canadian Air Force, having served with the Royal Flying Corps in World War I. It was on his return to the Museum after the war that he was appointed head of the newly established Division of Extension. Within a few months he was seconded by the Ontario Department of Education for a special two-year project, but he continued to advise and direct the Museum division until the end of his two years' leave of absence, when he found it necessary to withdraw altogether from his Museum work. He died suddenly while attending a conference of UNESCO in Denmark.

Cross's short span of work in the Museum after 1946, when he sat by invitation on the committee of directors, coincided with the time when the relationship between the University of Toronto and the Royal Ontario Museum was coming under strain. Cross played a large part in presenting the case of the directors to the board of trustees of the Museum; his experience both as a University instructor and as a Museum director and his gift for organization and planning were invaluable.

Soon after his appointment to the Division of Extension, Cross was able to persuade the Ontario Department of Education to appoint two qualified teachers to the Museum and to have a sum earmarked for the Saturday Morning Club included in the Museum budget. In 1946 Miss Catherine Steele was appointed supervisor of education, and when she relinquished her post in 1952, she was succeeded by Miss Norma Heakes, who served until 1971.

In those postwar years education in the Museum exploded. School groups proliferated; they came on foot, by automobile, bus, streetcar, and train to throng the galleries. To reach schoolchildren who could not come to the Museum, the teachers embarked on a visiting program, which was planned in detail with provincial school inspectors and local schools. And for schools the teachers were unable to visit, or with which they wished to maintain contact, the Division of Extension devised travelling cases, which were circulated throughout the province. They contained Museum material relevant to the curriculum and notes for the teachers. Typical titles were *Shakespeare's England, Roman Everyday Life, Bird Adaptations, Science in the Rocks.*

Thus from tentative beginnings grew today's wide-ranging Education and Extension (now Outreach) services, which reach tens of thousands of Ontarians each year, both inside the Museum and throughout the province. In addition to ever-increasing numbers of school classes, taught both in English and in French, Education Services provides lecture/discussion series for adults and a variety of other continuing education programs. In 1984/1985 Extension Services circulated forty travelling cases to forty-one Ontario school boards, for use in the public and separate schools under their jurisdictions. Two museumobiles, *Fossils of Ontario* and *Man in Ontario,* travelled 12 000 kilometres, visiting schools, community museums, libraries, and special events. And the programs of both departments are enriched year by year.

8

Gaining Ground

Sir Edmund Walker's pleas, during the last years of his life, for the alleviation of conditions in the Royal Ontario Museum that he described in a letter to Premier Ernest Charles Drury in 1921 as "distressing and really impossible of continuance" had been met by the Ontario government with nothing but promises and postponements. After Walker's death the government continued to turn a deaf ear to the complaints of the directors, in their annual reports, of the crowding and congestion that impeded their work.

Then, in 1929, just before the financial crisis that was to mark the beginning of the Great Depression, the decision to go ahead with expansion was taken. Perhaps the determining factor was the economic boom of the later 1920s. If so, a different rationale very quickly became necessary. By the time the work was started in the spring of 1931, the country was in the grip of the Depression and the Museum's expansion had become a make-work project. The government insisted that as far as possible Ontario labour and Ontario materials should be employed in the construction. The exterior walls were faced with Credit Valley and Queenston limestone; all the interior decorative marble flooring and trim were of Bancroft marble. Brick from the Toronto yards in the Don Valley was used for the walls facing the old building so that they would match the original construction, and because it was hoped eventually—a hope deferred for a further fifty years—to fill the spaces between the old and the new buildings with other buildings and connecting floors.

The plan of the expanded building was the one for which provision had been made from the beginning. To the east of the existing building, and parallel to it, a new wing was built, so that what had originally been the entire Museum now became a "west wing". A connecting building

66

between the two wings gave the whole the form of the letter H, the two wings representing the uprights. The new main entrance was in the centre of the new wing's eastern façade.

All the excavation for the new building was done with pick and shovel, and horse-drawn wagons were used instead of tractors. Men worked shortened shifts so that more workers could be drawn from the army of the unemployed. The carved decorations with their symbolic figures were all modelled in clay by the sculptor Charles McKechnie. Plaster casts made from the clay models were set up on the scaffolding for skilled stone-carvers to copy. When it was finished, this almost handmade great building, dominating the northern approach to the circular sweep of Queen's Park Crescent, was a thing of beauty.

There had been no attempt on the part of the architects, Chapman and Oxley, to follow the traditional museum façade exemplified by the British Museum and the Metropolitan Museum of Art in New York. Loren Oxley, the son of one of the architects of the new wing, and himself an architect, traces the design to an earlier and simpler precedent found in University College and the old main library of the University of Toronto. Whatever the source, the effect was imposing; the carved figures, and the symbolism conveyed in their grouping, imparted something of the grandeur of a medieval cathedral, while the long sweep of the east front was reminiscent of an Oxford or Cambridge college. Inscribed in the stone on either side of the massive central entrance were the legends THE RECORD OF NATURE THROUGH COUNTLESS AGES and THE ARTS OF MAN THROUGH ALL THE YEARS.

Entering the Museum, visitors found themselves in a large rotunda, thirteen metres in diameter, under a domed ceiling of Venetian glass mosaic designed and executed in Toronto. Standing there, they were provided with a magnificent vista through the Armour Court—the long hall connecting the two wings—to a large west window, through which light poured into the old wing. Beyond the Rotunda, stairways built around square stairwells on either side led to the upper floors. The plan made it possible to enter each of the five museums from the new main entrance without going through any of the others. The earth sciences were, appropriately, on the ground floor of the new wing, geology and mineralogy facing one another on either side of the Rotunda.

Geological features and processes are on such a tremendous scale that it is difficult to encompass them within the scope of a gallery. The Royal Ontario Museum of Geology met this difficulty by showing many features with the aid of models. These were used to illustrate such phenomena as Niagara Falls, and even the glacial and interglacial deposits exposed in the Don Valley, within walking distance of the city. Models were also used to demonstrate methods of mining and of extracting oil from deep underground. There were specimens of rocks, as well as magnificent specimens of gold and silver and nickel ores. Included in the geology gallery was a column of coal 2.3 metres high which the Dominion Steel and Coal Corporation had mined from beneath the sea.

The second floor of the new wing was given over to palaeontology, vertebrate on one side, invertebrate on the other. Since palaeontology provided a link between the earth sciences and the life sciences, it was natural for the top floor to become the domain of zoology. Archaeology now occupied all three floors of the west wing, as well as almost the whole of the building connecting the two wings. A special extension had been built to house the Ming tomb.

The four giant totem poles obtained for the ethnological collection some years earlier were now immediately visible to Museum visitors when they moved out of the Rotunda towards the Armour Court. The transportation of the poles from British Columbia to Toronto had not been accomplished without much toil and ingenuity. They were first floated down the Portland Canal to the ocean and then towed to Prince Rupert. The largest of them, the Sakau'wan pole, twenty-four metres in length, had to be cut into three sections while still afloat before it could be loaded onto a railway car.

There had been no room for the poles in the original Museum building. Currelly had been told that they would not last for more than one hundred years in the open air, and so eventually a home would have to be found for them in a new wing. Meanwhile some method of preservation had to be applied to prevent their deterioration. Currelly had not forgotten Flinders Petrie's lesson that the archaeologist faced with a problem must often invent his own tools and procedures; his prescription in this case was to soak the sections of the poles in petroleum until they were thoroughly saturated, and then to pour gallon after gallon of ordinary floor wax on them. They were then wrapped in protective bandages and burlap and lay outside the Museum for several years until the east wing was under construction. They emerged from their wrappings perfectly preserved and were erected in two back-to-back pairs between the Rotunda and the Armour Court, with the stairways twining around them. The architects had calculated nicely. When the building was completed, these great works of art of the native people of Canada's Pacific Coast, with their carved symbols articulating complex cultural meanings, seemed in this position like twin stems around which the other museums were wound.

In the autumn of 1931, when construction of the new wing was well advanced, two distinguished visitors from Britain arrived in Toronto to inspect the Museum. They were Sir Henry Miers, a trustee of the British Museum and president of the British Museums Association, and S. F. Markham, secretary of the association. They had been commissioned by the Carnegie Corporation to report on the museums of Canada, on the strength of the well-received report they had already done on the museums of Britain. In all they visited 125 museums recorded as existing in Canada at that time.

The thoroughness of the Miers-Markham investigation tended to throw the picture out of focus, for many of the "museums" visited were no more than local historical societies preserving relics of their own past, their collections consisting of faded photographs of early pioneers, military uniforms, and primitive agricultural tools with which the pioneers had broken the land. No more than a dozen institutions from coast to coast met the strict qualifications of Miers and Markham for recognition as true museums. The two men were full of good will and anxious to be helpful; their final report not only noted the shortcomings in what they had seen but offered advice as to how these might be overcome. What baffled them was the difficulty they had in extracting information. "Paralytic modesty is a common museum disease from Calgary to Halifax," they remarked. Summarizing the defects, they wrote:

> Few objects are exhibited with a definite purpose behind them; overcrowding and reduplication are common; direction notices, instructive labels, guides and handbooks are conspicuous by their almost entire absence; and last, but not least, it is made as difficult as possible for any one to find the museum, and when found, to be able to see it as it should be seen.

From this charge the Royal Ontario Museum was specifically exempted: "Its collections cannot fail to be of educational value to all visitors. Many of the exhibits are definitely arranged with an educational purpose in view, and it performs very fully the offices both of a university and a public museum."

Some apprehension had been expressed in the committee of directors over the impression the visitors had received of the Museum, which at the time of their visit was structurally complete, but with galleries not yet furnished. Miers and Markham had observed that very few Canadian museums had reserve collections that could be lent to schools or other teaching institutions or used for the purposes of research. The Royal Ontario Museum had a large reserve stored outside the Museum in other parts of the city, for conditions had been so crowded inside the Museum that there was simply not sufficient space for storing all the material that was not on display. The visitors had had it explained to them that when the collections were brought in from their depositories, the storage space available now to the museums would enable them to make frequent changes in their displays. The collections would be available for research and, where suitable, for sending out to schools on loan.

But Currelly in particular was worried, and he wrote to Sir Henry Miers in December to say that he wanted to see a proof of the Royal Ontario Museum entry in the report before it was printed. The report could not be held up for that, but the directors must have been agreeably surprised by the generally enthusiastic comments about the Museum in the published report, which found it "situated on a splendid site ... the largest museum building in the Dominion, and the new extensions render fair to make this one of the largest museums on the American continent".

Like all British commentators on museum management, Miers and Markham emphasized the importance of properly trained, fully equipped, and well-paid curators. A knowledge of "languages, biology, history, science, etc." was among the requirements they listed as essential. "Moreover," they went on, "a university training gives that insight into research which is so needful if a museum is to keep abreast of modern ideas, and if its treasures are to be made useful and available." The fact was, however, that at the time of their visit curators were ill-paid compared with university instructors in the same subject, and some of the most gifted of them did not have all of these "essential" requirements.

Miers and Markham remarked that "university collections tend to remain under the direction of professors long after a qualified director for the whole museum is needed", and urged the replacement of the professors with professionally trained museum specialists. Though the five component museums of the Royal Ontario Museum each had its own qualified director, Miers and Markham noted also another departure from British practice in the relationship between the directors and the board of trustees. In Britain, museum trustees were totally removed from the day-to-day management of the museum. In North America, by contrast, trustees often assumed that because it was they who appointed the director, they had a right to interfere with his administrative decisions. This practice was becoming increasingly common, sometimes to the point where the situation developed into an open struggle for control between powerful boards on the one hand and ambitious directors on the other.

In the case of the Royal Ontario Museum the chairman of the board was entitled to sit on the committee of directors, and the board made final decisions. This overlapping of roles was eventually to lead to a crisis of management in which vocal Museum specialists advocated the reduction of the board to an advisory role so that the Museum staff could run their own institution. There was to be much turmoil before a satisfactory accommodation was finally achieved.

The Miers-Markham report was valuable for drawing attention to certain disparities between the treatment of museums in Canada and that accorded to similar institutions in Great Britain, Germany, and the United States. Of the more than one hundred museums listed in the *Directory of Museums in Canada,* only three, the National Gallery of Canada and the National Museum of Canada in Ottawa and the Royal Ontario Museum in Toronto, had an income of more than $100 000 a year, and only seven other museums in all Canada had an annual income of $10 000 or more. By contrast, the yearly museum expenditure of the cities of London and New York was well over $5 million each; two museums, the British Museum (including the Natural History Museum) and the Field Museum in Chicago, each spent more than twice as much in a single year as all the museums and art galleries in Canada put together.

Comparisons of the cultural affairs of Canada and the United States at that stage in history are always unfavourable to Canada, implying that in cultural matters Canada was relatively a wasteland. This judgement overlooks the fact that endowments are as necessary to cultural development as breath is to life, and that private wealth flowers chiefly in great cities. The half-dozen largest centres of population across the wide expanse of Canada at that time were still small compared with the great cities spread across the United States. Although the sizes of the populations of the two countries have remained roughly proportional, both private and government support for cultural institutions in Canada have vastly increased, and the discrepancy would now be less marked.

~~~

Buoyed up by the favourable impression made on the distinguished British visitors, which would be communicated to the international community of museums, and rejoicing in the spacious new quarters, nearly everyone in the Royal Ontario Museum felt happy. Currelly alone seemed discontented. The area of the Royal Ontario Museum of Archaeology had been more than doubled, but he was not satisfied with the arrangement. "Rocks to the right of me, rocks to the left," he grumbled, pointing to the favoured position of geology and mineralogy at the entrance. "No one cares about my collection, which is hidden away at the back."

It is impossible to recapture the tone in which this remark was made. It may have been a humorous aside to one of his staff. Or it may have sprung from the sudden recognition that in the end science would come into its own in the Museum. The science collections were no longer teaching sets from a university but were internationally recognized as part of the community of scientific museums. Or it may have been a symptom of the strain he was under at this time in amassing one of the finest collections of Chinese antiquities in the world.

Currelly had laid the foundations of the Chinese collection in Cairo in 1908 and in London between 1909 and 1911; then George Crofts had made his great contribution. Not long before Crofts died in a London hospital in 1925, Currelly had had another visitor at the Museum, William C. White, bishop in Honan (Henan) in China, who was to crown the achievement and to be both a boon and a burden to Currelly in the years ahead.

9

Bishop as Archaeologist

William Charles White was sent to China as a missionary by the Church of England in Canada in 1897. In his early days there he often lived in remote districts, rarely seeing anyone of his own race, other than an occasional missionary on his way to another posting. He had been advised by the church authorities at the start of his mission "to sail to China alone". He left behind the girl with whom he had an "understanding", Annie Ray, a student at the Church of England Deaconess and Missionary Training House. His loneliness and sense of isolation at first must have been intense, but Annie Ray joined him ten months later, and they were married in Shanghai in October 1897.

White earnestly set about learning the Chinese language, and in order to identify himself as closely as possible with the people among whom he was to work he started to dress in Chinese clothes and even to wear his hair in a queue. This was not an unusual practice for missionaries in isolated districts, where European dress attracted curiosity that was not always friendly.

In 1907 White was posted to Foochow (Fuzhou) and there he found himself in an ancient capital where mandarins had been established in authority for centuries. Their exquisite manners revealed to him how uncouth he must appear to these civilized Confucians. These men were scholars and intellectuals who knew the history of their ancient civilization and lived in splendid surroundings. It was White's contact with these scholars that first turned his mind and interest to Chinese history and culture.

When White had served in China for ten years, the Church of England in Canada instructed him to survey the huge province of Honan, south of the Yellow River (Huanghe). This was one of the last areas in China to be opened to Western influence, and White was asked for advice on where the headquarters of a new mission might be established. He recommended that the headquarters should be in Kaifeng, the capital of the province, and should be under the supervision of a bishop. His report was accepted, and in 1909 he was recalled to Toronto to be elevated to the rank of bishop.

Bishop White arrived in Kaifeng in March 1910. Not only was the background changed, but White himself had begun to change, perhaps without being fully aware of it. Conscious now of his princely rank in the church, he was no longer the humble suppliant for God's forgiveness who had filled so many of the early pages of the diary he had started to keep at the age of twenty. Humility was something he could demand from those working under him. Not everyone was ready to comply; there was trouble with some of the young missionaries who asked to be moved to other jurisdictions. He drove other people hard, as he had driven himself.

From the time of his arrival in Kaifeng, Chinese archaeology constituted a growing interest in White's life, but his work for the Royal Ontario Museum should not be allowed to obscure the reality and the magnitude of his accomplishments in the missionary field. Through his effective organization, he made a substantial contribution to the growth of the Chinese Christian church in Honan. Before he left China in 1934, there were eleven churches in his area, each with a Chinese pastor. Although the main thrust of his work was evangelical, he was from the beginning preoccupied with the health, welfare, and education of the Chinese peasants. Lewis C. Walmsley, White's biographer, notes that "over the years the foodstuffs and financial assistance which he [Bishop White] obtained from abroad for famine relief saved tens of thousands of lives".

〰〰

In the early centuries of the Christian era Kaifeng had been the site of a colony of Jews who may have migrated there, either for trade in silk or for freedom from persecution. Some centuries later their descendants had been permitted to build a synagogue in Kaifeng. The Jews had intermarried with the Chinese and had gradually been assimilated into the culture. Two stone stelae were still to be seen on the site of the synagogue. These and other relics fired White's interest in archaeological remains, and with his mission work well established, he began to devote more and more time to the study of Chinese archaeology.

Kaifeng had been the capital of the Chinese Empire during part of the Sung (Song) dynasty (A.D. 960–1279). Anyang, some hundred kilometres north of Kaifeng and famous for the ancient royal tombs discovered there, and Loyang (Luoyang), another ancient capital about the same distance to the west, were both within reach by newly constructed railway lines. These places were proving rich in finds excavated during the construction of the railway, and Kaifeng had become the central market in North China for dealers in antiquities. Chinese archaeology had just begun to attract interest around the world. By the end of the 1920s wealthy collectors would be driving prices sky-high, but at the beginning of the decade Bishop White, like Currelly in Egypt twenty years before, was to find himself at the right spot at the right time.

In his position as bishop, White was a man of note in the community. He met Dr John Ferguson, a Canadian who had spent nearly all his life in China and had been appointed first president of the University of Nanking (Nanjing), one of the mission universities. Ferguson was a sinologist of international repute who had for many years served as an adviser to the Chinese government. He helped White by introducing him to noted Chinese scholars engaged in archaeology. Soon after his arrival in Honan, White also met Dr James Menzies, a Canadian Presbyterian missionary at Anyang, who had made a special study of the late Shang dynasty culture (14th–11th century B.C.), particularly of the form of script incised on bones used for divination.

An ancient form of Chinese writing, oracle-bone script is extremely difficult to decipher. Menzies was a scholar of the highest order, the only non-Chinese to have made a significant contribution to early studies in this field. Years later he was to join the Royal Ontario Museum when Bishop White had gained prominence as keeper of the Museum's East Asiatic collection and professor of Chinese studies in the University of Toronto. Menzies, a shy, unassertive scholar, who had given the Museum some fine early bronzes of the Shang period, and who had helped Bishop White with his knowledge and connections when White was making his first ventures in the archaeological field, could never have felt happy in his subordinate position under Bishop White. Fortunately Menzies' war duties kept him away from the Museum for much of the time. His collection of oracle bones was to be added after his death to those which Crofts and White acquired, making the Museum the most important depository of these records outside China.

~~~

After the 1911 revolution, which overthrew the Ch'ing dynasty and marked the beginning of a prolonged period of civil war, anti-foreign feeling in China grew rapidly. But the bishop seemed to be oblivious to it.

When World War I ended, he felt that his work as a bishop was nearly done, and it was then that he threw himself into his passion for collecting. By the time in 1924 when, on leave in Toronto, White came to call on Currelly, with a fine Chinese painting under his arm, he knew a great deal about archaeology and about the value of the finds being excavated in his area. He also knew what he wanted. It was precisely what Currelly had wanted twenty years before: recognition as an official collector for the Royal Ontario Museum. White knew George Crofts, and would have been aware of Crofts's present misfortunes. It was an appropriate moment to make the approach to the Museum. White and Currelly discovered that they had been at the University of Toronto at the same time, White at Wycliffe College, a Church of England establishment, and Currelly at Victoria, a Methodist one. They had both begun their careers as missionaries, but they came from quite different backgrounds. Currelly had had a secure, happy upbringing, White a narrow, puritanical one.

Currelly does not say much about their first meeting in *I Brought the Ages Home*, and curiously, in his annual reports, he does not acknowledge Bishop White as the source from which flowed year by year huge shipments of immensely valuable Chinese artifacts. This may well have been at the bishop's own request. The church authorities in Toronto might not have been pleased to know that their bishop had been spending so much of his time in archaeological pursuits. It was not until ten years later in 1934, when the bishop was driven out of China by the civil war and the increasing anti-foreign feeling and returned to become a professor in the University of Toronto and keeper of the East Asiatic collection in the Museum, that his great contribution was openly acknowledged. The hundreds of letters the two men exchanged, preserved now in the Museum's archives, show how closely they worked together. But what Currelly was seeing at that first meeting was someone who for fourteen years had been a bishop. He was quick to recognize that the area in which Bishop White would be working was yielding artifacts of a much earlier period, the Bronze and Iron ages, and could add immensely to the value of the Museum's already extensive collection. He encouraged White to send back whatever he could, especially early bronzes of the Shang period.

Both men had found what they were looking for. In the next ten years, before White was forced to flee from China, he was to send back to the Museum a steady stream of valuable artifacts. Currelly's encouragement had let loose his driving ambition. White now dreamed not of high ecclesiastical office, but of fame as the builder of the greatest collection of Chinese art outside the mainland of China.

In the passion for collecting which had seized him, Bishop White no

longer felt bound by the limits that Currelly had placed on his acquisitions. Unconsciously echoing Currelly's triumphant letters to Sir
Edmund Walker, White wrote to Currelly, "I have practically cleaned out
the collections in the city shops." The two men were united in their desire
to get everything they could while the going was good. Reading the
hundreds of letters that passed between them, one sometimes has the eerie
feeling of listening in to the whispered conversation of conspirators. On
20 January 1926 the bishop wrote to Currelly.

> I was somewhat worried about what a dealer said today. He asked me not to
> let people see the good Shang bowl, and I gather there is criticism of the
> best things being bought by foreigners, and sent away from China. The
> present nationalistic feeling in China is really anti-foreign and it is going to
> hinder the exportation of Chinese antiquities.

Currelly replied on 15 February: "There is no doubt that a settled
China would try to make it difficult to export the antiquities. I feel
therefore there is all the more need to make hay while the sun shines."
When the Legislative Yuan in Nanking passed a new law in May 1930
dealing with the "preservation of all antiques and ancient relics of the
country" and stated that "exportation to foreign countries is strictly
prohibited", the bishop was indignant about "the present selfish and
narrow anti-foreign attitude".

Some of the treasures the bishop acquired were unique. The great
Buddhist wall-painting which can be seen in the gallery bearing his name
came from a temple in Shansi (Shanxi) province. It is considered one of
the world's major art treasures. The description in Currelly's memoir of
how the fresco was taken apart into eighty pieces is an exciting account;
its reassembly on the wall of a gallery in Toronto, its preservation, and
finally its recent conservation treatment constitute a magnificent example
of science coming to the aid of art.

Two bronze bells from a royal tomb, cast about the time of Confucius; a
stone sundial incised to give not only the hour but the precise segment of
it which would have lapsed at any particular moment; and the more than
forty thousand volumes of the H. H. Mu Library—cheaply though the
bishop had acquired these treasures, the cost was far beyond the Museum's
capacity to pay. But he could not resist them. They extended the scope of
the Museum's acquisitions until, in the words of Lewis Walmsley, the
Chinese galleries of the Museum displayed "all the fascination inherent in
the development of Chinese culture through thousands of years".

As always, donors came to the rescue, recognizing that White had had to seize his chances and could not wait for authorization. The donors were not all wealthy; some were scholars like Sir Robert Falconer, the president of the University of Toronto, and the bishop himself contributed. White's greatest period of collecting began at the time of the Wall Street crash in 1929 and continued with increasing investment through the earliest and worst years of the Depression when ready money was scarce. The bishop remained jaunty throughout. At one point when he had run the Museum bank account into an overdraft of ninety thousand dollars he wrote to Miss Greenaway, Currelly's executive assistant: "Tell the professor not to worry in the slightest on my account with regard to payment. Although I am sorry for the embarrassment I have caused you, I am greatly elated that the Museum has these priceless things."

White assured the chairman of the board of trustees of the Museum that the objects he had acquired in the past two years were no financial risk. He instanced: "One bronze jar which cost the Museum $1200 if returned to me here could probably sell for $10 000." Having been informed by Currelly that the board remained uneasy, he immediately wrote a charming letter to the chairman, assuring him that he was in no hurry for the money: "The question of payment does not concern me much but I am concerned that the Museum should retain these valuable articles." He recommended that the board should repay him in instalments, a certain sum annually—he was obviously not pressed for money. He was advised on 23 November 1932 that his letter, when read at the board meeting, "created the greatest interest and every member of the Board expressed his deep appreciation over your generous offer to carry over your claim against the Museum on annual payments". How White managed to carry the huge sums involved on a bishop's salary is a mystery that remains unexplained.

Before White's purchasing had been completed, all accounts with the Museum had been settled. In his passion for collection he appeared as clever and as ruthless as any gifted dealer. He knew about people who had fallen on hard times and might be prepared to part with their treasures for a small price. He kept his eye on people who were ailing and might die soon, at which time certain pieces he desired might be easy to obtain. The H. H. Mu Library had been collected by a Chinese scholar, Mu Hsüeh-hsün (Mu Xuexun), who had been Chinese secretary to the German legation in Peking until his death in 1929. The bishop had heard of the library on a missionary trip to Peking. The family had decided to sell it, but only to an institution of learning that would keep it intact and maintain the association with the Mu name. The bishop lost no time. Without consulting Currelly, he immediately made an offer, which was accepted, of approximately $9000, about one-third of the price normally paid at that time for a collection of such magnitude. He then wrote to Dr H. J. Cody, president of the University of Toronto, on 27 March 1933.

> I cannot begin to tell you all the good things of this library. . . . It seems a bad way of doing things, to go ahead and buy a large library and then solicit subscriptions from you. But I know it will be of outstanding importance to Toronto and to Canada in the future and I doubt whether I shall be able to do any greater thing for Toronto than that of getting this Library.

Bishop White himself proposed to bear part of the cost of the library, and Dr Ferguson, who was instrumental in obtaining an export permit for it, had already made a contribution towards the purchase price. Dr Cody lost no time in obtaining further subscriptions from Sir Robert Mond and Sigmund Samuel, two old friends who had always given generously to the Museum. Soon after the purchase the Chinese government brought in very strict regulations concerning the export of Chinese books, and prohibited altogether the export of books published before 1851. Dr Ferguson's influence with the Chinese government enabled him to work out a suitable compromise whereby the Committee on the Preservation of Antiquities accepted three volumes, published in the Ming dynasty, for presentation to the National Library of Peking, and "some tens of volumes" to be donated to the Documents Department of the Palace Museum.

But Bishop White's days as a collector were drawing to an end. All the world was now after Chinese treasures, and he was encountering increasing competition from wealthy connoisseurs and their agents. At the same time Chinese officials had awakened to the flood of antiquities making their way to the West, and the government in Nanking had enacted a ban on all exports of antiquities. Civil war had broken out again, and Japan was threatening invasion from Manchuria. In 1933 missionaries and foreigners were advised by their governments to leave China.

White was ready. He felt that the future of the mission was clouded and, in any case, his interest in it had been waning as the passion for collecting dominated him. He was always to remain devoted to his religion. But for the moment it was subordinated to another element in his nature, ambition for fame. He had risen as far as he could in the service of the church, to the princely rank of bishop. Circumstances, not wilful desire on his part, had brought his career in China to a conclusion. Moreover, by 1933 his wife's health was concerning him and made a return to Canada necessary. Even before this, however, he had conceived the idea of using the considerable knowledge he had acquired of Chinese history and culture to promote a new career for himself as a museum curator and a university professor.

The man who had taught White at Wycliffe, Dr H. J. Cody, had become president of the University in 1932 on Sir Robert Falconer's retirement. When White had been on leave in Toronto in 1931, no doubt to discuss with the Mission Board the future of the mission in China, he had consulted Cody about his project for the establishment in the University of Toronto of a School of Chinese Studies, for which the remarkable collections in the Museum would be a working laboratory. It was part of the plan that the keeper of the Chinese collection should act as associate professor of Chinese studies in the University. Cody thought the suggestion sound and asked White to prepare a brief memorandum of the proposal which he could introduce at a meeting of the board of governors of the University. He must also have asked what Currelly thought of the proposal, since nothing that affected the Royal Ontario Museum of Archaeology could be discussed without the director's knowledge. It can be assumed that Currelly wholeheartedly approved; perhaps he even collaborated in the wording of the memorandum, a draft of which, undated and unsigned, is in the Museum archives.

Currelly brought pressure to bear on the Museum's trustees to make the submission an official one from the board, rather than a self-seeking one from an applicant not yet a member of the Museum's staff. The memorandum laid emphasis on the economic advantage of the proposal to Canada, as well as on the benefits to the thought and general culture of the people of Canada. It then set out in seven clauses the advantages of founding a School of Chinese Studies in the University. Its author marshalled the arguments. The Royal Ontario Museum's collection of Chinese antiquities was already acknowledged to be one of the greatest in the world. No Chinese department existed in any other university in Canada, whereas in Europe, and in England particularly, several chairs and professorships had been established, most notably in Cambridge University and at the Courtauld Institute of Art, affiliated with the University of London. The close association of the Royal Ontario Museum and the University of Toronto offered the ideal combination of a university course and a laboratory for the study of Chinese life and culture. The function of the new department would be to bridge the Pacific and to enable the cultures of the East and of the West to be better understood by their respective peoples.

The application in the first instance was unsuccessful, Dr Cody advising the chairman of the Museum's board on 22 June 1932 that there was "no hope of establishing a Chinese chair in the University" at that time. As a campaigner of long experience, Currelly knew that "no hope" could be turned to inviting prospects if someone could be persuaded to endow the chair. He recalled that the retiring president of the University, Sir Robert Falconer, was a trustee of the Carnegie Corporation of New York.

It took a little time, but on 17 January 1933, about a year before the bishop was forced by the rapid approach of the Communists to leave Kaifeng, Currelly was able to write to him:

> I have been in New York trying to drum up money for a Chinese professorship, and I have every reason to think that the Carnegie Corporation will give it. I am to see Dr Cody in a few days, and he will then make a specific request for the money.
>
> The Carnegie people propose a three years' trial to see if the plan is successful, in other words, to see if you're a success, with the understanding that if things are then all right, the department will be endowed.

The bishop took up his duties at the University of Toronto in 1934, and in the beginning conscientiously reported to his director on every move he proposed to make in his master-plan, even asking humbly for leaves of absence to attend the General Synod of the Church of England in Montreal and to give three lectures on Chinese archaeological subjects in connection with an exhibition of Chinese art in San Francisco. On 29 October 1934 he gave his inaugural address as associate professor of archaeology (Chinese) in the University of Toronto.

It was the beginning of term, but there were as yet no students registered for the course. The Museum collections had to be organized, and there was a great mass of material which had to be examined, classified, and recorded before it could function as the essential laboratory for the study of Chinese life and culture.

When in 1936 the course opened, White proved to be an inspired teacher. One of his students recollected:

> When we were under his instruction we went into another world away from the stress and strain of the work-a-day world.... One felt in his presence a sense of complete and intense involvement in the subject under discussion. His enthusiasm carried a contagion.

But outside the classroom, among his colleagues at the University and the Museum, it was not long before there were signs of strain and abrasion. To those aware only of the bishop's supreme contribution to the

Museum's famous collection, this comes as a shock. Reading his diary and letters, one is impressed by the genuine spiritual humility of the man. That a bishop should have had this spare-time fascination with archaeology seemed a pleasantly harmless addiction. That he should have learnt the Chinese language so thoroughly as to have become a master of the country's history and to have acquired a knowledge of its culture seemed to make him an ideal curator of a museum's collection and, granted the necessary scholarship, a suitable head of a department in a university concerned with Chinese art and culture.

What this overlooks is that Bishop White was trained neither as a scholar nor an archaeologist. Currelly had had field experience under a famous archaeologist. He had had to struggle to acquire a scholar's knowledge of all the processes a valuable artifact goes through from its first emergence from darkness to the marketplace, and eventually to its place in a museum. The bishop had none of these advantages. Moreover, while most of his missionaries had not questioned his authority as a bishop, his subordinates in the academic world felt perfectly free to express their own opinions.

F. St George Spendlove, who had joined the Museum as an assistant to Bishop White, was a scholar who had completed the diploma course in Chinese archaeology at the Courtauld Institute of Art in 1935/1936. He had been appointed assistant secretary and editor of the catalogue of the very successful international exhibition of Chinese art at the Royal Academy in London. Returning to Canada, he had written to Bishop White from his home in Montreal, asking if they could meet to discuss the future of Chinese studies in Canada. The meeting had taken place; the bishop had been impressed and subsequently wrote to ask Spendlove if he would like to assist him in the Museum and in his course at the University at a very small salary. This offer was confirmed by Currelly as director, the "nominal" salary being six hundred dollars a year. Spendlove had means of his own, although not substantial ones. He agreed to accept the offer, provided the six hundred dollars was designated a subsistence allowance and not a salary. He took up his duties at the end of November 1936.

It seems possible that White thought he had found the ideal assistant in Spendlove, a scholar with experience in lecturing on Chinese art. The bishop had just commenced his course at the University, which had taken a full year to organize, and he was finding the work of composing his lectures and keeping up with the cataloguing of the collection too much for him. The arrangement did not work out as he had fondly hoped. Spendlove was happy to be part of the Museum and soon became completely immersed in the riches of the collection, acting towards it more as an independent researcher than an assistant to the keeper. And he was not to prove as submissive to the bishop's views as some of the young missionaries in Kaifeng had been. Disputes between the two men soon began, growing more acrimonious as time went on. In the end there was an all-out row, which could be heard up and down the corridor, "so that we all," as one listener recollects, "ducked for cover". This was in 1942, when Spendlove was forty-five years old. He could stand it no longer and told Currelly that he wished to resign.

Currelly liked Spendlove and realized his great potential as a curator. Too well by this time he knew the bishop's character. He moved Spendlove, giving him the title of assistant keeper of the Modern European collection, thereby bringing Spendlove directly under his authority as director over all the archaeological collections. Some years later Spendlove became the first curator of the Canadiana collections in the new building for which Sigmund Samuel and the Province of Ontario had shared the costs; it opened to the public in 1951. He made this change at the special and warm invitation of Sigmund Samuel himself, and with Currelly's approval. Between Spendlove and Samuel there grew to be a complete understanding, which had proved impossible with Bishop White.

～～

The chair of Chinese studies at the University of Toronto had been formally endowed in 1942, with Bishop White as the first occupant. Between then and the end of World War II was a time of strain for everybody. With the end of hostilities in 1945 there came a call for help from Honan, where the Chinese bishop who had succeeded White found himself overwhelmed by the strain of reconstruction. He appealed to the primate of the Church of England in Canada, asking that Bishop White should be sent back to help. It was an appeal that White could not resist. He was granted a year's leave of absence from the School of Chinese Studies and the Museum, and he left for Honan in the spring of 1946. His place was temporarily taken by Dr Richard C. Rudolph who had become assistant keeper of the East Asiatic collection in July 1945, and in April 1946 was named acting director of the School of Chinese Studies.

White had been eager to get back to the place where he had lived so long, not altogether forgetting his now burning archaeological interest and the opportunities the return seemed to offer of further enriching the Museum's collection. He seems to have been as oblivious to the actual state of affairs in China at that moment as he had been to the growing anti-foreign feeling in the years after the revolution of 1911. There was to be little time or opportunity for archaeological acquisitions. China was boiling over.

White was seventy-three when he reached Honan. He found everything in a state of complete confusion. War had swept over the countryside, leaving a people suffering from disease and hunger. He tackled with surprising energy in a man of his age the problem of relief work, but runaway inflation and flagging morale on the Nationalist side, as Mao Tse-tung's (Mao Zedong) Communist forces advanced towards the north, made every effort useless. White soon saw that nothing could be done to save the situation.

The war in China and the ascendancy of the Chinese Communists over the Nationalist forces of Chiang Kai-shek had changed everything. As early as 1942 Mao Tse-tung had exhorted his supporters to "take over all the fine things in our literary and artistic history, critically assimilate whatever is beneficial and use them as examples when we create works out of the literary and artistic raw materials in the life of the people of our own time and place". Henceforth Chinese archaeology was to be firmly in Chinese hands.

Chinese archaeologists were specially encouraged. Foreign intervention in this field was forbidden; the day of the collector was over. When White left Kaifeng in 1947, it was as though a door had slammed behind him. The Museum would have to depend for any additions to its extensive collection on private gifts and benefactions. The pace of acquisition was to slow considerably, although some important accessions were made at intervals. In 1955 Major James E. Hahn presented a collection of Ming and Ch'ing dynasty lacquers, for which the lacquer court was built. Mrs Edgar J. Stone, who for fifteen years was a member of the board of trustees of the Museum and who travelled extensively with her husband, was also a generous donor. Among her many gifts was a collection of Chinese textiles and furniture. She greatly admired Bishop White and after his death organized the Bishop White Fund in his memory to provide assistance to the Far Eastern Department.

White left to return to Toronto in May 1947, a few weeks before the Communist forces launched their attack on Kaifeng. He had written ahead to the board secretary, Miss Helen Reynar, to tell her of his early return: "If Dr Rudolph is getting along all right I do not want to disturb him. All I shall need is a corner in the Museum where I can pursue my research."

But Rudolph had already left when the bishop returned, and in any event the University had become dissatisfied with the results of the course on Chinese art and archaeology organized by the bishop in May 1943, when Statute No. 1592 of the senate of the University of Toronto had authorized the establishment of a School of Chinese Studies. Sixty-one students had registered for the first year's courses, but in 1946 only three had registered. The University saw the need of change and, in Walmsley's words, realized that "the time had arrived when the scope of instruction must expand and shift in emphasis from archaeological studies to more intensive courses in language, history and civilization, religion, and culture". And White himself was ready to retire.

A new Department of East Asiatic (later Asian) Studies was established by the University in place of the School of Chinese Studies, and Lewis C. Walmsley was put in charge of it. Meanwhile Helen Fernald was named curator of the Far Eastern Department (formerly the East Asiatic Department) of the Museum. Bishop White's status was recognized by the title "Keeper Emeritus". White was to devote the rest of his life to writing and to church work.

~~~

White and Currelly stand out as two major figures in the early history of the Royal Ontario Museum. Currelly's contribution was unquestionably the larger; he covered the whole field of art and archaeology and had the supreme quality of the museum director, the ability to get the best out of all who worked with him. White was totally lacking in this ability; he had an unfortunate capacity for irritating his subordinates. Both men had the sensitivity of artists, another quality instinctive with curators who look upon their collections as the instruments through which they project their vision.

Bishop White was the more complex personality. The fierce intensity of his character was remarkable. It is reflected in the diary he had kept since he was a student, into which, in the loneliness of his first years in China, he had poured out all his inmost thoughts, his longing for humility, his detestation of his own pride. "Spiritual self-flagellation," one of his biographers was to call it. But nobody could question his faith or his longing to serve. Only later—the diary goes on for years—does it seem possible that such intense concentration might have been disguised ambition, and that the temptation he was finally unable to overcome was the ambition for fame, even the fame of a martyr, rather than nothingness. He had become a bishop before he became an archaeologist. It was on the recommendation in his report that he had been elevated to the position of head of the Church of England mission in a huge province of North Central China. We know that he gloried in the pomp and panoply that went with the rank; the figure of the young missionary in isolated posts who grew a queue and dressed in Chinese clothes vanishes like a wisp of smoke in the presence of the bishop in the more sophisticated surroundings of Kaifeng, proud of his robes and decorations and rank, lording it over the young missionaries under his control. But even the episcopate palled as, finding himself in an area rich in archaeological treasures, his interest in China's history and culture grew, and ambition of another kind took control—the desire to become a scholar like the mandarins whose manner and bearing and intellectual command had so much impressed him.

White's visit to Currelly in 1924 had been speculative, but it was in line with his ambition for wider fame. Currelly had the gift for igniting latent enthusiasms in those capable of serving his Museum. Though he did not much like White at their first meeting, he saw in him someone ideally placed to complete the work which Crofts had begun; and he became quite attached to him in the next ten years as they exchanged long and frequent letters. These letters make strange reading today, when ethical attitudes towards acquisitions make past practices seem heinous, the more so because they were written by a man of the cloth and a man who had begun his career as a missionary. What Currelly had been doing in Egypt twenty years earlier was what the bishop was then doing in China. The Museum's life, like that of all museums, even the great and world-famous ones whose collections had been built in the 19th century, depended on snatching these treasures while there was still time.

The Royal Ontario Museum owes a part of its fame to the endeavours of Bishop White, whose complex character has attracted the attention of biographers. There have been two searching studies of his life and character. Lewis C. Walmsley's *Bishop in Honan* was commissioned by the bishop's admirers, and could have been merely adulatory. But Walmsley is too much a scholar not to plumb the depths of White's character, and while the book praises the bishop it also misses none of the defects which, as much as the praiseworthy elements, are the explanation for his ultimate fame. Charles Taylor's study of White in *Six Journeys: A Canadian Pattern* has deeper psychological perceptions, although it owes something to paths which Walmsley had to tread more lightly. Both books are essential to a full understanding of a complex character.

~~

With Mao Tse-tung's final victory and the expulsion of Chiang Kai-shek in 1949, the door on foreign archaeological work in China was firmly shut. From 1949 onwards, and especially in the years of the Cultural Revolution from 1966 to 1976, the scale of field work carried out by

Sir Edmund Walker. (Photo: Ashley & Crippen.)

Right: Charles Trick Currelly. (Photo: Ashley & Crippen.)

Below: A meeting of the Royal Commission of 1905/1906. *Left to right:* the Reverend D. Bruce Macdonald, the Reverend H. J. Cody, Sir William Meredith, Joseph Flavelle, A. H. U. Colquhoun, Goldwin Smith, Edmund Walker. (Photo: Courtesy Archives of Ontario, Ref. S800.)

Group of Torontonians at the Pyramids in 1909; some of them went on to visit Charles Currelly at Deir el-Bahri. The party included (*left to right*) Charles Cockshutt, Mrs H. D. Warren, Gordon Osler, Mrs G. Osler, and Edmund Osler.

A field expedition of the Royal Ontario Museum of Zoology to Port Sydney, Ontario, in July 1919. *Left to right:* E. M. Walker, L. L. Snyder, E. B. S. Logier, N. K. Bigelow.

W. A. Parks (*right*) and Levi Sternberg on a field trip to the Alberta Badlands in 1921. (Photo: National Museum of Natural Sciences, National Museums of Canada, Ottawa, Neg. 46586.)

A. P. Coleman (*right*), at an annual camp of the Canadian Alpine Club at Maligne Lake, Jasper National Park, Alberta, with Captain C. G. Crawford who was a member of the second Mount Everest expedition.

TOURNAMENT (1475) KNIGHTS CLAD IN CAP A PIE SUITS OF PLATE ARMOUR JOUSTING AT THE BARRIER

A mural in the Armour Court, painted by the artist Sylvia Hahn in the early 1940s. The artist modelled her medieval figures on members of the Museum staff. *Left to right:* Mr Fortune, Alfred Petrie, Bishop W. C. White, unidentified man, James M. Menzies, Katharine B. Maw (later Brett), Ella Martin, Ruth Home, Homer Thompson, J. H. Classey, T. F. McIlwraith, Charles Trick Currelly, Mary Campbell.

Left: George Crofts. (Photo: Louis Langfier, London.)

Below: Bishop W. C. White in Honan province, China.

MUSEUM BUILDING

A the Chairman
of the Board of
Trustees of the

ROYAL
ONTARIO
MUSEUM

it is my great privilege
to offer to Your Royal
Highness our sincere thanks for your gracious
kindness in honouring the proceedings of the day by
your presence.

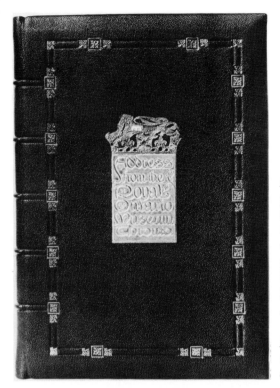

Left: Inlaid and tooled leather cover of the presentation copy of the chairman of the board's address at the official opening of the Royal Ontario Museum on 19 March 1914. The copy was presented to the Duke of Connaught, the governor general of Canada.

Opposite is a page of the presentation copy, hand-lettered and illuminated by Toronto artist A. H. Howard.

Below: View of the 1914 building of the Royal Ontario Museum, showing the front entrance on Bloor Street.

Right: One of many photographs sent from Tientsin by George Crofts to Charles Currelly illustrating objects available to him in China. The objects in the photographs were numbered for identification. These two T'ang dynasty (A.D. 618–906) ceramic tomb figures of guardians were acquired for the Far Eastern collections, along with several others, through a gift of Mrs H. D. Warren.

Below: A gallery of the Royal Ontario Museum of Archaeology in the 1914 building, with crowded cases of Chinese artifacts.

Opposite: The construction site of the 1931/1933 addition to the Royal Ontario Museum on 14 April 1931, with the east wing rising in the foreground and the building connecting it to the west wing visible at the extreme right of the photograph.
Below is a view of the façade and front entrance after completion.

Above: The Rotunda of the 1931/1933 addition, with its Venetian glass mosaic ceiling and view into the Armour Court.

Right: "Mountain Chief" totem pole made by the Tsimshian Indians from Geetiks, Lower Nass River, British Columbia. The pole was installed in the north stairwell of the 1931/1933 addition to the Museum.

THIS IS THE LAST WORD IN MUSEUM DESIGNING

The technique of museum showmanship has made immense strides in the last few years, and the Royal Ontario Museum embodies every device for making exhibits more interesting and instructive. Almost all of the new exhibition halls are now open to the public.

The pictures in the top row show exhibits in the Zoological Section.

The middle picture in the second row is from the same section, and shows an exceptionally lifelike posing and grouping of grown lions and very young cubs.

The other second row pictures show the beautiful architecture of the main entrance hall and its stairways, the one on the left giving a glimpse of the top of the totem pole which is set up in the staircase well.

Bottom left, the Chinese funerary monuments, probably the finest exhibit of this kind of art in the world. Bottom right, "Venus the Mother" at the entry to the hall of ancient sculpture, pottery and armor.

—*Leica Camera Studies by "Ess", exclusive to Saturday Night. Copyright.*

A page in the 15 July 1933 issue of *Saturday Night,* highlighting the new galleries of the 1931/1933 east wing of the Museum. (Photo: Courtesy *Saturday Night.*)

Right: Saturday Morning Club members drawing in the Armour Court in 1949.

Below: Ella Martin conducting a tour in the Egyptian galleries. She is showing the children the casts of the wall-reliefs made by Charles Currelly at Deir el-Bahri in 1909.

The Sigmund Samuel Canadiana Gallery, on Queen's Park Crescent, which officially opened to the public in 1951. The façade sculptures, done by the artist Jacobine Jones, depict Samuel de Champlain, Major General James Wolfe, John Graves Simcoe, and General Isaac Brock.

Right: The expanding Bickell Globe in the geology gallery after the 1957 renovation. The globe, named after J. P. Bickell, whose foundation made the gallery possible, took three years to build.

Below: The McLaughlin Planetarium, on Queen's Park just south of the Museum building, which opened to the public in 1968. The planetarium was made possible by a very generous gift from Colonel R. S. McLaughlin.

Chinese archaeologists was immense. In the opinion of Barbara Stephen, who was acting head of the Far Eastern Department before becoming associate director of the Museum, the achievements and drama of these years were comparable with those of the earlier days of Western archaeology, when the riches of classical antiquity and of the biblical lands were being unearthed.

Much of this new archaeological work was concentrated in the area near Anyang and Loyang, where Bishop White had been active. All his eager collecting had not blinded him to the fact that the excavations of his day were only scratching the surface of buried wealth beneath. Charles Taylor records that in 1943 White had predicted that a great day for archaeology in China would dawn with the end of the war, and that what had been dug up thus far was "but tokens of further treasures to be uncovered, and deeper revelations to be unfolded".

After twenty-five years of silence Chinese archaeology burst upon the Western scene with the *Exhibition of Archaeological Finds of the People's Republic of China,* which visited Toronto in 1974 following long stays in London and Paris. This was flattering recognition of the international standing of the Royal Ontario Museum's Chinese collection.

The Chinese had organized an exhibition of objects from the period of Early Man in China to the 14th century A.D. Following Marxist analysis, they see human history to date as marked by five consecutive social systems—primitive, slaveholding, feudal, capitalist, and socialist. In this scheme "primitive society" covers the long span of human development from the earliest times to the late Neolithic period, at which point class society developed, together with a pattern of exploitation of the labour of the working people, leading at last to the advent of socialism.

What Chinese archaeology has thus provided is a magnification of the view of China's past to which all of us are heirs. Human history is pushed back beyond the Shang dynasty to the Hsia (Xia) period of the 20th to the 16th century B.C. when China first advanced to statehood. A balance is restored, to some extent, between what the West first discovered about its historical roots in ancient Mesopotamia and Egypt and what the East has now revealed through its intense and specialized archaeological researches.

10

In Search of an Identity

The Royal Ontario Museum, which had been closed to the public during the process of renovation and the building of the new wing, was officially reopened on 12 October 1933. The cost of the work had been $1.8 million, compared with $400 000 for the west wing twenty years before. With the addition in 1937 of two upper floors to the small extension that abutted the southern end of the original wing, the Museum became the largest museum in the British Commonwealth outside London.

Now that the unbearable congestion from which the Museum had been suffering was relieved, it was possible to see in the enlarged gallery space the remarkable growth that had taken place in all the collections. What the Museum visitor could not see was the greater convenience and elbow-room each of the departments now enjoyed—the workrooms, laboratories, storage spaces, and offices, all close to the collections, making possible frequent changes of display. This was a museum that could bear comparison with any in the leading cities in the United States, and with all but the most illustrious of the famous museums of Europe.

In the twenty years since its opening, the Royal Ontario Museum had come of age. But the administrative structure to manage this hydra-headed beast had not kept pace. The committee of directors met monthly as it had done in Sir Edmund Walker's time. The minutes were kept by the secretary of the board of trustees, Helen Reynar. Most of the matters dealt with by the four professor/directors and Currelly were mere housekeeping details. The directors had no powers of decision; all they could do was to pass resolutions and forward recommendations, which the secretary would present to the board at its next meeting.

The passage of time had brought changes among the directors who reigned over the scientific collections. Dr A. P. Coleman had retired from the Royal Ontario Museum of Geology in 1922 and had been succeeded by Dr E. S. Moore, who was to remain director through 1945. At the beginning of 1946 the museums of geology and mineralogy, which had been closely related for many years, were merged to become the Royal Ontario Museum of Geology and Mineralogy. Moore continued as director of the combined museum until 1949, when he retired and was succeeded by Dr V. B. Meen.

Dr T. L. Walker, a shy, reserved scholar who had been appointed the first director of the Royal Ontario Museum of Mineralogy, had not had the temperament for contact with the public, and though he did not retire until 1937, ill health made his last years inactive. But he was a distinguished mineralogist, and it was during his directorship that the mineralogy museum experienced the first rapid growth that was to make it a world leader in its field. Walker was succeeded by Dr A. L. Parsons, who had been appointed assistant director in 1921. In a brief history of the mineralogy museum written in 1939, Parsons admitted that the collection could not have grown as it had done without extensive research, but that most of the research had been carried out in the University, not in the Museum, which had only recently been equipped with a laboratory for the chemical examination of minerals. When Parsons had joined the Royal Ontario Museum of Mineralogy in 1920 as unofficial (unpaid) assistant, the staff had consisted of "the director, one assistant for cataloguing and stenographic work, and a part-time preparator". By the mid-1930s the staff had increased only by the addition of one lecturer.

Dr W. A. Parks, first director of the Royal Ontario Museum of Palaeontology, had become much more of a "museum man" than some of his scientific colleagues, responding vigorously to the enormous public interest shown in his collection and display. Parks had been the strongest supporter of Sir Edmund Walker's plan for a university museum with a public face. He too had a large University department to supervise, but his mind was constantly involved with the problems of the growing Museum. On his sudden death in 1936, his favourite pupil, Dr Madeleine A. Fritz, who had come into the Museum when she obtained her Ph.D. in 1927, had been appointed acting director of the large vertebrate collection, as well as of the invertebrate collection in which her training and interest chiefly lay. This was soon found to be too much for one director to look after, and Dr Loris S. Russell, who was on the staff of the Geological Survey of Canada, joined the Museum in 1937 as assistant director of vertebrate palaeontology; Dr Fritz became assistant director of invertebrate palaeontology.

Presiding over departments that were understaffed and underequipped for scientific research, all of these people were overworked. Those who survived the strain best were men like Parks, buoyed up perhaps by the almost annual expeditions to the Red Deer River district of Alberta and the resulting haul of dinosaurs brought back to fascinate the public, and Dr B. A. Bensley, first director of the Royal Ontario Museum of Zoology. Amiable, cheerful, and capable, Bensley had entrusted to his young assistants—L. L. Snyder, E. B. S. Logier, T. B. Kurata, J. L. Baillie, and T. M. Shortt—the work of cataloguing the specimens that flowed in in increasing numbers from nature lovers in Ontario.

On Bensley's death in 1934 Dr J. R. Dymond, who had joined the zoological museum as "secretary" in 1922, and had become assistant director in 1931, succeeded to the directorship. From the beginning he had identified himself with Bensley's group of gifted assistants, joining their expeditions as they collected specimens, drew and painted them, prepared them for exhibition, and in the process became experts in their particular interests. These men built up an enthusiastic following for the Museum, becoming in effect the first curators, although often without the title.

The University still held sway over the scientific collections, and at this turning-point in the Museum's history, praiseworthy though their growth had been, the collections remained chiefly representative of Ontario's and Canada's resources. This had been the charter for research in each of the science museums: in zoology to study the flora and fauna, in palaeontology to uncover the fossil record, and in the earth sciences to provide a comprehensive collection of rocks and minerals, and, in general, to carry out a more detailed examination of Ontario's resources than the Geological Survey of Canada had been able to do in its steady advance in the mapping of half a continent. The Geological Survey, in addition to its cartographic function, had had the secondary task of advising mine operators about the possibility of metal-bearing formations. As the Geological Survey's historian, Morris Zaslow, wrote: "They not only mapped the geology, they collected materials from every phase of life they encountered—samples of rocks and minerals, plants, animals, fishes, birds, Indian and Eskimo artifacts, even languages and legends."

But the members of the Geological Survey could not pause to research each region in depth. They were the pioneers. Their heroic efforts brought into being what was to become the National Museum of Canada at very little cost to the taxpayers. Towards the end of the 19th century the Ontario Bureau of Mines became very actively involved in the detailed examination and mapping of northern Ontario.

The close attachment of the science museums to their corresponding university departments had two effects. Where research and expenditure on staff were concerned, the museums came second, not first. And curatorship, a word not yet in use, but meaning the responsibility for the growth and interpretation of a collection, came to depend on the possession of a postgraduate degree. The technicians, who were carrying out the duties of curators, were largely precluded by this barrier from advancement beyond a certain point, and consequently from the recognition and the salary levels to which they felt entitled by their accomplishments. The specialists, for their part, comparing their salaries with those of their University counterparts, also considered themselves to be underpaid; and they had difficulty in defining their place in the administrative system. The dissatisfaction and resentments thus generated were to increase with time, particularly when the administrators appeared on the scene in increasing numbers.

~~

There is little doubt that by the mid-1930s the international recognition that was beginning to be accorded to the Royal Ontario Museum came both from its reputation as a research institution and from the riches of its growing collections. While it is not easy to keep the limelight away from Currelly, it must be remembered that international recognition came from acceptance by world scholars in related fields of study, as exhibited material became correctly and fully documented, acceptably organized and labelled, and published in the special journals of related disciplines.

Currelly deserves total credit for the energy, boldness, self-confidence, and enthusiasm which had won him in his younger days the affection of influential older men like Flinders Petrie, Holman Hunt, and C. G. Seligman and the support and trust of important collectors like Dr Allen Sturge and famous archaeologists like Sir William Ridgeway of Cambridge University. All called him Carlo, and their letters show the warmth of their interest in him. This ability to win people's trust, which Currelly appeared quite unconscious of possessing, added to the luck which all successful collectors must have—such as the luck of his accidental encounter with George C. Crofts—had given his collection a scope and a value far beyond what might have been expected. The scope came from his aim—to show how man had lived in the past; the value from the intensity of his passion to acquire what the Museum needed, not what it could afford to have.

Such a self-confident young man was unlikely to have acquired modesty when he found himself at the age of thirty-eight director of his own museum, the largest of its kind in Canada. His ambition was to make it a museum of world rank. His genius—it was nothing less—for remembering prices and the intricate network of connections he kept up with traders in London and Europe justified him in believing that he was in competition with New York's Metropolitan Museum of Art, the Smithsonian Institution in Washington, and the British Museum and the Victoria and Albert Museum in London. And he was. Though these institutions would not have acknowledged him as a rival, they were after the same things, and he kept crossing their paths. In 1934 the poet Laurence Binyon, who for forty years had been with the British Museum and was an acknowledged authority on oriental art, had written that the Royal Ontario Museum's Chinese collection was second only to the British Museum's, and in some respects was superior to it.

But on the face of it, to claim parity with such majestic institutions was ridiculous. The Smithsonian Institution, for example, had inherited almost $600 000 in gold sovereigns and a fine collection of art from a natural son of the Duke of Northumberland who had taken the name Smithson. Smithson lived in Paris during the French Revolution and had acquired republican sympathies. He became an ardent admirer of Benjamin Franklin, the first ambassador of the new American republic to the new French republic. In his will he left the gold and his art collection to the United States Congress for the specific purpose of founding an institution, which was to be called the Smithsonian Institution and was to be devoted to "the increase and diffusion of knowledge among men". The Smithsonian's financial position was guaranteed by the United States government, as was that of the British Museum by the British government.

In sharp contrast, the Royal Ontario Museum had obtained its collections piece by piece. For thirty-five years it was to remain the ward jointly of the Ontario government and the University of Toronto, never quite sure whose child it really was. The science collections had been bred in academic stringency, aimed in the beginning at graduate and undergraduate students. The collections of the Royal Ontario Museum of Archaeology, apart from an inheritance from an older provincial museum, were the work of one man, incurably extravagant in acquiring anything his museum must have, yet almost painfully frugal in what he spent on himself. Backed by a few well-to-do rather than wealthy patrons, and with grants from the University of Toronto and the Province of Ontario, living year by year on a modest budget, he had accumulated a collection that was little short of miraculous.

Currelly's methods were not unlike those of the notorious Sir Sydney

Cockerell, who had become director of the Fitzwilliam Museum in Cambridge in 1908, and who is said to have "scrounged, bullied and begged his way to countless bequests that immeasurably enriched the holdings of the Museum". So single-minded was Cockerell in his pursuit of funds or objects that his acquisitive powers became legendary, and the chancellor of the university declared, "There is no collector in the world who feels his treasures safe so long as Sir Sydney is in the land."

The speed with which Currelly pounced on the wills of people from whom he had already received a great deal, to see what testamentary provision had been made for his museum, tells much. He was deeply attached to Sir Robert Mond, as Mond was to him. On 10 December 1936, little more than a year before Mond's death, he had written Mond about a discovery, describing the find as "one of the most dramatic things that has happened in the history of the Museum". The letter goes on, "Every time anything really important happens, as well as the joy of getting the material for the country, which is the main thing, I feel a great personal sense of satisfaction that your extraordinary blind trust in me is being justified—because you had mighty little to go on, my friend, when you started backing me." Within a month of Sir Robert Mond's death, Currelly was writing to his friend's lawyers in London:

> I had a letter that you had been asked to allocate the things of the late Sir Robert Mond. I daresay you know that Sir Robert was one of the Board of Governors of this Museum. I most sincerely hope that we may come in for a good slice.

There is no doubt that Mond was his closest confidant and that the two men were on affectionate terms. We learn more from Currelly's letters to Mond of how and why he acquired particular objects or collections year by year than the bare descriptions on the acquisition cards in the Registration Department of the Royal Ontario Museum could possibly reveal. The references vary from "80 pieces of arms and armour, mainly arms of course, but four remarkably fine suits", to "two most amazing Chinese pictures, each 40 feet by 10 feet ... [which] together with our great central picture will make something simply wonderful". Elsewhere he records:

> We have also just received away over ten thousand specimens of Stone Age material from Saskatchewan.... The tremendous drought and the dust storms have blown a lot of the surface topsoil away in certain areas, and have revealed literally thousands of knives, arrowheads, scrapers, spearheads, etc. of the very finest workmanship in America.

An acquisition that brought a more ambiguous renown to the Royal Ontario Museum was the Beardmore relics. Deriving their name from the place north of Lake Superior where they had purportedly been found, these consisted of an ancient sword broken about in half, an axe, and what was perhaps the iron grip of a shield. They were said to have been unearthed when a prospector put a charge of dynamite under the roots of a tree which impeded a trench he was digging in following a vein of ore.

The find had allegedly been made in 1930, but it was brought to the attention of the Museum only in 1936. Currelly wrote Sir Robert Mond that the axe was almost identical with one in the London Museum which had been dredged up from the Thames and that the sword had been identified as a Viking weapon of about A.D. 1000. Currelly added that this would be the very first find of a Viking presence in the interior of North America and would "add at least a paragraph to the early history of the continent". He told Mond that the discovery had been made on an ancient trade route that ran from James Bay to Lake Superior.

Currelly sent Professor T. F. McIlwraith to inspect the site of the discovery and to obtain possession of the relics, which had been found stored in the cellar of a house at Port Arthur in which the prospector had lived. The Museum secured the relics for five hundred dollars and Currelly set about authenticating them. Finally, after corresponding with Norse archaeologists and the director of the National Museum of Iceland and receiving their assurance that sword and axe were of the period of A.D. 1000, Currelly in a short article in the *Canadian Historical Review* of March 1939 declared the Museum's notable find and put it on exhibition.

Subsequently the authenticity of the discovery was called in question. It was not the genuineness of the objects that was in doubt, but whether they had actually been discovered on the northern Ontario site. In 1941 Currelly and a Mr O. C. Elliott, who had read a paper on the subject to Academy II of the Royal Society of Canada, jointly issued a pamphlet in which their differences of opinion were politely aired. In 1956, concerned with the fact that the relics were being used uncritically, even in text-books, as evidence that the Norsemen had indeed penetrated the Upper Great Lakes region almost one thousand years earlier, and hearing that the press was about to raise the question of authenticity, the Museum announced that the whole matter was to be reopened. To absolve itself from any suggestion of bias and to give full publicity to the new inquiry, the Museum asked the Toronto *Globe and Mail* to assign an experienced reporter to assess all the known data and seek new evidence. When the first article appeared in the *Globe and Mail,* a telephone call was made to the Museum by a man who turned out to be the step-son of the man who had claimed to find the relics. He came to the Museum and in Dr A. D. Tushingham's office told his story, which was recorded, and finally made a sworn statement that his earlier affidavit, supporting his step-father's account of the discovery, was false, and that the weapons had in fact been taken to the alleged discovery site from their house in Port Arthur. As a result, the Museum removed the relics from exhibition. A full account of the affair was published by Dr Tushingham in 1966.

If Currelly's enthusiasm seems sometimes to have precipitated commitment to a premature judgement, it has to be remembered that he had gone as far as he could to authenticate the historicity of the relics. But perhaps not far enough to allow for the temptation to which a few hundred dollars can subject human veracity.

~~~

In the meantime World War II had come, temporarily shelving all problems, including the mystery of the Beardmore relics, imposing salary cuts that forced a number of staff members to resign, and suppressing for the duration any question of the relations between the University and the Museum.

Some archaeological research was undertaken. In 1941/1942, at the request of the Society of Jesus, the Museum excavated the ancient site of Fort Ste Marie on the Wye River at Midland, Ontario. This had been the centre of the Jesuit missions in Huronia between 1639 and 1649 and a key position in the attempt of the French in the 17th century to establish an empire in North America. During the war years also the famous Indian site of Cahiague, in Huronia, where the French explorer Champlain spent the winter of 1615, was identified by Margaret Thomson, the assistant to both Professor Homer Thompson and Professor McIlwraith. She began an excavation there which, on and off, has provided a training ground for many of the students in the Department of Anthropology of the University of Toronto.

But shortage of staff and resources stilled nearly all activity that did not directly contribute to the war effort. Many of the men who were to head divisions or curatorial departments in the postwar years were on active service overseas. A number of them had had to abandon graduate studies towards the higher degrees now considered essential for museum work. After the war, coming home fresh from contact with the great European museums, many of them saw their future not so much in the University as in the Museum, more in research than in teaching. It was not until between 1948 and 1950, when they had acquired their Ph.D. degrees, that they came into the Museum.

The return of these scholars was to shed a twilight on the first generation of remarkable men who had come to the Museum in the early years as technicians or draftsmen, and who now held positions of some responsibility. L. L. Snyder, a man of considerable learning but lacking a postgraduate degree, had joined the Museum in 1917 as a draftsman and in 1935 had been appointed head of the division of birds in the Royal Ontario Museum of Zoology. James L. Baillie had come to the Museum in 1922 as a junior assistant in zoology. In the years that followed, Baillie won renown as a popular writer and lecturer and for some years taught ornithology in university extension courses. His hour of greatest fame came when he acquired for the Royal Ontario Museum of Zoology a specimen of the great auk, the flightless seabird of the North Atlantic that had become extinct in 1844, seven years before Audubon's death. The famous painting of the great auk in Audubon's *Birds of America* had been done from a specimen Audubon had obtained in London. It was this specimen which Baillie acquired from Vassar College, in whose possession it had been since 1867. The two other extinct Canadian species that Baillie acquired for the Museum were the Labrador duck and some of the 140 passenger pigeons in the collection.

Baillie was in failing health for the last ten years of his life, and the University's reluctance to promote technicians to full curatorial rank somewhat embittered his end. He had been made an assistant curator in 1960, and the fact that he was passed over for head of the department was not due entirely to academic arrogance. A new period of museum development had arrived. Dr Jon Barlow, who was appointed head of the Department of Ornithology in 1965, acknowledges how much these early self-made specialists had contributed to making the Museum the home of the largest ornithological collection in Canada, and one of the largest in the British Commonwealth, second only to that of the British Museum, which in 1972 had 1 250 000 specimens. The J. H. Fleming bequest to the Museum in 1940 of 33 000 specimens had added enormously to the importance of the collection. Fleming was a Toronto businessman who had devoted much of his life to collecting and acquiring bird specimens and publishing his collections.

The Museum's ornithological collection had been well managed, but the department had lacked the instruments necessary for advancing the level of complexity of the research work in avian biology, such as a spectrophotometer (for quantitative analysis of colour differences), an up-to-date binocular dissecting-scope with its necessary attachments, and an automatic calculator. And little had been done in field research on other continents, essential if the collection was to reach world standards.

There was now a new appreciation of the archival role of the ornithological department in the preservation and study of extinct birds. Several
specimens had formed part of the J. H. Fleming bequest, and others had
been acquired by exchange. The great auk and the Labrador duck had
been species native to Canada, but extinct species that had had their
habitat in distant parts of the world were also represented. In the collection were very rare examples of the New Zealand huia and quail and
several specimens of the Carolina parakeet.

And the field work of the Department of Ornithology had now passed
beyond the general collection of birds to mission-oriented expeditions on
which only particular species were collected for studies of their biology
and evolution. A typical year's field work outside Canada is described in
the annual report of 1970/1971: "We were able to collect generally and to
study vireos, warblers or Savannah sparrows in Jamaica, Grand Cayman
Island, Puerto Rico, St Vincent Island, Costa Rica, British Honduras and
in the Mexican states of Durango, Sinaloa, Jalisco, Oaxaca, Nayarit and
Mexico, as well as in the territory of Baja California and on Guadalupe
Island." Much of this work was financed by the National Research
Council of Canada.

We have come a long way from the time of Charles Darwin, who had
become interested in the study of birds while still at school at Shrewsbury
by reading Gilbert White's *The Natural History of Selborne,* and had
wondered why every gentleman did not become an ornithologist. We are
a long way, too, even from the time of Terry Shortt's three-month Arctic
voyage in 1938 in the Hudson's Bay icebreaker, *Nascopie,* when he
brought out a collection for the Museum that the Dominion of Canada
ornithologist described as "the finest so far brought out of the Arctic by
one man in one year".

That had been a memorable voyage. Shortt had shared a cabin with
Frederick Varley, who was painting Arctic scenes. An occasional visitor to
the gatherings aboard ship had been Bishop Armand Clabaut, Roman
Catholic bishop of the Vicariate Apostolic of Hudson Bay, "a megalithic
man with a back as straight and as flat as an oaken door. . . . [who] wore a
cross that was so big that it was referred to as 'the *Nascopie*'s spare anchor'.
The chain on which it was suspended would have tethered an Eskimo
dog."

The biological study associated with microscopes and fine instruments
brought with it sobriety and earnestness, and we miss the humour of the
pioneers in the field. All of them—Snyder, Logier, Shortt, Baillie, and
Kurata—had worked first for Professor Bensley and then for his equally
amiable successor Professor Dymond. Their field expeditions had been

run on a shoestring. Their work was their training, and they covered all Ontario and eventually all Canada. The early faunal surveys of Ontario, started in 1919, had been the foundation of what were to become the separate departments of ornithology, ichthyology and herpetology, mammalogy, and entomology. Logier's interest in herpetology led to his taking charge under Professor Bensley of the Museum's small collection of snakes, much of which had been acquired by the University from J. H. Garnier, a physician of Lucknow, Ontario, whose collection included snakes from around the world.

The arrival of the scientifically trained men of the next generation, just as the study of evolution in action was beginning to push aside the study of local fauna, heralded a change in emphasis in the work of the Life Sciences departments. Biology offered a new approach, the study of evolution through systematics, which involves the study of speciation, the diversity and differentiation of organisms, and the relationship between them, together with a systematic classification of knowledge concerning them. The first generation of the Museum's scientific workers did not have the advanced training necessary for this research. The most able of them was L. L. Snyder, a born leader who had worked more closely with Professor Dymond than any of the others and had been made assistant director of the Royal Ontario Museum of Zoology in 1938.

~~~

A protest against the changing character of the Museum was bound to be made. It was initiated by Snyder. In 1946 Professor Dymond, then director of the Royal Ontario Museum of Zoology, reported to his fellow directors that he had received a lengthy memorandum from Snyder proposing a five-year plan for the Museum's board. A motion was carried by the committee of directors that the memorandum should be considered at the next meeting, and a committee was set up consisting of Currelly, Snyder, McIlwraith, and the new chairman of the committee of directors, Professor Loris Russell of the Royal Ontario Museum of Palaeontology, to report back on Snyder's proposal.

At the next monthly meeting of the directors in June, McIlwraith brought in the report of the committee. The report was favourable to Snyder's recommendations: that the Museum Act be revised to make the Museum more self-managing; that the new act should provide for the maintenance grant to be paid directly to the Museum instead of through the University; that the executive body of the Museum should be the committee of directors, who would be given full administrative power; and that the board should be enlarged to represent all parts of the province and should assume the status of a consultative body, meeting twice a year to settle matters of policy. Snyder's memorandum pointed out that the classification of staff into Museum employees paid wholly by the Museum, employees shared by the University and Museum and paid by both institutions, and University employees paid wholly by the University, was bound to lead to inequality in pay, confusion of duties, and divided loyalties.

Nearly a year of meetings and discussions followed. Finally in 1947 Snyder's original recommendations, revised by Professor Dymond, were ready for submission to the board. Robert Fennell, the newly elected chairman of the board of trustees, suggested that they should be discussed over dinner at his house, which he would ask President Sidney Smith of the University to attend. Professors Dymond, Meen, and Fritz were nominated by the committee of directors as their representatives to attend this meeting, and to see that copies of the recommendations were sent in advance to Fennell and President Smith.

The dinner took place on 5 March 1947. No record of the discussion was kept, but Smith and Fennell undertook to see that copies of the recommendations were also sent to all members of the board of trustees before the board's next meeting, at which the proposals would be discussed.

Meanwhile, however, an alarm bell had been rung. President Smith had lost no time in getting in touch with the premier of Ontario. At the March meeting of the University's board of governors, the chairman announced that he had heard from the premier in the following terms: "A meeting will be held in the near future in connection with the University of Toronto absorbing the Royal Ontario Museum on a similar basis to the Toronto Conservatory of Music."

At a meeting of the Museum's board of trustees on 19 March, Fennell and Dymond reported on the discussion that had taken place at the dinner meeting on 5 March, but it was not until a special meeting on 30 April that the board was informed of the new arrangements for financing and administering the Museum, as determined jointly by the Ontario government and the University of Toronto. These arrangements were enacted later in the year by the Royal Ontario Museum Act 1947.

The main provisions of the act were a complete repudiation and reversal of what Snyder's five-year plan had sought to accomplish. The membership of the Museum's board of trustees was increased to twelve, of whom four, including the chairman, were to be appointees of the University's board of governors from among its own members. With three *ex officio* members also officials of the University—the chancellor, the president, and the chairman of the University's board—the University now had firm control of the Museum's board and of the institution itself. In addition, the Museum's entire budget, instead of only half of it, was to be incorporated in the University's budget, and the University assumed full responsibility for the Museum's management, as one of its own departments.

Some parts of the directors' recommendations were accepted in the new dispensation. The University undertook to make some revision of Museum salary scales to bring them more into line with University salaries; and it agreed that two places on the new board should be reserved for members appointed by Queen's University and the University of Western Ontario, to meet the proposal for wider representation from the province. But the overall effect of the new arrangement was not only to strike down the aspirations of those who chafed at the Museum's subordinate status and were eager for its independence, but also to ensure that any further challenge to the University's supremacy would be defeated.

In a severely worded memorandum the Museum's board of trustees and its committee of directors were reminded:

> The University and the Museum should be regarded as a "community of scholars". If this ideal is to be realized the Museum staff must win their place in the esteem of their University confrères through the carrying out of more and better research and publication.

Snyder's memorandum had been intended to remind the Museum, now in its thirty-fifth year, of its constitutional duty as a public museum. But instead of achieving the independence of the Museum and the transfer of executive power from the trustees to the working directors, at which it had aimed, the Museum's attempt to control its own destiny had ended in a take-over. Twenty years were to pass before most of Snyder's recommendations were adopted and the Museum was granted the independence for which Snyder and the committee of directors had so earnestly pleaded.

11

A Time of Transition

Currelly had considered retiring in 1939. Nearly thirty years had passed since he had moved into the basement of the original wing of the Royal Ontario Museum and now, as he turned sixty-three, the prospect of country ease at his home in Welcome, while he finished writing his memoirs, almost overcame his reluctance to hand over his museum to another's keeping.

The approach of war postponed these hopes. The Ontario government was forced in 1939 to reduce its subsidy to the Museum, and the resulting salary cuts caused some members of the staff to resign. Others left to join the armed forces. Yet the detailed work of cataloguing the collections had to go on. Here Currelly had his usual good fortune. Dorothy Macdonald (later Burnham), whom he had known since she was a child, had joined the Museum as a draftsman in 1929 and by 1936 had become chief draftsman and cataloguer. Now she was able to take over the textile collection. And Winifred Needler, who had joined the Museum in 1935, also as a draftsman and cataloguer, and who had worked under Currelly from that time on, was available to take charge of the work of identifying, classifying, and documenting the great Near Eastern collection, a project for which Currelly managed to obtain a grant of five thousand dollars. Dorothy Burnham was to become keeper of the textile collection, and Winifred Needler head of the Near Eastern Department, and later of the Egyptian Department when it was formed in 1967.

Currelly's memory was phenomenal, and he was proud of it. He carried everything in his head. Nothing was written down. Ethel Greenaway, his secretary and later his executive assistant, kept him tidy, and his papers in some semblance of order. She had started him on his memoirs, chiefly by urging on him how important to the history of the Museum the record of

101

its beginning would be. Her sudden death on 28 April 1941 was a blow
from which it took time for him to recover. He had dictated to her five
full notebooks of his memoirs, but he could not take up the task again. In
Miss Greenaway he had lost the ideal channel of communication, for she
had shared so great a part of those early years. The war, in any case,
allowed him no spare time. When he did retire in 1946, the notebooks
could not be found, but he was to see his memoirs, *I Brought the Ages Home,*
published before his death in 1956.

By 1946 there was no longer any pressing reason for Currelly to
continue. In his view, an ideal successor was already at hand in Professor
Homer Thompson, who in 1933 had joined the University of Toronto as
associate professor of archaeology and had become keeper of the Greek
and Roman collections in the Museum. Thompson had already established a reputation as a member of an ambitious project of the American
School of Classical Studies to excavate and, as far as possible, restore the
Agora in Athens. He was later to become assistant director of the project,
and still later director. There he had met and married his wife, Dorothy
Burr, who was also a field archaeologist working on the Agora project.
During the war this work had had to be suspended. Thompson had served
in the Royal Canadian Navy and had returned to the University and the
Museum in 1945, continuing the excavation in Athens the next year.

Shortly before Currelly told the board of trustees of the Museum of his
intention to resign, the Institute for Advanced Study in Princeton had
invited Thompson to join its permanent staff. The freedom from teaching
duties, as well as the opportunity to spend part of each year in Athens,
which this appointment afforded, induced Thompson to accept, and he
had to decline the offer of the post of director of the Royal Ontario
Museum of Archaeology as Currelly's successor. He was in Athens at the
time, preparing for the start of the spring excavations at the Agora, which
in the years ahead were to bring him and his wife international fame. But
he agreed to head a search committee for a suitable successor to Currelly.
The board also nominated Currelly himself and the associate director of
the Royal Ontario Museum of Archaeology, Professor T. F. McIlwraith, to
the committee. Dorothy Thompson offered her services as temporary
director of the Museum until a new appointment could be made. Vincent
Massey, just returned from England where he had been Canadian high
commissioner during the war, and now a trustee of the Museum, offered
the use of his London connections to find a suitable director.

A confidential memorandum prepared for a later board of governors of
the University of Toronto, which traces the history of the relationship
between the Museum and the University, leaves no doubt as to the kind of

man they were looking for to succeed Currelly: a scholar, not a "museum man". As they saw it, a scholar would give the Museum prestige in the outside world. He would pick the right staff, not the type of publicity man that had taken over command of other museums when they cut loose from scholarly connections. A scholar would encourage research and publication, the prime functions, in their view, of a museum which ideally should provide a laboratory in which university scholars could test their findings. The Museum had become additionally important because of the rapidly increasing growth of the University's graduate school.

There can be little doubt that it was through Vincent Massey, who shared the University's view, that the choice for the directorship finally fell on Gerard Brett, a young archaeologist from the Victoria and Albert Museum in London. After a brilliant school and university career, during which he spent his undergraduate vacations working on archaeological digs, Brett had made a grand tour of European museums and had joined the Victoria and Albert Museum a year before the outbreak of World War II. During the war he had served with the commandos and had been awarded the Military Cross for a particularly hazardous exploit in the 1942 attack on the German submarine base at Saint-Nazaire. He had been taken prisoner and in 1945, with other prisoners from the Saint-Nazaire and Dieppe raids, had been forced by the retreating German army to accompany it as a hostage. Following his release from the army after the war, he had rejoined the Victoria and Albert Museum as keeper of the textile collections and assistant to the director of the museum.

It could not have been easy for a gifted young man who had advanced so far and so fast in the hierarchy of one of London's leading museums—the one, in fact, on which Currelly had modelled his own archaeological museum—to abandon a promising future there to come to Canada. In one way, however, the move would be an advancement: he would be director of his own museum. And after the claustrophobia induced by three years in prison camps, no doubt Canada offered an attractive prospect.

Before accepting the directorship, Brett paid a visit to Toronto in September 1947. He met the president of the University of Toronto, Sidney Smith, and the chairman and members of the board of trustees of the Royal Ontario Museum. He talked to the directors of the now four component museums and learnt the details of their proposed five-year plan which the University had just largely rejected in favour of its own plan to make the Museum a department of the University. That decision did not seem to Brett to be a threat; the Ashmolean at Oxford and the Fitzwilliam at Cambridge were shining examples of how naturally a great museum could fit into a great university without losing its public.

In talking to the curators, Brett quickly sensed the sources of their dissatisfactions: the frustration of being asked to do too much for too little and the sense of inferiority which the difference in salaries induced. A few days before his return to London he wrote a long letter to President Smith dated 3 October 1947, making his acceptance of the post conditional upon the University's rectifying this situation.

> The Museum of Archaeology covers in its collections a field which is roughly equivalent to, say, those of the British and the Victoria and Albert Museums combined—its smaller size in this immediate connection [being] largely irrelevant; it is engaged in a formidable amount of field-work in Ontario, and this is giving a lead to many smaller bodies; in the Extension and Teaching work it carries a load which few English museums do; and on top of this, many members of its staff have teaching duties in the University. It is proper that the leading Museum of Archaeology and Fine Art in Canada should attempt this programme, but I do not feel that the attempt can be made with hope of permanent success with a staff as low as at present. Coming from outside I have been greatly shocked and alarmed by the staff position, which is as bad as, or worse than, that of the understaffed British museums of today. I mean no disrespect to the Board when I say that I do not think they can possibly have realised how much work is involved in carrying on the Museum's many activities, or how much the Museum is really getting for what it is giving.

Among other assurances Brett asked for was that Bishop White would be retired before he took up his office. He had heard enough about the bishop to know that he tended to dominate the scene and would not take kindly to having a younger man over him.

President Smith and Vincent Massey had been nominated by the Museum's board of trustees to deal with the appointment. They recommended that Brett's conditions should be accepted, and the board concurred. Just before he left for England, Brett was called in to be warmly felicitated. He was to take up his appointment on 1 January 1948.

It was something of a shock for the board to receive a letter from Brett soon after his return to say that the Victoria and Albert was not yet ready to part with him forever. It had agreed to grant him a five-years' leave of absence, at the end of which time he would have to make up his mind whether to remain in Canada or to return to England. Notwithstanding the shock, the Victoria and Albert's reluctance to lose Brett reassured the board that they had chosen the right man.

Brett had been impressed on his visit by the Museum's textile collection, since textiles were his own field of specialization. The collection had been founded by Currelly during the period when he was still attached to the Egypt Exploration Fund. He had acquired some important examples of linens from Pharaonic Egypt of the second millennium B.C. and later many early Christian textiles from Egypt. To these he had added systematically during his years in London, when his acquisition allowance had been greatly increased, and when he had had the additional windfall benefits arising from the frequent London visits of Sir Edmund Walker and Mrs H. D. Warren, as well as those of the ever-generous Robert Mond and Sigmund Samuel. In his travels through Europe and the Middle East on his honeymoon, he had been able to add decorative silks, embroideries, and rugs, so that when the Museum opened in 1914 the textile display was already an impressive part of the Royal Ontario Museum of Archaeology.

The collection of Chinese costumes was outstanding. The core of the collection had been purchased by George Crofts on the Peking market. An early supporter had been the Robert Simpson Company of Toronto, which in 1919 donated to the Museum a shipment of 173 items described by Crofts as "rare to usual", among them a very rare early Ch'ing dragon coat. Over the years the collection had been built up through the efforts and generosity of many private donors, including Mrs W. C. White and Mrs Edgar J. Stone.

Then in 1934 a unique collection of Indian chintzes and French and English 18th-century woodblock- and copperplate-printed textiles had come into the possession of the Museum. It consisted of more than eight hundred items from the private collection of Harry Wearne, an English textile designer, and was given to the Museum by his widow.

The textiles that were to captivate Gerard Brett after he came to the Museum were the unique early Ontario woven coverlets. The first of these had arrived at the Museum as an unsolicited gift in 1941. Dorothy Macdonald, who was then keeper of textiles, was convinced that if one coverlet had survived there must surely be others tucked away in rural Ontario. In 1944 she married Harold Burnham, a banker who since boyhood had had a keen interest in museums and in woven textiles. Fourteen years later he was to accept an invitation to join the Textile Department, of which he subsequently became curator.

From the beginning of their marriage, Harold Burnham shared his wife's enthusiasm for early Ontario spinning and weaving. In 1947 the Textile Department took a booth at the Canadian National Exhibition, where visitors were asked if they had any knowledge of existing samples of Ontario weaving. The response was so positive that the department decided that a research project would be very worthwhile. In the next few years Dorothy and Harold Burnham, often accompanied by their children, were to travel hundreds of kilometres in their search for early Ontario coverlets.

Common interests drew Gerard Brett and the Burnhams together. A year after his arrival at the Museum, Brett married Katharine B. Maw, who had succeeded Dorothy Burnham as keeper of textiles when Mrs Burnham left the Museum for a period to devote more time to her growing family. Mrs Brett continued the project, which resulted in the accumulation and documentation of an outstanding collection of Ontario coverlets, most of them woven between 1840 and 1860.

~~~

Gerard Brett had taken up his post as director at an unpropitious time. The years from 1948 to 1951 were a period of severe financial stress for all Canadian universities. The money that had been poured into the universities by the Department of Veterans' Affairs shrank as the veterans graduated. Inflation was eating into the value of the dollar; salaries, except for those of full-time University staff, were frozen. For Museum staff, whose salaries were still below University level even after the increase granted when the University took over the Museum, this situation simply made more acute the existing sense of inequity.

By 1949 the situation was desperate at all Canadian universities, and on 8 April the Privy Council of Canada appointed a Royal Commission, naming Vincent Massey, who was now chancellor of the University of Toronto, as chairman, to inquire into and report on "certain matters related to the arts, letters and sciences in Canada". The report, which was published in 1951 and which came to be known as the Massey Report, was to revolutionize the cultural life of Canada, and in helping to shape government policy towards museums Gerard Brett was to play a not insignificant part.

It is possible that no Royal Commission before or since has had so wide a range of reference or has accomplished so much in less than two years. The record was remarkable. The commission held hearings in 16 cities in the 10 provinces, travelled nearly 15 000 kilometres, and held 224 meetings, 114 of them in public session. It received 462 briefs, including 13 from federal government institutions, 7 from provincial governments, 87 from national organizations, 262 from local bodies, and 35 from private commercial radio stations.

The five commissioners appointed could not possibly digest so large a mass of material, dealing with so many forms of art, letters, and the sciences, many of which required some technical knowledge of the processes involved, as well as some knowledge of the historical background. Specialized committees, each with five or six prominent and experienced members, were formed to analyse the briefs and to advise the Royal Commission. The committee on museums consisted of Dr Kaye Lamb, Dominion archivist; Colonel C. P. Stacey, military historian attached to the Department of Defence; H. O. McCurry, director of the National Gallery of Canada; Dr F. J. Alcock, chief curator of the National Museum of Canada; and Gerard Brett, director of the Royal Ontario Museum of Archaeology. As the Royal Ontario Museum was the largest museum in Canada, it was appropriate that its voice should be heard. But it is significant that Vincent Massey, as chairman of the Royal Commission, should have selected as an expert on this Canadian problem a qualified man who had been in Canada only a year.

Brett, who had been elected chairman of the Museum's committee of directors for 1949, had been asked by his colleagues at a meeting on 5 October 1949 to draft a brief for submission to the commission, which was to hold hearings in Toronto from 15 to 19 November. He had had only a few weeks to prepare it, but it was a masterpiece of conciseness. It began with a brief history of the Royal Ontario Museum from its beginnings in 1914, reviewing the various changes of control it had gone through, and recapitulating its purposes, which were not very different from those of the National Museum and the National Gallery. The chief difference was that in the thirty-five years since its founding the Royal Ontario Museum had become not only the largest museum in Canada, but the largest in the Commonwealth, outside London. It had been visited since its opening by more than five million people. It served a large university, as well as the public. Although only provincially financed, it had collections of international reputation. Its brief, therefore, would be of special interest to the commission.

Fortunately for the commission, the Museum spokesman was articulate and was not biased in favour of his own institution. Brett particularly impressed the commission because he spoke from a very broad point of view that took the interests of the entire Canadian museum community into account. His prognostications of the future for Canadian museums were echoed repeatedly in the section of the report that dealt with this topic, where the hand and style of Vincent Massey were clearly apparent.

In its second part Brett's brief particularized the three functions that had been the Museum's aim: to build its collections, to carry out study and research on these collections, and to interpret and use them for education. Inside the Museum, education was to be carried on by exhibits and lectures to visitors and schoolchildren; outside the Museum, by the circulation to schools of small displays, by publications, both scholarly and popular, and by assistance to local museums through loans of objects and technical assistance in the preparation and mounting of their own exhibits. The Royal Ontario Museum, therefore, from its unique position and the wealth of its collections, could reach out to inform or inspire people in communities too distant to make visits to Toronto possible.

The third part of the brief expressed content that the National Museum and National Gallery should be the leaders. For this purpose those institutions crowded together in the old Victoria block in Ottawa would need new buildings and independent boards of trustees to release them from the ignominious position in which they were now placed as sections of government departments. The brief proposed that the national institutions should join with the Royal Ontario Museum and other large museums in Canada to form a galaxy of museums from which the smaller museums of Canada could borrow skills and objects and from which their staffs could also obtain museum training. For this last purpose the large museums would have to initiate courses in museum subjects. Once a satisfactory level of expertise had been reached, it would be possible to establish a chain of well-staffed museums of worthwhile quality right across the country. The national and the large provincial museums and galleries would then feel much readier to send exhibits from their collections on tour or on permanent loan.

The whole brief was set forth impressively in less than two thousand words. It correctly foreshadowed the actual development of museums in Canada. Of the seven recommendations contained in the Royal Commission's report in regard to museums, five, including the proposal for the training of museum curators, were taken from the Royal Ontario Museum brief. However, it was to take another seventeen years to produce the National Museums Act of 1968, which established the National Museums of Canada as a corporation, and to bring about the "chain of museums of worthwhile quality" which Brett's brief had called for.

The Massey Report could not have appeared at a more appropriate moment. In the previous fifteen years Canada had become one of the world's most important industrial nations. It was seen that the country's prospects depended to a large extent on developments in science and technology; the Massey Report was a timely reminder that the humanities and the liberal arts were an essential complement of the development of science and technology.

What was needed was a new body, something different from the National Research Council already in existence. The model chosen was the Arts Council of Great Britain, and the final recommendation of the

Massey Report was for the establishment of the Canada Council, a body independent of the government but financed by it, whose function would be to encourage research and publication, writing, and the fine and the performing arts.

It was to take six years to get this proposal implemented by Parliament and to establish the funds that would put the new body's continued existence beyond the reach of government's periodical fits of economy. When the Canada Council was established by Act of Parliament in 1957, its independence was assured by making it a crown corporation, and its financial security guaranteed by an initial grant of $100 million, $50 million of which was designated as an endowment fund, and $50 million as a capital grants fund. The money came from the windfall succession duties on the estates of two wealthy Canadians.

~~~

That more easeful future was still only a vision. Meanwhile the changes embodied in the Royal Ontario Museum Act 1947 were affecting every level in the Royal Ontario Museum from the board of trustees down. The new Museum board was firmly under the control of the University's board of governors. The Museum trustees who were not also members of the University's board, and who included benefactors like Mrs H. D. Warren and Sigmund Samuel, were annoyed when the University members, busy with University affairs, did not turn up for meetings. There were occasions when there were not enough members present to form a quorum. This apparent slight added to the feeling of resentment that all decisions of the trustees now had to be referred to the board of governors for confirmation. These frustrations filtered through to the staff of the Museum, increasing the sense of tension which was perceptible in the annual reports of all the directors. It was reflected also in the resignation of Dr Loris Russell in 1950 from his position as director of the Royal Ontario Museum of Palaeontology, to which he had been appointed on his return from war service in 1945, to become chief of the Division of Zoology at the National Museum of Canada and subsequently the museum's director.

After Russell's departure the palaeontological and zoological museums were combined to become the Royal Ontario Museum of Zoology and Palaeontology, under the directorship of Dr F. A. Urquhart, an entomologist who had begun his career in the Museum in 1935 as a lecturer, and after war service had been appointed to the Royal Ontario Museum of Zoology as keeper of the collection of insects. Urquhart had become assistant director of the zoological museum under Dr J. R. Dymond in

1948 and had succeeded Dymond as director in 1949. Following the amalgamation of the two museums, Dr Madeleine A. Fritz, who had been associate director of the Royal Ontario Museum of Palaeontology, became associate director of the combined museums, but she cannot have welcomed the imposition over her of someone who was not a palaeontologist. In 1955 when the component museums were amalgamated under a single director, Dr Fritz was made curator of the Department of Invertebrate Palaeontology. Two years later she resigned her curatorship and became a research associate of the Royal Ontario Museum, while remaining a professor in the Department of Geology of the University of Toronto.

This period of unsettlement and imposed economy contributed to the tensions in all ranks of the Museum's staff. It coincided with the beginning of a breakdown in Gerard Brett's health.

Meanwhile Brett's reports on the research undertaken by the Royal Ontario Museum of Archaeology carried a despondent note. He mentions only the excavations by Professor T. F. McIlwraith, associate director of the Royal Ontario Museum of Archaeology and K. E. Kidd, deputy keeper of the ethnology collection. In 1950 no excavation work was possible because of lack of funds. The renewed flow of funds promised for 1951 turned out in the end to allow for one small excavation at Lake Scugog, financed by the University. There were no excavations in 1953/1954, and in 1954/1955 "excavation was not possible".

On the brighter side, Brett had some gifts and loans to report. Sigmund Samuel's Canadiana collection had grown steadily in importance and by 1947 already far exceeded the space available to it. At the time the Archives of Ontario were looking for new premises and had been contemplating building in the space west of the original wing of the Museum, a move that would have restricted the Museum's hopes of a future extension in that direction if it became necessary. However, an admirable space was available on University property a short distance south of the Museum building on Queen's Park Crescent. Since the Archives of Ontario were a branch of the government, and since his own collection of Canadiana was mainly historical, Samuel conferred with the University of Toronto and the Province of Ontario and the decision was taken to put up a building on this site, in which the Archives would have the accommodation they needed and the Canadiana collection a permanent home while remaining a part of the Royal Ontario Museum.

The building was completed in 1951 and was opened on 19 June by Vincent Massey. The other collections in the archaeological museum—they were not called departments until the amalgamation of all the museums under a single director in 1955—were as active as limited budgets allowed. They were the Greek and Roman, the Near Eastern, the European, the Far Eastern, the textile, and the ethnology collections. The last two grew rapidly because of their easier access to fields of research. Ethnology was stimulated also by the activity of the University's Department of Anthropology.

There were gifts, some of them substantial, to all these collections. Brett, strapped for money, planned a series of small exhibitions mounted for short periods of eight weeks. What he created with virtually no funds, and no particular interest or support from the parent body, the University, is remarkable. His training at the Victoria and Albert Museum, where frequent changes of exhibitions and the modernizing of galleries were constant preoccupations, served him and the Museum well, as the titles of some of these special exhibitions indicate: *English and Canadian Silver; Books of the Middle Ages; Animals in Art; Early Canadian Guns and Gunsmiths; Industrial Design 1951* B.C.–A.D. *1951; East and West*, an attempt to demonstrate the cultural impact of one-half of the world on the other; and in the following year *West and East*, designed to show the process in reverse.

The University was itself going through a difficult financial phase. It had been generous to the Museum in the first two years following the Museum's incorporation in the University as a department. But it now had pressing needs for new buildings, beside which the question of modernizing the Museum's galleries and brightening its public image by well-planned but costly public relations must have had a low priority. Falling public attendance testified to the waning of public interest in the Museum, which not even Brett's economical but well-designed exhibitions could sufficiently revive. In truth, the Museum was out of tune with the times—exciting times, as a rich province developed its magnificent resources, and industrial growth and rapidly expanding immigration cast the future in a rosy glow. Seen in these circumstances, the Royal Ontario Museum appeared an early 20th-century museum in a world that had changed.

Brett had experienced the first symptoms of multiple sclerosis in 1949, the year in which he had prepared the brief for the Massey Commission. At the end of 1952 the illness was so far advanced that he felt compelled to write to the chairman of the board, Robert Fennell, to reveal the state of his health. The disease, he explained, manifested itself in a steadily increasing loss of energy, but left the mind perfectly clear. Intellectually he remained as active and articulate as before, and he felt perfectly capable of carrying on the directorship if he could be given an experienced assistant, and if the keepers of the collections were encouraged to take more responsibility. There was a possibility that the disease could be arrested, but the cause was unknown and research had not yet found a cure. Given time, he might get back his normal strength, but there could be no certainty of it.

The board could hardly do anything but wait and see, though privately it seems to have decided to look about for a possible replacement, in case that should become necessary. As they were accustomed to do in an emergency, the trustees consulted the Museum's best friend, Homer Thompson. Thompson paid a visit to Toronto at the end of that year, saw Brett, talked to Toronto friends and former colleagues, and wrote to his friend Francis Henry Taylor at the Metropolitan Museum of Art in New York asking if he had any suggestions for a replacement. He added that he had been shocked at the deterioration in Brett's physical condition.

The relations between the University and the Museum had been steadily worsening during the financial difficulties of the early 1950s. The science museums had accommodated themselves quite well to the University connection, but the relations between the Royal Ontario Museum of Archaeology and the Faculty of Arts and Sciences of the University were very much less cooperative. Hard times contributed to sensitivity on both sides. The Museum curators complained that it was virtually impossible to persuade any member of the University staff to use the Museum. President Sidney Smith and Moffat Woodside, dean of arts and sciences, were concerned about what they thought was a conspiracy on the part of the archaeological museum to separate the Museum from the University. When the University had taken over the Museum's budget and incorporated it in its own, the Ontario government had ceased to pay the annual subsidy of fifty thousand dollars for acquisitions it had been making since 1921. This deprivation increased the financial burden on the University. Morale in the Museum was reported to be low, and Thompson confirmed this in his letter to Taylor; he wrote that he was "sickened by the spectacle of Currelly's great work coming to a standstill".

This state of alarm, added to the steadily increasing financial burden of supporting the Museum, prompted the president and the board of governors of the University in October 1953 to call in their accountants, Clarkson, Gordon & Co., and to ask for an analysis of the problems and recommendations for their relief. The terms of reference called for "a survey of the Royal Ontario Museum in its relation to the University of Toronto, the schools of Ontario, and the public".

12

Taking Stock

The report on the condition of the Royal Ontario Museum by Clark-son, Gordon & Co., which became known as the Glassco Report after the partner responsible for it, was issued in 1954. A large part of its value lay in its historical survey of the origins and development of the Royal Ontario Museum and its orderly presentation of attendance figures, sources of funds, and expenditures over the years, which touchingly revealed the heroic endeavour to create out of limited financial resources one of the great museums of North America.

The figures produced by J. Grant Glassco's analysis recorded some impressive facts. They showed that from 1921 until 1948, when the Museum was wholly taken over by the University of Toronto, the Ontario government, in addition to bearing half the cost of the Museum's maintenance, had given the institution "special funds" totalling almost a million dollars ($993 333), a record that elicited from Glassco the comment that "support by public authority on such a generous scale is decidedly rare in the history of museums generally". In the same period private benefactions had totalled $558 411. Between 1921 and 1953 approximately $7 million altogether had been spent on the Museum, of which the Province of Ontario had contributed $2.7 million and the University $3.4 million; the balance of almost $1 million had come mainly in the form of bequests, projects paid for by generous benefactors, and acquisitions purchased for the Museum by individuals. It was a record of which every participant could be proud; and since the University's contribution came ultimately from the province, the government had certainly acquitted itself nobly in the undertaking it had been pushed into in 1909 by Edmund Walker and Edmund Osler.

His review of the Museum's history completed, Glassco formulated his

conclusions and recommendations. The first of his "central conclusions
... upon which all other conclusions and recommendations must rest"
was startling. It was "that the Royal Ontario Museum must be regarded as
a Museum of Natural Science and its long-term objectives should be to
develop its collections and conduct its research in a manner consistent
with that concept". When he went on to speak of "certain portions of the
collections [that are] somewhat redundant", it must have seemed, at first
sight at least, as if the great collections of art and archaeology that had
been the glory of the Museum had no place in his concept of the
Museum's future, and that Walker's vision of a museum of archaeology
and science "under one academical roof" was in peril.

But that, apparently, was not what Glassco had intended, for when he
came to describe in detail the organization that he envisaged for the
Museum, the first of the three main divisions that he listed was a Division
of Anthropological Sciences, comprising five sections or departments: (1)
a department of Eastern archaeology, with a curator of oriental art and
archaeology, an assistant curator in charge of the Near Eastern collections,
and perhaps also a curator of Middle Eastern archaeology; (2) a department of classical archaeology under a curator; (3) a department of
ethnology and American archaeology, with a curator of American archaeology and an assistant curator of ethnology; (4) a department of decorative
arts, with a curator of decorative arts and an associate curator of textiles;
and (5) Canadian Archives, under a curator. It was recommended "that
deliberate emphasis should be laid upon the ethnology and archaeology of
the Western hemisphere and, in particular, North America", but Glassco
saw his proposed organization as embracing almost all the existing
collections. "The only one of any consequence whose continuance is
inconsistent with this concept [a Museum of Natural Science]," he wrote,
"is the print collection and the happiest solution would be to entrust it to
the Art Gallery or some other fine arts institution."

All this is a far cry from a Museum of Natural Science in the recognized
sense, and the ambiguity in the report remains unresolved. But there is no
doubt that this strained and rather ridiculous attempt, for the sake of a
formal and schematic neatness, to bring all the collections of the Royal
Ontario Museum under the rubric of natural science, shows the influence
of Dr Robert T. Hatt, director of the Cranbrook Institute of Science of
Bloomfield Hills, Michigan, who was reputed to be experienced in
museum consultancy and who assisted Glassco in his survey. In the preface
to his report, Glassco acknowledged that its central conclusions and
recommendations reflected the observations and views of Dr Hatt. At all
events, the Museum's board of trustees gave this particular recommenda-

tion short shrift. Dr Hatt, it noted, was a scientist. "A similar authority," it contended, "should have been consulted concerning the requirements of the Museum of Archaeology." Then it dismissed the whole matter with the lofty statement, "The History of Man cannot be confined to North America, as suggested." The University's board of governors was equally firmly opposed to the recommendation.

The second of the report's central conclusions was that the Museum was and must continue to be a public museum. While the Museum would still serve the special needs of the University of Toronto, the claims of the elementary and secondary schools and of the general public to its services were no less important. It was therefore in every way desirable that the Museum should have a governing body that was representative of the general public—one that would devote itself exclusively to the welfare of the Museum, without a bias in favour of the University.

The implementation of this proposal was not thought to involve the complete separation of the Museum from the University. The interests of the two institutions had become inextricably interwoven over the years, and while there was considerable dissatisfaction with the relationship between their staffs, the connection was now so close and intricate that to dissolve it suddenly would inflict a loss on both. Continued integration and cooperation was therefore foreseen both at the academic level (the teaching of graduate students, cross-appointments) and at the functional level (the operation and maintenance of buildings and premises). But in two crucial areas, Glassco recommended fundamental change.

The first of these areas was finance. The report recommended that the Ontario government should make annual operating grants to the Museum, in place of the grants hitherto made by the University. These grants might be routed through the University for administrative convenience, "but the responsibility for dealing with the Province with regard to such annual grants should lie with the Museum's Board of Trustees".

Secondly, if the Royal Ontario Museum was to be a public museum financed by the Ontario government, it was clearly illogical that the board of trustees should continue to be controlled by the University. The pattern established by the Royal Ontario Museum Act 1947, Glassco declared, had not been successful. He therefore recommended that the board of trustees should have twenty members, fifteen of whom would be appointed by the Ontario government and only five by the University. Even these five were represented as a concession to the University for the sake of "maintaining the closest possible liaison".

Perhaps the most important of the report's major recommendations— inasmuch as it was the only proposal for fundamental change that was forthwith adopted—was the appointment of a single director who would have authority over all three museums—the Royal Ontario Museum of Archaeology, the Royal Ontario Museum of Geology and Mineralogy, the Royal Ontario Museum of Zoology and Palaeontology—which would thus become the separate divisions of a single museum. Glassco had effectively exposed the inadequacy and unworkability in the 1950s of an ideal conceived in the first decade of the century. The association of three administratively independent museums each under its own director, two of them scientific institutions headed by leading professors with a dominant interest in scholarship, the third concerned chiefly with educating the public in the history of man and his arts, was bound to lead to some uncertainty of aim. Other obvious defects, as Glassco noted, were the extreme dispersal of authority and the lack of well-defined lines of responsibility. It was Currelly's genius that had launched the Royal Ontario Museum on the course that was to bring it worldwide renown; but at this point in its fortunes, that course had brought it to crisis. "The greatest single need," observed Glassco, "is an administrative head [for the institution as a whole] of suitable stature and competence. Without such leadership it is difficult to see how the apparent deterioration in the Museum's fortunes can be arrested."

The Glassco Report was delivered to President Smith of the University on 29 July 1954. By September its contents had become generally known, but as the board of governors, sphinx-like, had made no public response, the already touchy relationship between the University and the Museum was only aggravated.

Finally, in October, the Museum's board of trustees issued a tentative statement commenting on what was by that time general knowledge. Since the board of governors of the University controlled the Museum board, this could not have been done without their approval. But the board of trustees had another constituency, the curators, pressing for reform. The statement was a suitably guarded one, made, as the Museum board acknowledged, "pending further development of plans", and meekly offering "to report further on these points if the Board of Governors of the University so desires".

The board of governors themselves had not been pleased with some of the recommendations of the report. The chairman wrote to the president:

> I don't think it reasonable to expect any decision on a large scale on Glassco's report for a long time.... I did think we were faced with the necessity of implementing certain things which we know should be done at the Museum, one director to run the separate divisions, etc. I have arranged to

talk with Mr Frost [the premier of Ontario] within the next two weeks. But I know it will be fruitless. As a matter of fact I must tell you that I do not agree with the conclusions reached in the report, and I suggest that we should sit down with one or two of our colleagues and go over the whole thing privately, so that there may be an exchange of views.

President Smith replied by sending the chairman a six-page letter from Dean Moffat Woodside, with pros and cons concerning Glassco's recommendations. The effect of the whole was decidedly negative.

On the other hand, there was much in the report to please the non-University trustees of the Museum, particularly the recommendation that the Museum should be recognized as a public museum, the University being included amongst the elements in society to which it rendered a particular service, but having no special claim exceeding that of elementary and secondary schools and of the public itself. Glassco's recommendations, if implemented, would have meant virtual administrative independence for the Museum. That had been the aim of L. L. Snyder's original five-year plan proposed in 1946. The University had answered that challenge with an outright take-over; but another six years had now gone by and it was still not clear what the most fruitful relationship between the Museum and the University might be. Complete independence would largely destroy the Museum's usefulness to the University. The unification of the museums under one director offered a more promising prospect; but here wisdom dictated silence until the man to fill the post could be found.

Meanwhile, following Homer Thompson's alarming report on Gerard Brett's condition, the Museum board had accelerated the search for his successor as director of the Royal Ontario Museum of Archaeology. A number of candidates had been recommended, and had been reduced to a short-list of three: Mr Aschwin-Lippe, a brother of Prince Bernhard of the Netherlands and an archaeologist of experience attached to the Metropolitan Museum of Art in New York and strongly recommended by its director, Francis Henry Taylor; a young professor of Old Testament history at Queen's University, A. D. Tushingham, who had had extensive archaeological experience in the Middle East, where he had been director of the American School of Oriental Research in Jerusalem; and Peter Swann, a young keeper of oriental art at the Ashmolean, nominated by Dean Moffat Woodside who had met him the year before at Oxford. It is possible that Swann was unaware of his nomination, since there is no record of his application. But a letter from the dean to President Smith makes it clear that Swann's nomination was discussed.

Tushingham had been strongly recommended by Mrs O. D. Vaughan, an active and influential member of the board of trustees of the Museum, whose husband was a member of the University's board of governors and was later to become its chairman. Mrs Vaughan had heard Tushingham lecture on archaeology and had been most impressed. She urged President Smith to contact him to see if he would be available if the position were offered him. President Smith had done so in the fall of 1953, only to find that Tushingham had just been offered a post at Princeton University, where he would have a greater chance to do archaeological work than at Queen's. Moreover, his friend Homer Thompson was at the Princeton Institute for Advanced Study. But Tushingham replied to President Smith that, having returned from Jerusalem for the sake of his children's education, he would prefer to remain in Canada. In the end Tushingham was chosen; he accepted the post of director of the Royal Ontario Museum of Archaeology, starting on 1 July 1955.

In the meantime the University had brought itself to accept some of the recommendations of the Glassco Report, including the all-important one to appoint a single director to have authority over all three museums, which would become amalgamated in a single institution. The candidate for this important office was another recommendation of Francis Henry Taylor of the Metropolitan Museum of Art. His name was Theodore A. Heinrich. At the time Heinrich was associate curator of paintings at the Metropolitan, under the most distinguished of all that museum's curators, Theodore Rousseau, and had been with the institution just a year.

Again Mrs Vaughan was the agent. She and her husband visited New York frequently, and she had told Taylor that the Royal Ontario Museum was looking for an overall director. Had he any suggestions or recommendations to make? Taylor mentioned Heinrich as a bright and pleasant young man whose future Rousseau was blocking, since he had no plans for retirement. Heinrich turned out to be as pleasant as his superior had said. Of course, the war had checked the careers of all men of his age, but all the same he seemed to have crowded into his years more experiences than most. He was a Californian who, after graduating from the University of California, had taken his doctorate in fine art at Cambridge. Following a tour of European museums, interrupted by some further postgraduate study in Tours and in Bonn, he had spent a year in Hollywood as adviser to a film company on accuracy in historical film furnishings. He had been called up when the United States entered the war, and in the postwar occupation of Germany had served on the American High Commissioner's staff as a civilian, in which role he was engaged in recovering paintings that had been looted by the Nazis and restoring them to their rightful owners. He had then spent two years as curator of art collections at the Huntingdon Library, Art Gallery and Botanical Gardens in San Marino, California, before joining the Metropolitan Museum of Art in 1953. All this in the end counted for less than his suave and confident manner and the flow of his eloquence as he modestly suggested plans to restore the sunken morale in the Royal Ontario Museum, to re-establish harmony, and to turn around the declining attendance figures by holding exhibitions on a scale that would draw the public in large numbers.

These plans were not unfolded all at once but in a series of meetings over several days. Mrs Vaughan returned to Toronto impressed. With President Smith's approval, she invited Heinrich to visit Toronto where she arranged a series of lunches and dinners at which he met senior members of the Museum staff and influential members of the board of trustees, ending up with a meeting with President Smith. All were charmed, even mesmerized, including the president. The contract was signed and the Museum had its first overall director.

Tushingham had to be advised immediately, since the title, at least, of director of the Royal Ontario Museum of Archaeology had now vanished, and instead of being responsible directly to a board of trustees he would be responsible to a director placed over him. He was invited to go to New York to meet Heinrich, to see if he could get along with him. After the meeting he reported that he thought they could get along well enough.

Under the new organization the former three museums became the three divisions of a single unified Royal Ontario Museum. The three divisions were Art and Archaeology; Geology and Mineralogy, later changed to Earth Sciences; and Zoology and Palaeontology, later changed to Life Sciences. The existing Education Division made a fourth. The heads of the divisions were to be consulted by the director and together they were to constitute an advisory council on whose wisdom the director would rely in making his decisions.

The new dispensation was to begin on 1 July 1955. For its inauguration it was thought necessary by the University of Toronto's lawyers to amend the Royal Ontario Museum Act 1947 by the addition of clauses empowering the Museum's board of trustees to carry on the management and to make such rules and regulations as were approved from time to time by the board of governors of the University. Thus the Royal Ontario Museum still remained an integral part of the University of Toronto, but it maintained its status as a public institution. Theodore Heinrich's appointment as director, however, and the changes it entailed, signalled the beginning of a new era in the life of the Museum.

13

A New Era

All this time, beyond the walls of the Royal Ontario Museum as well as within them, there had been change. World War II had left the United States a superpower; and Canada, living in its shadow, emerged as the fourth industrial nation in the world, with Toronto as its financial capital. Since the Museum existed to serve the needs of the community, these changes were reflected within the institution, as the excitement of the early years of collecting and classifying gave place to a professional earnestness, with research and publication the proclaimed priorities.

While building the collections remained an important aim of the Museum, the industrial and commercial worlds, faced with new demands and challenges opened up by the scientific and technological developments of the war, were ready to encourage, and frequently to support, the researches of the scientific departments of the Museum. Museums were reference libraries where facts were stored, laboratories where experiments could be tested. Among the briefs submitted to the Massey Commission in 1950 had been one from the National Gallery of Canada in Ottawa, pressing for a museum of industrial art. Gerard Brett's brief pointed out that the improvement of industrial design had been one of the proposed functions of the Royal Ontario Museum from the beginning, and that the Museum had great resources, especially in the Royal Ontario Museum of Archaeology, for this purpose.

Under this pressure from the outside world there was ever less time for teaching. In 1957 the head of the Earth Sciences Division for the first time was not carrying any teaching duties, and only Walter Tovell, who had recently joined the division, continued undergraduate teaching. The new generation of curators increasingly looked to industry to finance their projects, often on a scale that the University of Toronto would have

found itself unable to match in the period of financial dislocation that
followed the return to peace. In mineralogy, the work of identifying
minerals for government agencies and for private concerns occupied
much of the time not given to research.

Support came not only for the development of natural resources. The
Toronto *Globe and Mail* provided financial assistance for the excavations at
Jericho, and for the ethnological studies at Round Lake, Ontario, in
several succeeding years. Foundations were springing up, and professional, commercial, and art bodies, and associations or guilds of craftsmen
were ready to identify themselves with discoveries in foreign fields by
offering professional or financial assistance.

The Museum had again become badly overcrowded. The new wing,
which had seemed so spacious and up-to-date in 1933, with its laboratories and storerooms adjacent to the galleries, could now display only a
small part of the collections, swollen as they were by the gifts and
acquisitions of the twenty years since. Much of the rest mouldered away
in warehouses in the city, some of them environmentally unsuitable and
doubtfully fireproof. Too much in the early days had been accepted as
gifts, some of which had duplicated material the Museum already had, or
were not worthy of a first-class museum's collections. But it is sometimes
difficult to refuse a gift in a small community where to offend a donor
might be to lose a desired bequest at some future date. Metropolitan
Toronto was growing rapidly, but one did not have to look back many
years to the time when it had been small. In those early days the
generosity of the well-to-do had procured many of the Museum's finest
treasures. They had been well represented on the old board, these self-
made individuals with a philanthropic turn—people like Sir Joseph
Flavelle, Sir Edmund Osler, and Mrs H. D. Warren, whose fortunes came
from industry and finance. Like Sigmund Samuel, whose autobiography
was entitled *In Return,* they wanted to give something to the community
in return for what they had gained from it.

The new generation of trustees were executives like Harold Turner, the
chairman of General Electric, who became chairman of the Museum's
board of trustees in 1955. Turner was followed by Richard Meech, a
prominent lawyer who was a director of a number of leading corporations. These were as much self-made men as Flavelle and Samuel; but they
were well aware of the value of research to industry, from which their
fortunes came. As businessmen they were conscious also of the Museum's
responsibility for serving the public.

The growth in attendance at the Museum had been remarkable.
Between July 1957 and June 1958 the number topped half a million, and

in that same year the eleven-millionth visitor to the Museum passed unnoticed through the turnstiles. The Ontario Department of Education was now supplying the Museum with full-time trained teachers; school classes came daily in busloads, making a substantial contribution to the attendance figures. At the end of World War I Margaret MacLean had had to force her way into the Museum; after World War II education became so important a part of the Museum's functions that a separate Education Division was created. In 1957/1958 the number of children coming to the Museum in organized classes was almost seventy thousand. The annual increase in numbers as the school population grew added to the space problem in an already badly overcrowded building. The Saturday Morning Club could take only two hundred children in the Museum theatre. There was always a long waiting list for the privilege of joining, and each year the registration list was closed half an hour after it was opened.

~~~

It was to this scene that Theodore Heinrich came, and almost immediately there was a sense of bustle and change, not all of it welcome to the Museum staff. It had been assumed by the board of trustees of the Museum, and no doubt made plain to Heinrich by President Smith of the University, that the director was expected to act in effect as the chairman of a committee composed of the four division heads, an arrangement that would have resembled the committee of directors, chaired by one of their own number, that had existed in the days when the museums were autonomous. But this Heinrich chose not to do. He consulted the division heads individually, but even that step was sometimes omitted when the director felt unsure of support for some plan of his own, and a division head might hear only after the event of an initiative that had been taken affecting one of the collections for which he was responsible.

The weakness of the new Museum organization was that nothing had been done to divide responsibility between the director and the new heads of divisions. Heinrich worsened the situation by his lack of knowledge of and interest in the natural sciences and his overpowering interest in the Art and Archaeology Division, which frequently resulted in the purchase of objects without consultation with the divisional head or the curators in the division. Some of these objects were excellent, but some were duplicates of what the Museum already held; and unfortunately some were fakes. It was the lack of definition of powers that was responsible for the growing disenchantment of the professional curators with a director whose interests were too specialized for an institution with the scope and range of the Royal Ontario Museum.

The misgivings, however, did not come until later. The board of trustees, at this stage, seemed to have every reason to be pleased with its choice. Heinrich had his first meeting with the board of trustees in October, three months after his installation. He took to it a number of recommendations, most of which Glassco had made in his report: the setting up of exhibits and publications departments, the institution of a wide-ranging membership drive, the establishment of a central Museum library, plans for more modern display methods, the removal of the Chinese tomb to a garden outside the Museum, where it would have a more naturalistic setting, and the use of the space thus vacated for other pressing needs.

These laudable proposals for expanding the services of the Museum had hardly been noticed by the board of trustees amid the shocks that the Glassco Report had administered. Now the satisfaction of having an experienced man in charge gave the proposals a new and promising glow. There was, besides, the considerable comfort of knowing that all these changes would be centralized in the director's office and would not become the subject of argument among the four contending divisions.

Briskly Heinrich set out to the board his priorities for the process of revamping the Museum. He anticipated normal increments to the science collections in the years immediately ahead. But in the collections of what had now become the Art and Archaeology Division there were notable gaps which needed to be filled. This could be done through gifts, by trading duplicate materials, and by purchase; and economical purchasing could be achieved by ingenuity, by encouraging local private collectors to take an interest in the Museum, and by the creation of endowment funds. Heinrich also had plans for alleviating the crowded condition of the Museum by building an administrative wing over the parking lot; this would accommodate the board, the director, the administrative staff, and the library, and would also contain lecture and seminar rooms.

The battle cry was "Action now!" A fresh wind was blowing through the Museum. Anything seemed possible under such an inspired leader. The surface bustle at this stage helped to mute the murmurs of discontent from some of the curators. But Heinrich's assumption—put half-humorously in the self-deprecating manner with which he disarmed opposition—that, while he knew next to nothing about science, he knew everything there was need to know about art brought him into frequent brushes with the divisional heads; and especially with Douglas Tushing-ham, who as head of the Art and Archaeology Division, was responsible for most of the departments most dangerously exposed to Heinrich's enthusiastic forays in the role of expert.

In the excitement aroused by Heinrich's plans the University of Toronto seemed to have forgotten its determination to have a scholar, not a publicity man, in charge. Heinrich was not a dedicated scholar, but he knew that the way to get the crowds in was by publicity, and the effect of the rash of notices about the Museum and its new director that followed his arrival was quickly seen in the public attendance figures. The steady decline in these figures, which had been disguised by the greatly increased school attendances, was now arrested.

Ted Heinrich was a rare phenomenon in Toronto, a professional with international experience in the popularization of culture. He was a bachelor who loved society and dining out, and was eloquent on the subject of art without being overpowering, pouring out ideas and plans for raising Toronto to the level of New York and Los Angeles as a centre of art and culture on the North American continent. Its temple would be the Royal Ontario Museum. Heinrich welcomed being interviewed, ostensibly disparaging the interest his own previous career aroused and directing attention instead to the Museum of which he had become the first overall director. But the interviews were largely taken up with his own past achievements, recounted with an attractive air of humorous self-deprecation that endeared him to the interviewer and ensured the flattering tone of the story.

Heinrich did not present an annual report for his first year of office, 1955/1956, probably because much of his time was taken up with reorganizing the Museum. His report for 1956/1957 covered his first two years. It appeared in President Sidney Smith's annual report to the board of governors on the state of the University of Toronto, and it came with a laudatory preface from the president, reminding his readers that two years earlier he had prophesied that a new and exciting chapter was about to be written in the splendid record of the Museum. These last two years, he said, had proved the correctness of that forecast. Mr Heinrich and his staff were to be congratulated on their achievement in making the Museum "a great show window, through which one may observe a workshop of painstaking scholarship and research in the arts and sciences".

Heinrich's report did indeed break new ground in one respect. It was written in fluent, elegant prose, unlike the traditional plodding accounts of the past, which had listed accessions and the year's work in the space of a single page or two. Heinrich's report ran to seven pages, a striking feat of compression, since he was reporting now for the whole institution. It listed all the triumphs from new initiatives undertaken in the period, including the appointment of an information officer, Duncan Cameron, and the establishment under him of a central office for information

services and publications. The instant success of this measure was confirmed by the featuring of the Museum during the year on 53 television
and 52 radio programs, with the addition of the equivalent of 24.4 news
pages and 167 photographs in the Toronto papers alone.

There were aspects of Heinrich's personality and character that were
bound to attract criticism. His tendency to spend his leisure hours with
the rich and famous seemed to some people snobbish; his manner of
dressing suggested a Byronic elegance that was suspect in strait-laced
Toronto. Such criticisms, however, were unimportant and could be
dismissed; what counted was the impact Heinrich had on the Museum.
The chairman of the board of trustees, Harold Turner, was quoted as
saying with satisfaction, "Currelly created the Museum, but Heinrich has
sold it."

There had been an increase in public attendance of twenty per cent
since Heinrich had taken over. The Ontario government had made a grant
of one hundred thousand dollars for acquisitions needed to round out
some of the archaeological collections, evidently impressed by the criticisms of an art expert like Heinrich on significant gaps. The president of
the University reported in 1957 that a sympathetic study had been given
to the new director's estimates, and that an additional seventy-five
thousand dollars a year, guaranteed for three years, would be forthcoming
from the University's research fund. Turner announced that he had
deliberately given the new director a free hand since his appointment and
had been convinced that Heinrich had a firm grip of the situation when he
saw his budget. Even Mr F. R. Stone, representing the University's
accounts office, broke his habitual gloom to remark how well the
operations department had done in the first year of the director's management. The director, for his part, reported that there had been a notable
increase in archaeological excavations by the Royal Ontario Museum in
Canada, and that now, after the lean years, there were overseas expeditions
as well, giving the Museum an international status in archaeological
work. The good days of Currelly seemed to have come again.

The fact that the credit for the archaeological activity was really due to
Douglas Tushingham, the new head of the Art and Archaeology Division,
went largely unnoticed. Complaints from senior Museum staff that
Heinrich was buying objects for their artistic rather than their documentary value went unheard. What the board thought of their new director's
reply to an interviewer—"I am interested only in what is beautiful and I
don't care who made it, or where it comes from"—was not recorded.

Nevertheless, by 1959 the glamour was fading, and Harold Turner,
who had been Heinrich's strongest supporter, confirmed in answer to

press inquiries that he was currently holding consultations with Heinrich and, separately, with the heads of divisions and some twenty of the senior curators, to deal with differences that had arisen between the director and his staff. On 21 January 1959 Heinrich circulated a memorandum to the staff saying that a news story was to appear in the Toronto *Telegram* that day concerning staff problems in the Museum, and that this and subsequent reports might have a damaging effect on the Ontario government's grant for the coming fiscal year. The memo charged that the press report was the direct result of the "indiscretion of a member of the staff", who was left unnamed, and stated that it would be regarded as a serious matter if further indiscretions were added to those already committed. This was quickly followed by a second memorandum saying at some length that the prominence of Dr Tushingham's name in the news story might have given the impression that the director had had him in mind as the instigator of the "indiscretion". Heinrich was anxious to remove the impression: "Dr Tushingham was not the person referred to, and I wish to make this clear."

Heinrich's annual reports continued to list achievements but began also to record frustrations and disappointments stemming from space shortage and salary differentials. The Museum was crowded beyond endurance and curators' salaries were still only seventy-five per cent of those received by the University faculty. The director's reports for these years grew in length from seven pages to eighteen pages. The records of the work of the four divisions and a special section on the Office of Information Services give the impression of enormous activity. An analysis of the attendance figures for 1959/1960 showed that the half-million mark had again been passed.

The 1960/1961 report recorded "another year of virtual siege". The subway was being built in front of the entrance on Queen's Park and along Bloor Street, and the University's new Edward Johnson Building was rising on the third side. However, the perpetual din and the necessity of walking across planks or through mud had reduced the attendance of the public by less than six per cent; this in spite of the fact that this year saw the first imposition of an entrance fee of twenty-five cents. As to the subway, Heinrich was successful in having the station at the Museum's entrance named "Museum", following the example of the London Underground station near the British Museum.

Not reflected in the report was the growing dissatisfaction of the University representatives on the Museum board with the financial impact of all the new endeavours, and the mounting criticism by members of the staff. The director plainly was not an administrator. He had surrounded himself with an inner council of advisers, such as Duncan Cameron and Harley Parker, who had been appointed chief designer, and some curators who were impressed by his success in attracting the public to the Museum. Cameron and Parker were not responsible to the division heads, but to the director. Their task was to use the arts of publicity and design to popularize the Museum, but the curators felt that showmanship was taking precedence over scholarship, and they were inclined to resent the fact that decisions concerning their collections were being taken without their authority. Heinrich was also making the fatal error of prophesying results that were not borne out by events, leaving the bills to be settled in the University accounts office. The face of Mr Stone of that office, who attended all board meetings, now grew longer and longer.

In 1960 it became plain to the trustees of the Museum and to the board of governors of the University that an administrator would have to be appointed. Vincent Massey had just completed his term of office as governor general of Canada, and his son Lionel, who had acted as his aide at Rideau Hall, was now free. Lionel Massey had no administrative experience, but in his blood presumably ran the financial watchfulness that had made the Masseys for generations Canada's most successful manufacturers. Even if that should be missing in Lionel's case, he had through his father the right connections. He was firm and strong in character, while still maintaining an attractive modesty. He seemed to promise just the right check for the ebullient director, who was concocting costly plans for the Museum's approaching golden jubilee year in 1962.

Perhaps Heinrich suspected that something was in the wind. A few intimate friends he had made on the staff warned him of danger. He had not been asked to submit his usual budget for the year 1960/1961, which the University had to take into account in submitting its own budget to the provincial treasury. On 16 February 1960 he wrote to President Claude Bissell, who had now succeeded Sidney Smith, giving his estimates for the coming year. "This I do," he stated, "in the absence of the usual invitation and instructions for two reasons." One of these reasons was the necessity of appointing additional staff. The other was the ending in the previous year of the contributions of seventy-five thousand dollars a year from the University's research fund guaranteed by the University for three years in 1956, making "still larger the already depressing gap between vital needs and available funds", and broadening "the chasm of years between recognition of those needs and their fulfillment".

The estimates Heinrich submitted represented "months of soul-search-

ing and agonised reappraisal on the part of curators, service and administrative chiefs, Division Heads, the Chairman and myself". But it involved
an increase in expenditure in a year when economy was essential.
Acknowledging this, Heinrich added that all questions on the matter
could be dealt with in the discussion "necessary to reconcile this statement
of the Museum's current needs with the blunt facts of fiscal reality".

Lionel Massey's appointment as director of administration was
announced on 6 October 1960. It came as a surprise to Heinrich, who had
not been consulted. It was explained publicly as a measure designed to
take a great deal of the administrative burden from the shoulders of the
director. Massey appeared for the first time at a board meeting on 22
November 1960. It was not long before he made his presence felt,
recommending reductions in the Museum's plans for the 1962 jubilee
celebrations, the main feature of which was to be a major international
Arctic show, involving the cooperation of Russia and the Scandinavian
countries. Massey suggested that preparations for this should be postponed until the board heard from the University finance committee and
warned, "The Museum cannot proceed on credit."

In his annual report for 1960/1961 the director, in noting Lionel
Massey's appointment, attempted to diminish its significance by describing it as being equivalent to the office of a corporation secretary, adding
that Mr Massey had proved himself a very efficient aide to the director.
But the writing was already on the wall. The bright promise of 1955 was
fading rapidly, and the director's annual report for the following year,
1961/1962, recording the completion of the Museum's first half-century,
was to be the last written by Heinrich. It carried the announcement that
he was leaving the scene, expressed with great dignity and in his own
inimitable and graceful phrasing:

> The convenient landmark of its [the Museum's] fiftieth official anniversary
> therefore provides an opportune moment for the double-edged exercise of
> public congratulation for past achievement and private questioning as to
> future programme, development and support. This final report of the out-
> going director is not the place for the expression of opinions concerning the
> Museum's future course, but it is an appropriate occasion for him to join all
> those who are rejoicing in 1962 over its achievements of the past half-
> century.

Ending the final report of his stewardship with his belief that a
museum's duty was to constitute "a harmonious chord of the various
aspects of the world as it is known to its generation", he consciously or

unconsciously reiterated Sir Edmund Walker's faith that these aspects could only be effectively studied in depth in a museum and with the full orchestration of art and science. The Royal Ontario Museum, Heinrich declared, was one of the last great mixed museums in the world.

Heinrich had arrived at the Museum at just the right moment in its history to continue, in a very different way, the thrust imparted to it by Currelly. If he had not appeared when he did, the Museum, when Currelly had gone, might have become wholly absorbed in its scholarly pursuits, remaining a fine provincial museum, the largest in Canada, renowned for its close association with Canada's largest university. Its scholars would have gained for it international recognition, but not its reputation as one of the great public museums of North America. With his colourful personality and fervent vision, Heinrich recalled the memory of what the Museum had promised to become when Currelly in his early years had shouldered the science professors aside and claimed the attention of the public, not at all averse to being thought the director of the entire Royal Ontario Museum.

Heinrich had seen the Museum principally as a fine arts museum. This approach was important for the evolution of the Art and Archaeology Division of the Museum, and probably for the entire institution, and Heinrich may be said to have pointed in directions that had not been given enough thought. The Royal Ontario Museum continued firmly in the Currelly tradition. Currelly's vision was the stronger, but Heinrich added a new dimension to it.

Heinrich's failures were due to lack of stability in his own character; he could not sustain the weight of responsibility which the institution imposed on its director at this stage in its growth. He had brilliant perceptions; but he lacked the necessary sense of financial responsibility at a time when the Museum, still tied to the University administratively and financially, had grown to such proportions that it had to free itself from those ties if it was ever to flourish as a public museum. It was to take another six years for the Royal Ontario Museum to become an independent corporation and a partner rather than a dependant of the University.

There was no spite or envy in Heinrich, and those who got to know him well loved him in spite of his faults; they warned him that he was heading for disaster, but he laughed the warnings away. Both Theodore Heinrich and, at a later date, Peter Swann were very different characters from Currelly; but each in his way was to express the Museum's continual effort to free itself from the bonds in which the University of Toronto and the Ontario government, with the best intentions and the greatest generosity, had tried to keep it.

14

Calmer Waters

Before appointing a successor to Theodore Heinrich, the University of Toronto took time to consider. Having dismissed Heinrich, the board of governors now reflected that his appointment, made on the basis of a two-day visit to the Royal Ontario Museum, had been too hastily rushed into. Determined not to repeat this error, they announced that the chairman of the Museum board of trustees, Harold Turner, with the assistance of Lionel Massey, would temporarily assume the duties of the director, and that a committee chaired by Dr Claude Bissell, the president of the University, would be set up to consider the relationship between the Museum and other divisions of the University.

The committee reached its conclusions in the spring of 1963, although the Bissell Report, as it came to be called, was not published until September. One of its recommendations was that the divisions should be abolished and the curators be given direct access to the director.

In the matter of Museum salaries, the report announced that steps would be taken at the earliest date possible, and certainly within three years, to bring the salaries of curators, associate curators, and assistant curators level with those of their University counterparts. And further, the director and associate director of the Museum and the University personnel officer were instructed to initiate a study of the salaries of non-curatorial positions, particularly those requiring special skills, artistic ability, and expert judgement, with the purpose of bringing them into line with the curatorial increases.

Echoing proposals put forward in L. L. Snyder's five-year plan of 1946, the report proposed that the Museum's board of trustees should be turned into a Museum Advisory Board, "responsible for studying the needs, opportunities, and future development of the Museum, and giving guid-

130

ance and assistance to the Director". It further recommended the setting up of a Museum Council, to include all curatorial staff and the staff of the Education Division, under the chairmanship of the director of the Museum. The curators would thus be given a direct voice in the making of the Museum's policies.

The report was largely an attempt to pour oil on troubled waters. It seemed to herald great changes, but its effect was to lock the Museum more tightly into the University structure. The Bissell Committee included some of the most distinguished professors in the University. They held hearings; no one was barred from giving evidence even though it might be unpalatable to a university body. Bissell contributed an account of the committee's work and recommendations to the Museum's annual report for 1962/1963. In it he stated that the committee had satisfied themselves that it had become "increasingly clear that any conflict between the Museum's functions as a public agency and as a scholarly institution was largely the creation of outsiders with no real understanding either of the Museum or of the University".

Reading today these recommendations made by highly distinguished men, it is hard to remember that this was 1963, when Canada was on the verge of a museum explosion from coast to coast that was to be one of the major developments in its cultural history. The "museum age" was arriving all over North America. Stimulated by television documentaries and the greater leisure now enjoyed by many people, the demand for informal public education was growing. The result was a cultural environment entirely different from the one for which this report sought to provide. The Bissell Committee's recommendations seemed to be based on the notion that the Museum had gone slack. Under the right director, stimulated by an adjustment of salaries and differentials, encouraged to do research and to publish, it would recover its health. Bissell predicted that under the new director administrative appointments and new policies would "usher in a new period of achievement in the history of the Museum"—almost exactly the phrase used by his predecessor in extolling Heinrich's qualities.

By the time the committee's report was published, the new director had been appointed. He was William Elgin Swinton, who after a lifetime spent in the British Museum (Natural History) had joined the Royal Ontario Museum in 1961 as head of the Life Sciences Division. The contrast with Heinrich was not only in background, temperament, and training, but also in appearance and manner, and could not have been sharper. The aesthete who had arrived in Toronto in 1955, just at the right moment to awaken it to the claims of culture on the civilized mind, was now replaced by a scholar and scientist who had risen from museum assistant to become principal scientific officer of the British Museum (Natural History). Swinton was a world authority on dinosaurs, a scholar of repute who had done much to popularize science. His appointment promised a return to the principle on which the Museum had been founded, a union of science and art, under the guidance of a great university.

The list of Swinton's scientific publications was long and impressive, and his activity in the British Association for the Advancement of Science marked his continuous contribution to science. But it was as a popularizer of science that he was best known, his fame, in the words of the historian of the British Museum (Natural History), "spreading far beyond the museum". Swinton had the gift of natural eloquence combined with a mind clear of all clutter. A slight Scottish burr and the jolly appearance of a Mr Pickwick dispelled the natural apprehension a lay audience might feel on being addressed by a scholar. The Royal Ontario Museum had been lucky to acquire such a man as head of its Life Sciences Division when Professor F. A. Urquhart decided to return to university teaching. The relationship between Urquhart and Heinrich had not been happy. They were both ambitious, and scholar and aesthete had regarded one another with mutual lack of admiration.

Swinton had made a number of visits to North America for scientific congresses, and as president of the British Museums Association in 1958/1959 had been the guest of the American Association of Museums. Heinrich had always attended meetings of the British Museums Association on his annual visits to dealers and auctions in England, on his way to the villa he shared with three other men on the island of Giglio off the Italian coast north of Rome. On Urquhart's departure, Heinrich had written to the dean of arts and science of the University of Toronto strongly recommending Swinton for the vacancy.

In his sixtieth year Swinton could retire from the British Museum (Natural History). He had shared a house in London with his mother, whose death at this time dispelled any hesitation he might have had about moving abroad. He particularly liked Toronto because of its strong Scottish element.

Swinton had taken up his appointment as head of the Life Sciences Division in September 1961, eight months before Heinrich's resignation had been called for in May 1962. The last annual report of the outgoing director therefore included not only the announcement of his own imminent departure, but a welcome to the new head of the Life Sciences Division who would find, he feared, "a very different situation and set of problems in Toronto from those to which he has been accustomed in the less volatile ambience of the venerable British Museum of Natural History in London".

Swinton's appointment to the directorship of the Museum took effect from 1 July 1963. In making the appointment the board of governors of the University had calculated carefully. A second failure would be catastrophic. The board, acting on the Bissell Committee's recommendation, had therefore chosen a man who, it was convinced, could be relied upon to carry out its recommendations with tact and authority.

> We believe that there is no acceptable substitute for an academic Director who can represent and speak for the Museum; who can study its departmental structure, its problems, its weaknesses and its possibilities, and make the decisions about its component parts; who can give it imaginative leadership; and who can, above all, recommend appointments of high quality to the President for presentation to the Board of Governors. To merit the loyalty of his curators and the respect of the community, he must be a scholar of distinction, with Museum experience.

Swinton, for his part, was quite ready to carry out the first two of the three main recommendations of the Bissell Report which were, in general, to take steps to improve the relations between the Museum and the University, and to make such internal reorganization of the Museum as in his opinion would be necessary to give the curators direct access to him. One of his first acts produced some much-needed benefits. He obtained for all the curators an immediate salary increase of one thousand dollars a year, pending the raising of salaries to University levels, which was to be achieved within three years. The third recommendation, that the board should be restructured to become an advisory rather than an executive council, was a matter for settlement between the board of governors of the University and the Ontario government, in which he could play only a passive part.

Swinton's was to be a notable directorship in many ways, and if the intention of the board of governors had been to turn back the clock just at the moment when museums everywhere were being swept forward by a new interest on the part of the public, it was defeated to a certain extent by Swinton's own natural gifts. Television was becoming an ideal medium for introducing the collections to a public with a newly sharpened appetite for learning. Swinton's appearance, the timbre of his Scottish voice, and his talent for popularizing science, which had made his reputation in England as one of the British Museum's most admired lecturers, all helped him to establish and maintain a contact with the Canadian Broadcasting Corporation. He arranged a series of television programs which would give each curator and his particular collection public exposure. His experience enabled him to show them how the script should be written and how the objects should be presented. He was in effect a producer of programs as well as an outstanding performer himself. He could not understand why curators so generously helped in these matters should resent having their unexplained absences or regrettably late morning arrivals at the Museum drawn to their attention. There was a Scottish dominie hidden behind the bland appearance.

But those who got to know him well could make allowances for his mannerisms. He was elderly. He had been brought up in the British Museum where in his youth discipline had been strict and even eminent scholars had to keep museum hours. Beneath the mannered exterior they found a great boyish enthusiasm and an absolute freedom from jealousy of other people's achievements, a scholar and a first-rate museum man, stimulating to be with.

Simultaneously with Swinton's appointment as director, Lionel Massey had been appointed associate director. Massey's assistant, Ian Montagnes, had an excellent opportunity to observe both men. There was, he noted, a good deal of constraint in their feelings for one another. Swinton was not a good administrator, but he was the director, and final decisions had to be made by him. Massey had been appointed in Heinrich's time as the University's financial watchdog. Swinton thought that Massey may have hoped to be appointed director on Heinrich's departure and felt put out by Swinton's appointment. But Massey was no scholar and had had no museum experience. Perhaps Swinton, with his high reputation and brisk efficiency, and his mandate from the Bissell Report to straighten things out, rather awed him. Whatever Massey's feelings, he was a thoroughly decent man and quite incapable of jealousy. Sadly he was to die suddenly in office in 1965.

Montagnes says that Swinton had one of the most fertile minds he had ever encountered. He had no other interests than science and his work; when he found himself idle for a minute or two, some scientific problem of no possible application at that moment would float into his mind, and he would reach for paper and pencil to solve it—what, for example, was the maximum weight and wingspan beyond which a bird would be unable to fly? Speculations of this kind with scientific conclusions are to be found in numerous articles he contributed to journals and in books such as *Giants Past and Present,* which deals with all aspects of gigantism in fishes, birds of the air, reptiles, and human beings.

The growth of public attendance at the Museum accelerated every year in Swinton's three-year tenure, leaping from 580 726 to 729 536, an increase of almost forty per cent. Popularizing too often implies cheapening a subject by stripping it of its inner mystery so that it can be taken in even by people of limited education. But it is the duty of a public museum to instruct as well as awe the visitor. What draws the visitors is the visibility of the wonders they read about. Swinton was not a remote scholar concentrating on research. That came as a by-product of the interest of the subject itself. One of the most successful of the exhibitions put on in Swinton's time was the *International Aerospace Exhibition,* which opened in the summer of 1964, five years before the Apollo flight landed a man on the moon's surface. The National Aeronautics and Space Administration of the United States, which had been created in 1958 to test equipment and undertake research in and beyond earth's atmosphere, cooperated by lending spacesuits and other material. Smoke tunnels were created to provide a mock-up of a blast-off, and the entry into and re-entry from space were simulated with life-size figures. The first soft landing on the moon with probe, camera, and instruments had not yet been made, but it was already in preparation.

~~~

The exhibition may have been indirectly responsible for what Swinton called in the annual report for 1964/1965 "the most outstanding act of private generosity in the Museum's history", the gift of a planetarium and a fund to sustain it. Dr V. B. Meen, the chief mineralogist, had been trying for ten years to raise money for a planetarium, without success. But one day in October, when Meen was away from the Museum on an extended trip and Swinton himself was absent with a heavy cold, a man called at the Museum asking to see the director. Montagnes saw him, explaining the director's absence. The visitor gave his name as Mr English, and said he understood that the Museum was interested in establishing a planetarium and that he had a friend he thought might help. He obtained what particulars were available of the plans for a planetarium and disappeared. Two days later he reappeared with a letter from Colonel R. S. McLaughlin addressed to Dr Swinton undertaking to fund the project.

Mr English turned out to be Colonel McLaughlin's secretary. Colonel McLaughlin had been in Canadian automobile manufacturing, having turned his original carriage-building business to the manufacture of the McLaughlin car. In collaboration with General Motors, this had become the McLaughlin-Buick, and subsequently the Buick. McLaughlin had become many times a millionaire in the process and was a generous benefactor of many causes. His interest in a planetarium had been aroused during the war when he saw the Hayden Planetarium in New York, and later the Adler Planetarium in Chicago, and he determined that one day Canada should have a planetarium to rival them. He had had his own joke with the director when he telephoned after his emissary's first visit and revealed the identity of Mr English's "friend he thought might help". He asked how much a planetarium would cost, and Swinton, at a loss without even approximate figures, said "between one and two million dollars". In the event, the cost was $2.25 million, and in order to ensure that the planetarium could be maintained, developed, and improved, McLaughlin generously added an endowment fund of $1 million.

No gift could have been more timely. Public interest in the preparations being made for probing space and for enabling man to travel in it was evident in the attendance at the *International Aerospace Exhibition.* The fact that the gift followed so soon after the exhibition suggests that McLaughlin had visited it himself and had had his enthusiasm for a planetarium rekindled.

With the funding in hand, the University of Toronto provided the land, offering to demolish the Blood and Vascular Disease Building, just south of the Royal Ontario Museum on Queen's Park, to make room. There had been strong representation from the board of trustees of the Museum to place the planetarium on Bloor Street, where it could be seen to best advantage. But Swinton stood out strongly for the location on Queen's Park, where the dome would not clash with the northern ends of the parallel east and west wings. This proved fortunate; if the Bloor Street site had been chosen, the beautiful terrace galleries of the 1982 expansion would not have been possible.

But like everything else, plans for the planetarium moved slowly and a rising dissatisfaction with the ponderous pace with which any problem was approached had been making Swinton increasingly testy. The Museum had been grossly overcrowded for years, and although Heinrich had discussed a building plan, nothing had come of it. In his annual report for 1964/1965, after recording such highlights as the visits of the Queen Mother and the Empress of Iran and the *International Aerospace Exhibition,* Swinton went on to complain again of the lack of space.

> The demands of the public on our space and on curatorial time have so increased as to render serious research difficult in some departments. Our storage room is exhausted. There is no space for expansion of exhibits or for a single additional office. The Museum is almost literally bursting at its seams and the demand for increased space, staff and facilities, particularly laboratory facilities, is urgent.

The Museum cannot afford to cease adding to its collections, to forsake its research, to abandon its teaching, or to cease its interpretive function for the general public. No museum can stand still. The choice is to proceed or to recede. The Royal Ontario Museum is rapidly approaching the complete exhaustion of facilities that have served it well enough for the last fifty years but are no longer adequate for its present role or for the public's expectations of it.

Especially pressing were the demands of conservation—the endless work needed to preserve the Museum's collections in good condition. For this purpose laboratories, workshops, and temperature and humidity controls were essential if the collections of Canada's largest museum and the work of fifty years were not to be wasted.

Swinton went on to fortify his public statement by a long memorandum addressed to the chairman of the board of governors of the University, the president of the University, and the chairman of the board of trustees of the Museum, reminding them of the broad range of activities to which the Museum had become committed, largely in the past thirty years, during which time there had been virtually no increase in available space. On a Sunday afternoon, now, more than five thousand people might be in the building. In any one year well over a thousand new objects were added to the art and archaeological collections alone, ranging in size from small ceramics to an eight-metre kayak. It was estimated that the planetarium would add half-a-million annually to attendance, and yet as Swinton pointed out in his last annual report, for 1965/1966, eighteen months after Colonel McLaughlin's gift of the planetarium, "not a single trace of its creation is yet upon the ground and no steps have yet been taken towards the demolition of premises that must first be removed".

It must have been the memorandum from the director that made Henry Borden, the chairman of the board of governors of the University, write an eight-page letter on 16 October 1965 to William Davis, the Ontario minister of university affairs, giving detailed figures of the greatly enlarged scope of the Museum's work, and asking for a grant to build a new wing. Indeed Swinton probably drafted the letter, since Borden could hardly have been aware of specific details of the deplorable effect of crowding in the Museum building. The plan proposed for a new wing, to run east and west along Bloor Street between the old west wing and the newer east wing, was basically the one adopted ten years later for the Queen Elizabeth II Terrace Galleries.

The chairman of the board of governors assessed the cost of building the new wing at $4 million and estimated that it would add $250 000 to the existing annual operating cost of $1.25 million. Borden asked for this sum to be provided over three years so that construction might be started as soon as details of design and architectural plans could be prepared and agreed on. But no reply was forthcoming—perhaps because the Ontario government itself was already considering taking over the Museum. The situation worsened every month.

The problem of space had been a constant one almost since the Museum's beginning. The pressure had been only temporarily alleviated by the addition of the east wing in 1931/1933 and by the reduced activity of the war years. After this enforced pause, the need for space had soon accelerated again, and ten years after the war it had presented itself again to Heinrich as the Museum's major problem. With his talent for attracting attention, and with Duncan Cameron's assistance, Heinrich had seen to it that the matter received wide publicity both in the press and in a succession of speeches to such bodies as the Board of Trade and the Rotary Club, in which he hammered away at the theme of the need for space if the Museum was to fulfil its function.

But the project had not got further than the board of governors, probably because the University was preoccupied with its own expansion projects and regarded the Museum simply as another university department. That this was still how the Museum was viewed can be seen from the remarks of one of the most distinguished members of the Bissell Committee, who declared: "[The Museum] is primarily a research organization, and only after these purposes have been served is it a place for public amusement. . . . The Museum is rightly a part of the university community because of its teaching function." That this was the view of the committee as a whole was implicit in its recommendations and in Swinton's appointment to replace Heinrich, who had nettled the board of governors with his public statements about plans for the Museum's expansion.

If the University expected Swinton to be more compliant, it was in for a surprise. When the decision to abolish the three divisions gave all twenty-three departments direct access to him, Swinton was shocked into an awareness of how much of what the Museum should provide was being lost through tight-fisted financial policies and internal jealousy.

No one could express the Museum's needs better, but Swinton was not a born administrator. Nor could he easily work with anyone appointed to assist him who might attempt to exercise some form of constraint over his decisions. With many of the curators he got along excellently; they respected his scholarship and experience. But in the mass they bothered him. The Museum Council envisaged in the Bissell recommendations had met only once. That meeting had ended disastrously, because the director had lectured the curators and had rashly named those who had flouted or questioned his decisions; if they were not ready to acknowledge his authority, he told them, their resignations would be accepted.

Perhaps it had been a mistake to abolish the divisions; at least they had created a buffer between the growing power of the curators and the ambitions or shortcomings of a director. On the other hand, when power rested in the hands of divisional heads, the lack of their support could also weaken a director's authority.

Cross-appointments to the University meant that many of the most powerful curators were interlocked into the University system, where they could sow doubts that would weaken a director's position. It would be too much to imply that Heinrich's dismissal had been engineered by the division heads; but they did represent the curators, and Heinrich had made the mistake of acting independently of their advice. Swinton had not made that mistake, but he had not won the curators' unquestioning support, and the year 1965/1966 was to be the last of his directorship.

Yet there is no trace in the annual report for that year of any emotion. Swinton must have been saddened that his expiring three-year contract was not renewed, but a new University regulation had been passed, fixing the retirement age for administrators at sixty-five. His loyal service to the Museum and the University was rewarded by a full professorship in the University and a fellowship in Massey College, the new graduate college of the Toronto campus. Thus he was able to return to a life of scholarship, leaving the Museum a more popular place than it had been when he entered it. He was an essential element in restoring balance and in maintaining the Museum's growth between two regimes of extravagant innovation, not all of it beneficial or lasting.

15

Stormy Petrel

On 22 September 1965, when President Claude Bissell of the University of Toronto wrote to the members of the Museum's board of trustees conveying the news that the director of their institution was to retire at the end of June 1966, he added:

> As you will recall, the appointment of a Director of the Royal Ontario Museum is made by the University of Toronto Board of Governors on the recommendation of the President. I have appointed a small committee to advise me on this matter, and I have asked Dr Woodside, the Provost, to serve as its chairman. Sometime early in the New Year I hope to be able to announce Dr Swinton's successor.

It may be remembered that Moffat Woodside's recommendation for a director to succeed Gerard Brett had been a promising young keeper of Eastern art at the Ashmolean named Peter Swann, who was then being groomed for the headship of that department. In Woodside's view, Swann was "the sort of Englishman who would have no difficulty at all in accommodating himself to the Canadian scene".

While still an undergraduate at St Edmund Hall, Oxford, Peter Swann had joined the Royal Navy in 1939. He had volunteered to learn Japanese and had succeeded so well that when the United States entered the war he had been sent to Washington, where he had become head of an Anglo-American naval intelligence translation bureau. Returning to Oxford after the war, he had taken a first class degree in Classical Chinese and had then joined the Ashmolean, where Dean Woodside had first met him.

Swann's career had prospered. He had become editor of the journal *Oriental Art* and had been appointed an official adviser on Eastern art to the French government. As keeper at the Ashmolean, he had transformed the galleries to such a degree that the *Times* of London had declared that they should set an example of excellence for all British museums. He had also been retained by Princeton University to advise on the development of its museum.

Swann was quite plainly a man of energy and attainments, ambitious to get to the top. In 1965 he appeared highly suitable to head a museum that boasted one of the finest Chinese collections in the world. President Bissell did not have to wait for the New Year. On 5 November 1965, six weeks after his letter to the board of the Museum, he could tell them that the new director of the Royal Ontario Museum would be Peter Swann. In this way there entered the Museum's service the most controversial of all its directors, whose stormy passage can be seen in retrospect to have been as necessary to the Museum's great future as it seemed, at the end of his tenure, momentarily to threaten its continued development.

Swann's first act on taking office in August 1966 was to grapple with the crowded condition of the Museum. He began by asking all the department heads for a report on their space requirements. The response to this was immediate and enthusiastic. The curators were proud of their collections, and they were convinced that they would have been even better had there been adequate storage space, laboratories, conservation staff and facilities, and display areas. The reports necessarily included summary histories of the development of each department as part of the justification for larger space. The curators had been asked to be realistic in the estimate of their needs; some exaggeration may have occurred, but in the director's view this had been cancelled out by some over-modest estimates.

Swann had the 240 pages of reports and estimates put together in a binder and presented them as a brief to the Users' Committee. This committee had been appointed by the president of the University immediately following Swann's arrival specifically to consider the space requirements of the Museum. The statement accompanying the brief reminded the committee that no addition had been made to the building for thirty years and warned that the Royal Ontario Museum must expand or choke to death. The committee was equally prompt in giving consideration to the brief. By February 1967 it had accepted the brief in principle and had authorized a detailed study of the proposed space allocations.

At this point came a distraction of great importance, the separation of the Museum from the University. This was to postpone the detailed study of expansion for two more years. Then the matter had to be taken up by the Museum with an entirely new authority, the Ontario government.

The break had been inevitable for some years. The Royal Ontario Museum was getting too big and too expensive to be contained as a department of the University of Toronto. Yet the University was reluctant to let it go. The habit of authority which comes naturally to all great universities meant that it did not think it necessary to take the Museum authorities into its confidence. A defensive letter from President Bissell to members of the Museum board of trustees dated 10 March 1967 gave no hint of the impending change. It had been charged in the press that the University starved the Museum and that the Museum's wretchedly over-crowded state and lack of climatic control were due to parsimony on the University's part. Bissell's letter was meant to protest the charge and to document the University's generosity, which had frequently gone beyond the call of duty. The University, it pointed out, had always conveyed to the Ontario government the requests of the director and his associates without diminution. It had vigorously supported these requests and had been prepared to reduce its own needs in order to further the Museum's interests. Bissell protested that he had always taken great pride in the Museum and would always give it the strongest possible support, the more eagerly now "because in Mr Peter Swann we have a Director of international reputation who is working tirelessly on behalf of the Museum".

One has to remember that at this point all the Museum's accounts were settled by the University. The requirements put forward in Swann's brief, which included a new Bloor Street wing, were well beyond the powers of the University to fulfil, and there may have been a sense of relief for the president and the board of governors in the recognition that this was an appropriate occasion for a friendly divorce.

At what point did this change of view present itself to the board of governors? There was no hint of it in President Bissell's letter of 10 March. Yet on 26 April there is a memorandum from Peter Swann to President Bissell, reporting the outcome of an interview he had had with the Ontario minister of education and university affairs "regarding the divorce of Museum and University", which indicates an advanced stage in the negotiations. On 3 May, exactly a week later, a statement was issued by the director addressed "To All Departments", advising the staff of an impending change. It was briefly prefaced by an announcement: "This statement was issued by Dr Claude Bissell, President of the University of Toronto, today, to the *Toronto Star*."

Some changes in the relationship of the Museum with the University and the Ontario Government have been under discussion for some time. A number of details remain to be ironed out. But the close academic and research links between the ROM and the University will remain, and the system of cross-appointments whereby members of the curatorial staff also hold appointments in appropriate university departments will be maintained. The purpose of the change is to strengthen the Museum and thus extend its role academically and among the public.

"As the whole matter is still under close study," Bissell's statement concluded, "I would prefer to say nothing more at the moment."

No doubt all parties were willing the separation. For some time the Ontario government had been feeling that the University was getting all the credit for the Museum's growing fame, while the government was left to pay the bills. The director no doubt felt that his plans for expanding the Museum could more conveniently proceed under a new and vigorous board, particularly if he could exert some influence in choosing its members. In dealing with expansion, an informal relationship was infinitely to be preferred to an arm's length relationship with the University's board of governors.

The Ontario minister of education and university affairs was the Honourable William G. Davis, who was later to become the premier of the province. Soon the correspondence between minister and director was being conducted on terms of "Dear Bill" and "Dear Peter". By the year's end Swann was able to depart for a Christmas visit to England knowing that the legislation effecting the change was on the point of being approved by the board of governors. Only two sticky but revealing points remained to be settled, and about these he wrote to his friend Bill Davis. The director wanted the trustees' terms of office to be limited to three years, on the grounds that "many well-wishers would like to be able to participate and help the Museum". And he objected to the trustees' retention of the power to appoint, transfer, or remove a curator, officer, or member of the staff. He wanted this to be qualified by the proviso "except on the recommendation of the Director". It was not an unreasonable request. Some of Swann's requests were taken into account. The new board was to comprise twenty-one members, three of them *ex officio* —the chairman of the board of governors of the University of Toronto, the president of the University, and the director of the Royal Ontario Museum. Of the remaining eighteen, fifteen were to be appointed by the lieutenant governor in council and three elected by members of the Museum. And the terms of office were restricted. As to the jurisdictions of the board and director, the act stated that the director would "make recommendations to the Board as to all appointments to and all promo-

tions in, and removals from the staff of the Museum including the
Associate Director or Directors, curators and officers".

By July 1968 the new Royal Ontario Museum Act had been passed and
the formal separation was celebrated by an article by Peter Swann in
Rotunda, the journal of the Museum which he had founded on 1 January
1968, hailing "A New Era". The article was both a celebration of the
Museum's past history of difficulties overcome and triumphs achieved,
and a call to new action to throw off the restraints that had prevented the
Museum in the past from fully developing its public function.

> The ROM was not permitted to plead its cause independently before the
> bodies which recommend its funds. . . . Nor has the Museum been permit-
> ted to appeal directly to the public for funds and support. This sometimes
> resulted in frustration and resentment both on the part of the Museum and
> on the part of a segment of the public devoted to the ROM but unwilling to
> give to it in the mistaken conviction that the University would appropriate
> such gifts. As a relative newcomer it surprised me to find how widely and
> fiercely this conviction was held.

That Swann had something to celebrate cannot be doubted. Into this
overcrowded, unventilated old building, packed now with treasures of
which only a small part could be seen, the public had been coming in
rapidly increasing numbers. In 1958 the Museum had recorded its eleven-
millionth visitor since its opening. Ten years later Swann could record
that it had had another six million since that date. The attendance was
now well over 750 000 annually. This total included more than 110 000
schoolchildren receiving instruction from trained teachers attached to the
Museum staff, making the Museum the largest "school" in the country.
When the McLaughlin Planetarium opened in the autumn of 1968, it was
expected to bring tremendous crowds to the Museum. A new wing must
be built without delay, with public underground parking and the
desperately needed storage and study areas. "In a very short time," Swann
noted near the end of his article, "under the pressure of over one million
visitors per year we must remedy twenty years of insufficient support."

Another requirement was the establishment of a purchase fund large
enough to provide by its interest the acquisitions the Museum needed to
keep its primary place in the nation. A museum training program, which
it was hoped would lead to a university degree, was to begin in the next
year.

In tackling the problems caused by the lack of space, the expansion
plans produced for the Users' Committee two years earlier were brought

up-to-date and presented to E. E. Stewart, deputy minister of education and university affairs. The department remained responsible for the Museum even though it was now independent of the University. The essential space requirements were now set at 37 463 square metres, an addition of fifty per cent. The sum boldly asked for was $30 million, a large increase over the $4 million asked for by the chairman of the University board of governors in his appeal to the Ontario government in October 1965.

~~~

A new sense of active dynamism was coursing through the Museum. The case for expansion had been so boldly presented that everyone in the institution felt at last that something was going to be done. The prospect of a new wing lifted the spirits of the curators, and the director's popularity with them was unquestionable.

The Ontario government responded quickly. The estimates were approved in principle by the Department of Education and University Affairs in December 1969, and the Museum was authorized to proceed with an extension feasibility study. The firm of Moffat Moffat & Kinoshita, engaged as consulting architects, presented its feasibility study in December 1970, and in that same fiscal year the Ontario government earmarked $12.75 million for the Museum's expansion to be spent over the next ten years.

A diarist of the time lists some of Swann's successful initiatives; the construction of benches and showcases outside the Museum, the addition of a good restaurant and an attractive members' lounge, a vast increase in membership resulting from a well-directed and sustained drive in which the director himself played an active part, and above all the establishment of a purchase fund for acquisitions.

The Purchase Trust Fund had been one of the first of Swann's ventures. Such a fund was certainly needed, and the strategy he laid out for a campaign, if successful, would redound to his credit. The director initiated a search for a "Group of One Hundred", something like the "Group of Ten" who in Currelly's time had each pledged an annual contribution of $500. Swann's Group of One Hundred was to be a body of philanthropic and interested men and women who would each contribute up to $1000 a year for ten years. Other museums, the director pointed out, had purchase trusts ranging up to $100 million. That could hardly be expected in Toronto. But it was intolerable that Canada's greatest museum should be forced to refuse objects costing only $15 000 or less. The annual acquisition fund in the budget was $18 000 and that had to be spread over all departments.

In his report for 1967/1968 Swann could announce that the Purchase Trust Fund stood at $105 000. Only the interest could be used. If the interest could be brought up to $100 000 a year—$1 million would be needed to assure that—then a workable level would be reached. By the following year eighty-five people had enrolled in the Group of One Hundred, each contributing $1000 a year. The capital of the fund at that point stood at $230 000. In the next year it reached $400 000.

To a reader of the director's annual reports, these seem years of continual triumph. But behind the outward optimism there was growing unrest. Both the euphoria and the director's popularity were beginning to wane. He seemed uninterested in internal matters; his energy and drive were fixed on the need to raise money for expansion. Some of the curators still supported him strongly, but others were critical of his penny-pinching policy over necessary improvements inside the Museum. And while there was no doubt in anyone's mind that the Museum owed its independence to Peter Swann, the support that he had had earlier from the whole curatorial body was beginning to fall away.

The first board of the newly independent Museum, too, under its chairman, Richard Meech, was becoming critical of the high-handed manner in which the director ran the Museum. Of course, not all the problems that were surfacing were the fault of the director. He had taken over an organization that had been thrust into adulthood with no defined purposes or goals, no internal law or policies, no administrative structure, no personnel policy, no top management in the proper sense of the word, and no clearly established lines of authority. All the curators reported to the director, and all the rest of the staff reported to an administrator, who was ignored by a chosen few of the director's immediate friends. The Museum was disorganized and confused, and needed to be ruled with a strong hand.

In an attempt to set up a line of authority the board commissioned a report in 1970 from Price Waterhouse Associates, which was to undertake "an analysis of virtually every facet of the ROM's organization and operations". Included among its observations was the need to "dispel any ambiguity with regard to the relationship between the Board of Trustees on one hand and the Director on the other".

As Meech observed at the beginning of the 1970/1971 annual report, "The year under review has been a period of challenge, growth and self-analysis." "Challenge" was not an overstatement. It had begun when the curators asked, by virtue of their professional status, for representation on the board. This would require an amendment to the Royal Ontario Museum Act 1968 and the decision was deferred pending the receipt of

Price Waterhouse's report. The report consisted of seven volumes, the first of which was delivered in January and the last in August 1971.

~~~

In January 1971, in anticipation of possible opposition from the board to the renewal of his service agreement, the director's close friends among the curators had begun collecting signatures for a letter of curatorial support for the renewal of the appointment. The letter went on to say that if rumours of differences between the director and the board were to put in question his reappointment, the curators found it shocking that an issue so central to their lives should be settled without consultation with them. Thirty-seven curators signed the letter, which was delivered to the chairman on 29 January 1971.

Meech replied mildly to the curators' letter that the director's term of office did not end until 30 June 1971, and that the board would be discussing the matter at their next meeting. Their decision was to renew the contract until the end of the following Museum year, 30 June 1972. In October an announcement was released to the press to the effect that the director's contract had been renewed, but no mention was made of the brief duration of the renewal. The announcement said: "Dr Swann's reappointment as Director will provide the continuity that is so vital at this time in the Museum's development.... The Board of Trustees are most happy that he will continue in that capacity."

Meanwhile Price Waterhouse's report had been arriving in monthly instalments. Among its many recommendations was the appointment of an associate director. In December 1971 Walter H. Tovell, who had been with the Museum since 1949 and had been curator of the Department of Geology since 1964, was named associate director, responsible for curatorial affairs.

In January 1972 the director responded to this appointment in a memo to all staff, headed "Line of Authority", which said that at a meeting a few days earlier the board of trustees had agreed that the line of authority in the Museum would henceforth be director, associate director, business administrator. It went on to say: "I emphasized that, in my opinion, the genius of this place lay in its flexibility and this chain of command in no way interferes with the accessibility that everybody has to me, or vice versa. It is intended to come into operation mainly in the event of my absence." This was not the intention; the board had had a good deal more in mind than that when it made the appointment. However, at the same time it agreed that two curators, on a rotating basis, should be present at board meetings as observers.

Not surprisingly, two months before the end of his year's contract the director raised the question of its renewal, asking now that it should be renewed for another three years. He felt confident that he had the full support of the curators. The board had long been an obstruction to him. This was the time to challenge and defeat its authority.

The response of the board was to take up the challenge. They answered that they were not prepared to renew the contract, and offered to allow the director to resign at the end of June while receiving full salary for the remaining six months of the year, together with the generous severance sum which had been named in the year's contract.

Swann's immediate reaction was to summon all curators and department heads, curatorial and non-curatorial, to a meeting in the Museum theatre on 30 May 1972. The board was equally adroit. Noah Torno, who had succeeded Richard Meech as chairman, appeared to speak for the board. The director spoke first at some length, and with some emotion at the end, saying that if he had, as he thought, the deserved support of all the curators and staff his dismissal "for no cause" would not stand. Noah Torno spoke briefly and to the point, saying that if the staff supported the director the board would resign. Both men then left the room.

The staff discussion lasted for three hours. It revealed the identities of those whose reluctance in signing the previous year's letter of support now no longer needed to be hidden. Some of the curators said that they resented the constant pressure from the director to remove themselves from their discipline to engage in promotional activities for the Museum. Others who spoke felt the director had lost the ability to distinguish between himself and the institution. Still others who had attended the board meetings as observers said that the trustees were not the prehistoric dinosaurs the director had represented them as being.

A vote might still have swung the matter either way. But on the advice of the lawyer whom the staff had invited to the meeting that they should not be asked to vote on such a matter, the meeting broke up with no decision having been taken.

Meanwhile reports of the dissension inside the Museum had spilled into the press. Public spirit was aroused. A "Save-the-Museum Association" was formed which engaged in considerable activity, enlisting 850 members. Its officers were given a mandate to approach the government with a view to "broadening the board and reinstating the director". However, in face of all this the board maintained its resolution, and Swann's employment was terminated on 30 June 1972.

~~

Much had happened in the six years of Peter Swann's tenure. The Museum had broken free of University control, and the board had been revamped to suit Swann's plans for expansion, not only of the institution but of his own powers to direct it. He had not been tactful in his criticism of some elderly trustees. As early as February 1967, while the Museum was still under University control, he had written to the president of the University:

> For the sake of the record I think I should let you know that my relations with the Board seem to be deteriorating.
>
> Faced with inertia and disinterest on the one hand, I now find that, on the other, I am running into obstruction of things I would like to do to enliven the Museum, criticism of administrative and staff decisions which just had to be made, pressure from one member to fire curators whom she does not like, interference in matters which should not be the concern of the Board and petty needling on others. Some of this comes from the well-intentioned—some from the not so well-intentioned—and I need hardly say who that is.

Swann was plainly not a man who could work easily with others. His gifts and energy were undeniable, but he was impatient of restraint.

Though the board had been changed by the Royal Ontario Museum Act 1968, it still remained the supreme authority. Its members had made up their minds, with the advice and help of Price Waterhouse, that the director was not the man they wanted to be the chief administrative officer of a museum about to embark on a large-scale expansion, and with the authority of their office had said so.

16

Projecting the Future

The decade of the seventies, as the Royal Ontario Museum shook itself free from the heavy weight of the University of Toronto's paternalism and set out on its own as an independent corporation, was to prove one of the most dramatic and exciting in its history. This new era coincided with what amounted to a museum explosion all over the world. Museums had multiplied in the 20th century, particularly museums of science, which were now responding to the public interest in evolution and to the appetite for knowledge stimulated by increasing familiarity with science and advancing technology.

As the century wore on, many other factors contributed to the phenomenon—among them an aroused public consciousness about social issues, such as world hunger and concern about environmental damage and the pollution of our resources of air and water by the waste matter of technology. These were problems to whose understanding the research departments of museums could contribute. Thus museums had a new role thrust upon them; but at the same time they were expected to maintain their traditional role as treasure houses of the past history of man and his world.

In Canada the centenary celebrations of 1967 had aroused a sense of national pride and sharpened the nation's awareness of the dimensions of the task which its vast size and sparse population imposed upon it if it was to remain a united country. In 1968 Parliament had passed the National Museums Act. By this measure the national museums in Ottawa, including the National Gallery of Canada, the National Museum of Man, the National Museum of Natural Sciences, and the National Museum of Science and Technology, were organized into a corporation under a single board of trustees and enjoined to "demonstrate the products of nature and

150

the works of man". Four years later, in 1972, the federal government, through the secretary of state, Gérard Pelletier, announced a National Museum Policy aimed at involving the leading museums from sea to sea in a program for "the decentralization and democratization" of the arts. The participating museums were to become associate museums of the National Museums of Canada and, in return for federal government financial support, were to share their collections with the less well endowed museums in their areas and, through a fleet of museumobiles equipped as mobile galleries, to penetrate to remote areas whose inhabitants might never even have seen a museum.

For the Royal Ontario Museum, eligible to become an associate museum in this scheme, the time was unpropitious. The Museum was looking for a new director, and at the same time was studying the report from Price Waterhouse Associates on a suitable administrative organization for the institution—all this before resuming the expansion and renovation program vital to its continued existence. The Museum was also reliant upon the Ontario government for its operational funding. The traditional sensitivity of provincial governments to federal infringement upon their territory may have been an additional consideration in the Museum's decision to decline the invitation—a notable holdout from the new initiative.

~~~

A holding operation was necessary while a search was conducted for a new director. The board, free for the first time to make its own appointment, set up a search committee on which the Museum's staff had equal representation with trustees. Meanwhile, to fill the administrative gap, the board appointed the associate director, Walter Tovell, as director *pro tem*. But when after several months the committee reported that it had received two hundred applications for the directorship, many of them from abroad, and would need time to assess the qualifications of the candidates, the board removed the *pro tem* label from Tovell's position and appointed him director in June 1973, naming as his primary responsibilities curatorial and academic affairs. His service agreement was to run for two years, until 30 June 1975. At the same time Dr W. B. Scott, who had been curator in charge of the Department of Ichthyology and Herpetology, was appointed associate director.

Simultaneously, the board announced the appointment of a director (administration). This was a measure recommended in an early section of the Price Waterhouse Report. It came at a time when non-academic professionals—administrators, designers, display experts, communicators and public relations men, and others—were crowding into the museums of North America, sometimes to the discomfiture of some of the more academically inclined curators. An administrative authority with modern managerial skills was necessary to manage the wide range of activities in which a public museum was now necessarily involved.

There happened to be at hand an ideal candidate with the reputation, the authority, and the imagination to appreciate what the non-academic specialists could contribute to the shaping of an institution such as the Royal Ontario Museum. Maxwell Henderson, a well-known chartered accountant who had had experience with leading industrial firms, had just retired after thirteen years' service as Canada's first auditor general. In this position he had won national renown for his forceful criticism year by year of government extravagance. The simultaneous appointments of Tovell as director and Henderson as director (administration) were presented by the chairman of the board in the annual report of 1972/1973 as constituting a dual stewardship of the Museum.

The Museum's separation from the University during Peter Swann's directorship had made the board of the Museum aware of the ground the Museum had to make up to maintain its reputation as a great public museum. Heinrich had recognized the nature of the task as early as 1955 when he had appointed Duncan Cameron as the Museum's first public relations officer. Cameron shared Heinrich's vision of what a public museum should be and had quickly shown a talent for the role of what was to become a new type of museum officer, a professional without specialization in any particular collections area but involved in enhancing the image of them all. Among his many initiatives had been to make the first study of the museum visitor undertaken by any museum in North America.

Heinrich had wanted also a designer, someone who could design exhibits for the permanent galleries and for the splendid special exhibitions he planned to have, especially for the art and archaeology division. Douglas Tushingham, the head of the division, hired Harley Parker, a gifted painter who at that time was teaching at the Ontario College of Art. In collaboration with his friend Marshall McLuhan, who was much around the Museum in those days, Parker introduced a new notion of the manner in which design should involve the viewer. It was to be a process of total immersion. In an address to a seminar of museum directors in New York in 1967, he declared, "We need the help of sound and we need the help of film, in order to place these objects in their context. . . . I would even suggest that we move into the whole area of sound and light, with simultaneous projections of films and stills and possibly multi-tape-recorders to give an immediate sense of this."

But total immersion was not to everyone's taste. When Parker designed the invertebrate fossil gallery in 1967, complete with a "total environment" provided by films, stills, tapes, telephones, push-buttons, smells, and sounds, the resulting assault on the senses was so great that the display became known as the "discothèque gallery". Shortly after Swann's arrival, Parker resigned from the Museum to resume his career as a painter.

~~~

A major event in 1974 was the *Exhibition of Archaeological Finds of the People's Republic of China,* unquestionably the most successful and profitable exhibition in the history of the Museum. The renown of the exhibition had preceded the artifacts themselves. The board of trustees had authorized a budget of more than a million dollars for the Toronto showing and had set up the Chinese Exhibition Council. It included representatives not only of the Museum—Noah Torno, chairman of the board of trustees; Walter Tovell, director; Barbara Stephen, associate curator, Far Eastern Department; and Maxwell Henderson, director (administration) and controller—but also of a wide sector of public life— A. E. Ritchie, undersecretary of state for external affairs, representing the federal government; J. Gordon Parr, deputy minister of colleges and universities, representing the Ontario government; John Evans, president of the University of Toronto; Kenneth R. Thomson, chairman and president of Thomson Newspapers; and Chester Ronning, a distinguished diplomat who had had a long connection with the Far East.

The exhibition attracted vast crowds from every part of Canada, from the United States, and even from Europe. It ran for three months, and was visited by 435 000 people. After all expenses had been met, it had made a profit of $600 000 for the Museum, which was set aside as a fund to sustain future exhibitions.

The objects for the exhibition had been selected by the Chinese authorities and had to be displayed in the prescribed order and groupings. Mounting the exhibition in the Royal Ontario Museum had served incidentally to emphasize the crowded condition of the galleries surrounding it. By now, the overcrowding that had been in a desperate state for several years was approaching the point of disaster. The collections and the staff had not ceased to grow, creating the need not only for display space, but also for more storage space, more offices, and larger working areas. It had been possible to secure this only by invading and partitioning off already inadequate gallery space, and thus diminishing the public's access to the growing collections. The lack of any form of temperature or humidity control, even the elementary one of air-conditioning, was endangering treasures of great value, as well as putting visitors to great discomfort and intensifying the ailment that was now coming to be known as "museum fatigue".

~~~

A special grant in 1969 had enabled the board to commission the architects and planners Moffat Moffat & Kinoshita to undertake a survey of the Museum's requirements. Their report, *An Expansion Feasibility Study,* presented in December 1970, outlined several potential schemes for expansion. In the meantime the Ontario government had allocated $12.75 million for expansion of the Museum, to be paid over ten years. But it had become increasingly clear over the next four years, which saw the beginning of rapid inflation, that the amount earmarked for Museum expansion would be totally inadequate.

With the closing of the Chinese exhibition, planning for expansion was resumed in full earnest. The board set up a Project Control Group, with representation from the board, the administrative and curatorial departments, and the design consultants. In November 1974 the trustees decided to appoint a project director. Their choice fell on a professional consultant in private practice, David Scott, who had been director of physical resources at Guelph University, which had gone through a major expansion between 1965 and 1969. He had also been project director responsible for the management of the planning, design, and construction of the Metropolitan Toronto Zoo before his engagement by the Royal Ontario Museum.

Scott was by nature a visionary, a futurist, and the prospect of designing a museum built to last well into the next century must have particularly appealed to him. When he joined the Project Control Group as project director, it quickly became apparent that a clash between him and Henderson was inevitable. Each had authority as a coordinator. It was fairly plain that they did not see eye to eye on development, and equally clear that Scott had the confidence of the board. At the same time Henderson must have realized that his office, as one-half of a dual directorate, would not survive the appointment of a new overall director.

On 31 December 1974 Henderson resigned. He agreed to continue for a few months as consultant on financial matters to the board chairman, Gordon Wotherspoon; but shortly afterwards he was appointed audit adviser to the provincial government, a position from which by mere chance he was to be instrumental in bringing the Museum's expansion plans to a grinding halt. In 1975 he was appointed a trustee of the Museum in recognition for his services to it.

In January 1975 the firms of Mathers & Haldenby and Moffat Moffat & Kinoshita were appointed architects for the Royal Ontario Museum expansion. They began at once to make detailed investigations on matters related to physical planning constraints.

When David Scott had been appointed, he had been asked by the board to prepare a planning report. He had been given a wide mandate—"to look at everything, and to make recommendations for anything and everything as he saw fit". He lost no time, and by 15 April 1975 his report, called *Guidelines for Planning,* a little over one hundred pages in length, with some additional appendices, was submitted to the board.

Scott had indeed interpreted his mandate widely. The *Guidelines* began by presenting a profile of the Museum as it was and as it might become, examining every aspect of its obligations from the conservation of its collections to its responsibility for research, publication, and education. Against this it set a profile of the Museum of the future, continuing to proclaim THE RECORD OF NATURE THROUGH COUNTLESS AGES and THE ARTS OF MAN THROUGH ALL THE YEARS, but now emphasizing the Museum's involvement with the problems of the present and future, of survival in a threatened world.

The report argued that there should be a basic theme to express this concern. For an era in which the threat to the environment and the loss of the meaning formerly imparted to human existence by religious faith had invaded the public mind, it proposed as the theme "Meaningful Survival". The upheaval and destruction caused by half a century of world conflict, and the physical and sociological threats to human life posed by the technological and scientific discoveries of the century, had brought the human race to a point where even bare survival presented a challenge. A museum's duty was to preserve and nourish the values that would make survival meaningful.

The report also called for a restatement of the aims and objectives of the Museum in a changing world, and of the constraints and disciplines necessary to achieve these. The Museum would have to shift away from the ethic of perpetual growth; growth would have to become qualitative rather than quantitative. The suitability of research projects should be assessed in relation to the resources of the Museum; and although most research projects were financed by outside grants, they should be examined to determine whether they met a long list of criteria, including whether the research contributed any new knowledge or merely duplicated something already undertaken. Finally, there should be an internal organization competent to coordinate and exercise these controls.

There was much here to arouse the suspicion of the curators. They would unquestionably resent the restrictions imposed on their activities, and the emphasis the report put on the importance of gallery display in communicating with new and future generations of museum visitors foreshadowed an unwelcome invasion of their galleries by design specialists and other experts.

But whatever might be said of Scott's report, it was a brilliant imaginative thrust into the future. It spoke for the unease in the minds of people who could no longer find consolation or reassurance in the churches' teaching of another life to come. Through museums they had learnt about evolution and the universality of nature. Through museums they might discern where history had brought them and what the future might hold. But the onus was on museums to communicate their purpose and to preserve by example and demonstration an awareness of what was worth saving in a threatened world and of the values that must be protected to make salvation worthwhile. That is why the report laid particular stress on design and display. It went on to deal with the planning context in which the expansion program would operate and the amenities which the public of the eighties would expect. As compared with those that had satisfied past generations of museum visitors, these would involve not only an increased level of physical comfort but the new display methods and techniques to which the public had become accustomed in other public places.

All this, the report said, should be set in motion before the architects' designer was asked to submit plans and drawings and specifications. And to this end Scott called for a *Statement of Intent* and for the controls necessary to establish the prescribed conditions.

This was a challenge certain to arouse considerable opposition. The board, inured to shocks, thought this one might be timely. Wasting no time, it immediately sent a copy of the report to every department in the Museum, and set up a Report Review Committee co-chaired by Mrs Julie Rickerd, chairman of the board's Planning Committee, and H. Donald Guthrie, Jr, a distinguished lawyer and chairman of the board's Property Committee, to conduct hearings. The chairman of the board, four board members, the director and associate director, two curators, and the head of the Members' Committee and of the Staff Association made up the balance of the committee. It was announced that the committee would conduct hearings, and everyone with something to say on the subject was urged to express his or her views.

The hearings lasted six weeks and included one afternoon when Scott, at the request of the curators, faced the whole Museum staff in the Museum theatre. Alone on the stage, unsupported by any representative of the board or its committee, he submitted for two hours to mostly hostile questioning. He held his own, withdrew nothing, and insisted that he must have the *Statement of Intent* in principle, even if details such as the title of the "theme" had to be changed—a point on which the curators had been insistent. But "theme" there must be, if the Museum was to meet its responsibilities to the public of the future.

In the end Scott carried the day. At the conclusion of the hearings, the Report Review Committee was unanimous in its opinion. In submitting its report to the trustees it wrote: "Your Committee cannot say too emphatically what a splendid document it finds the Guidelines to be.... In our view, it is the most exciting, challenging and comprehensive report of its kind to be put before the Museum in living memory."

The committee went on to recommend a number of modifications. It liked the idea of a theme gallery but was not satisfied with the title "Meaningful Survival". Its report incorporated the *Statement of Intent* for which Scott had asked. The document was approved by the board and promulgated at its meeting on 17 September 1975. It thereby became a constitutional document, setting out the goal of the Museum as being "the furtherance of man's greater understanding of himself, his society and the natural world of which he is a part". This was to be achieved through its collections, by the employment of scholars as curators, by research, and by interpretation of knowledge through gallery exhibits, operation of a planetarium, and all other practicable means of communication. Finally the goal was to be identified by a theme expressing the main purpose of the Museum. Later the forty pages of the *Statement of Intent* were to be boiled down to a four-page summary by the new director, James E. Cruise, who had succeeded Walter Tovell on 1 July 1975.

~~

The five years in which Walter Tovell had served the Museum as associate director and director had unquestionably been the most tumultuous in the Museum's history, stretching as they did from the Swann crisis to the Museum's commitment to the extensive expansion and renovation program. At heart, Tovell was a curator, and he must often have been sympathetic to the curators' point of view. But as director and chief executive officer responsible to the board for administrative as well as curatorial matters, he was unquestionably impartial.

Tovell's great achievement had been to keep the peace. Looking back over the press of events—the Chinese exhibition, the building plans, the financial crises, Scott's *Guidelines for Planning,* the *Statement of Intent,* and the institution of the geochronology laboratory, the only one of its kind in Canada, which occurred in his final year of office—Walter Tovell's presence is always apparent. A director with too strong a desire to manage everything might have been a disaster in this period. But while museum development fascinated Tovell, strife did not. At the termination of his period of office, until his retirement in 1981, he turned, happily one suspects, to the care and development of the support and advisory services provided by the Royal Ontario Museum to other provincial museums. In this role he was also to give much time to the development of the museology program for the training of specialists in museum work, which had been initiated in the Museum in 1969 with an enrolment of six. By the time it was taken over by the University of Toronto in 1978 as a graduate department, it had graduated more than one hundred students.

17

Planning the Future

The new director, James E. Cruise, at the time of his appointment was associate dean of arts and sciences in the University of Toronto. He was a graduate of the University of Toronto, with postgraduate degrees in plant physiology and plant taxonomy, and his scholarly accomplishments, beginning with the award of the gold medal in science in his graduating year, were beyond question. He had taught at Cornell and Princeton universities, and for a number of years had provided liaison between the Museum and the University's Department of Botany. But it was his personal qualities, which included a toughness of character concealed beneath a charm of manner, and his organizing experience on the administrative staff of the University that recommended him in the eyes of the trustees at this particular juncture in the Museum's history. His appointment was unexpected, both to him and to the Museum staff. He had been notified in March 1975 that he was on a short list, but having received no further word by June, he had assumed that he had not been the final choice. He was in Halifax visiting his aunt, who was in hospital, when he received a telephone call on 5 June telling him that he was the new director and that he was to take office on 1 July.

At the very outset of his directorship, Cruise was faced with the need for absorbing at short notice the mass of figures and calculations concerning expansion plans that had accumulated since the feasibility report of 1970. He had been given a free hand to shape his own internal organization, the board having noted "the burden imposed on the director by some thirty or so curatorial and non-curatorial departments reporting to him directly". The quotation is from a lengthy memorandum addressed to the staff and dated 29 September 1975, setting out the divisions and relationships in the structure he had designed. He was able to quote David Scott's

159

reminder in *Guidelines for Planning* that "an organizational structure is intended to facilitate the attainment of objectives", a statement that had been incorporated also, in slightly altered form, in the *Statement of Intent.*

The organization Cruise developed was a relatively simple one. In its eventual form, it comprised three reporting streams: the Curatorial Stream under an associate director; Education and Communication, headed by an assistant director; and Administration and Facilities, also headed by an assistant director. A fourth stream, designed to include service departments such as the Conservation Department and the Registration Department and the library, vanished within a year when it was recognized that these were essentially curatorial services and they were attached to the Curatorial Stream. Barbara Stephen, a curator in the Far Eastern Department, was appointed associate director on 1 January 1976; in May Joseph Di Profio, who for three years had been director of the Communications Branch of the Ontario Ministry of Education, was appointed assistant director of Education and Communication, and in June Gordon Bristowe was appointed assistant director of Administration and Facilities.

By 29 September 1975 the director could report that the streams were in place, and on 3 November that preliminary planning for new galleries and displays was actively proceeding, as also were studies in the field of visitor orientation. These latter were embodied in a series of background papers prepared by the newly formed Communications Design Team, the successor to an informal group formed by Scott to study the topics that *Guidelines for Planning* had designated as essential to the design process. These papers, compressed and edited by Scott, were to be published in April 1976 under the title *Communicating with the Museum Visitor.* This publication, widely noticed in the museum community in Canada and abroad, quickly ran into a second printing and today is in its fifth printing.

~~~

Suddenly, on 4 December 1975, all these plans were shattered. The Honourable Robert Welch, minister of culture and recreation, to whom the Museum now reported, advised the chairman of the board, Gordon Wotherspoon, that capital funds for expansion could not be made available "in the foreseeable future". It had been known since June that the Ontario government was looking anxiously into its spending commitments with a view to retrenchment. At that time it had set up a Programme Review Committee under the chairmanship of its audit adviser, Maxwell Henderson, for the purpose of cutting $3 billion from its annual expenditure of $11 billion. The committee had made a total of 183 recommendations to this end, and among the victims was the Royal Ontario Museum. It was an ironic coincidence that not long before the committee got to work Maxwell Henderson had been appointed a trustee of the Museum. But considering the wide sweep of the scythe, and the large sum—$12.75 million—that the ministry had committed for expansion, the Museum could not escape the blade.

The news was conveyed to the staff in a director's memorandum dated 18 December, which forlornly noted that the $12.75 million which had been promised in 1970 could not now be counted on. By chance another lengthy memorandum from the director, an end-of-year review of all that had been achieved, bore the same date, and the contrast between high hopes and those hopes dashed is as painful to read now as it must have been at the time.

The shock was felt by everyone in the Museum. This edict meant that there was no relief in sight for the intolerable overcrowding. It also postponed any hopes that the staff had for pay increases long overdue. In the spring of 1975, conscious of the inadequate levels of pay in a period of rapidly increasing inflation, the board had commissioned Woods Gordon, management consultants, to provide a job classification plan that would bring rates of pay more closely into line with those both in the private sector and in other areas of the public sector, and to introduce a salary administration policy. As a result, one round of increases had already been made.

These initiatives could not now be maintained. The Ontario government's economy budget of spring 1976 restricted the operating budget of the Museum to a five per cent increase, not enough to keep pace with the growth in the Museum's fixed operating expenses, such as heating, insurance, and so on, which were increasing with everything else. The board had to dip into the Museum's reserves even to maintain the increases made in the previous year. Staff morale was understandably at a low level.

Once it had recovered from the initial shock of the financial setback, the board had taken the position that, in spite of the suspension of the project, expansion was inevitable and that sooner or later the Ontario government would redeem its promise. David Scott was asked to prepare an *Interim Planning Report* in which everything that had been achieved to date was documented, so that whenever the hoped-for moment arrived, work could be resumed without wasting the time, money, and effort already spent on the project.

Scott had his *Interim Planning Report* ready by March 1976. It revealed how much had already been accomplished. Alternative sites had been examined, and the pros and cons of relocation had been compared with those of adapting the existing site to provide the approximately 60 000 square metres of floor space deemed necessary to meet the needs of the Museum to the year 2000. Such an expansion meant nearly doubling the existing floor space, and would make the Royal Ontario Museum the second largest museum building in North America, surpassed only by the Metropolitan Museum of Art in New York with its 93 000 square metres.

The *Interim Planning Report,* more than half of it contributed by the architects, revealed that the expansion could be accomplished on the existing site by building on the areas to the north and south of the centre block that connected the east and west wings of the Museum. The northern area held the Ming tomb, a landmark familiar to Torontonians, and the Chinese garden in which it was set, and the Museum restaurant; the southern area was occupied by the exhibition hall and the Museum parking lot. There was justification for clearing both areas of their present contents. The Ming tomb was already showing signs of deterioration, the result of industrial pollution in a rapidly growing city, and had to be moved indoors to save further damage to a priceless relic. The Chinese garden could be dispensed with, and a place for the restaurant found in the renovated building. The area thus cleared could provide space for a new block of galleries facing Bloor Street. In the southern courtyard the exhibition hall could be demolished; space for large temporary exhibitions could be provided in the renovated building. The parking space, already quite inadequate, could be done away with altogether, since the Museum was excellently served by the buses and subway of the public transportation system. In this cleared southern area a new curatorial centre could be built.

The advantages of remaining on the site at the corner of Queen's Park and Bloor Street were, of course, immense. In the very heart of the city, the Museum was a familiar landmark, easily accessible. To renovate and expand the existing building would be a quicker operation than building from scratch elsewhere. Moreover, it was hoped that the Lillian Massey Building, a University of Toronto property almost directly opposite the main entrance to the Museum, could be acquired and connected to the main building by an underground passage. After a long suspense, however, while the University considered its own need for expansion, this hope had to be shelved.

The curatorial centre was to be an entirely new building contained within its own walls, but separated by only a few metres from the existing walls of the two wings. This was part of the designer's solution to the need for a building requiring a considerable variety of climatic controls while remaining unaffected by the temperature that had to be maintained in the public areas. With the curatorial centre fitted into the cleared area between the two southern arms of the original H-shaped structure, and the new terrace galleries embraced between the northern arms, the new Museum would have the outward appearance of a solid quadrangular block, while still retaining within its structure the original H-shaped building as a separate and distinct element.

~~

Several months were to pass following the *Interim Planning Report* before, in September 1976, the Ontario government reaffirmed its commitment to the $12.75 million grant originally promised, and a few months later added as compensation for the delay a grant of up to $10 million from its Wintario lottery fund, to be matched by private fund-raising. Encouraged by this and by hints of further capital funding from the Ontario government, the board asked the architects for two conceptual studies, one based on a budget of $36.75 million and the other on one of $42.5 million. The plans based on the larger figure were accepted, and in February 1977 a capital expenditure of $44 million was authorized. Three planning groups were set up, each concerned with a particular function. The architects and consultants formed one group; a second group was to deal with exhibits and gallery design; a third with fund-raising. During the course of construction the Ontario government was to commit another $14 million to the project, and the Metro Toronto Council to approve a grant of up to $5 million, to be matched by private fund-raising.

The prominence given to exhibit and gallery design in planning was a reflection of the emphasis placed on it in *Guidelines for Planning* and the *Statement of Intent.* In the stream structure set in place by the director, gallery design became the responsibility of the Education and Communication Stream under Joseph Di Profio, the assistant director for the stream, who had taken over the chairmanship of the Communications Design Team. This body had its origins in the informal group with which Scott had been working. But with bureaucratic sensitivity to rank, Di Profio could not be expected to take second place to a consultant. Scott had taken on large responsibilities as the architect of the concept of the new Museum, with its principles engraved in the *Statement of Intent.* These he now had to yield to the new director and his organization. Moreover, Scott could not have been unaware that he was resented as much by the curators as he was admired by the small group he had selected to write the background papers, which formed the substance of the manual *Communicating with the Museum Visitor.*

Di Profio was the exemplar *par excellence* of the new breed of management and professional people who had arrived at the Museum. He was young, well educated, talented, and ruthless as ambitious people often have to be. He did not give a fig for the élitism of the curators. His job was to popularize the Museum, and unquestionably he succeeded. He poured money into Extension Services for travelling exhibitions throughout Ontario and he enlarged Information Services. Having taken over the chairmanship of the Communications Design Team, he automatically became chairman of the Exhibits Communication Task Force that succeeded it in September 1976.

The Exhibits Communication Task Force was made up of six curators, experts from the Conservation Department, Education Services, Extension Services, and Exhibit Design Services, and a member of Urban Design Consultants, who acted as coordinator. It was a much more important task force than its predecessor. The curators, who, it must be remembered, had their own collections to look after during this period of rapid change, worked under great pressure to meet a deadline for the *Final Planning Report,* when the Museum would be committed and the architects could start work. The task force published its own report, *Opportunities and Constraints,* dealing with an overall plan for the galleries and the allocation of gallery space. The construction of the galleries and the mounting of exhibits would be a major factor in the expenditure. This was recognized by the board, which had set aside $3 million from the expansion funds—a sum which was to be increased to $4 million in the following year—for the start of the creation of new galleries and exhibits. The task force was also to provide for a "theme" gallery, one of the recommendations of *Guidelines for Planning* which had been accepted in the *Statement of Intent.*

~~~

During all this activity the figure who had set it all in motion vanished from the scene. The chairman's annual report for 1976/1977 makes no mention of the event, and the Renovation and Expansion Project Report records only that "upon the achievement of this benchmark in the planning process, and by long-standing arrangement, Mr David Scott asked to be relieved of his responsibilities". Scott returned to his private practice in Guelph, Ontario, leaving behind a Museum utterly changed by the impact of his vision and planning. He had a missionary's fervour for his task, and a visionary's conception of the goal to be reached that had bothered some people, just as it had inspired others who shared that vision. He had seen that interpretation could no longer be left to the curators alone; they needed the assistance of designers and artists, even psychologists (the "human engineers" of Scott's definition), and Scott may well have felt that with everything engraved now in the *Statement of Intent,* with the necessary funding assured, and the *Final Planning Report* approved, he might do his cause more harm than good by remaining on the scene. One may imagine that he would have liked to stay on, perhaps as the head of the stream responsible for the Museum's physical facilities, a position for which his experience particularly fitted him. But all the evidence shows that he was an extremely difficult man to work with, deaf to any argument that ran contrary to the course he had decided on. There was really no place for him in the structure his own *Guidelines for Planning* had envisioned. Having pointed to the Promised Land, the prophet was destined not to enter it.

Scott was succeeded as project director by Henry Graupner, who had been assistant project director for the previous six months. Scott agreed to stay on as a consultant for a few months, but there is no record of his having taken any part in the active planning of the exhibits.

18

Expansion and Renovation

Meanwhile the architects' design had been approved. Everything was to be fitted into the existing site, and the work was to proceed in three stages. The first stage would be the construction of the new curatorial centre to accommodate the offices and laboratories and storage areas, together with all the basic mechanical and electrical facilities. The second stage was to have been the construction of the new terrace galleries facing Bloor Street on the north side of the building. The third and final stage would then have been the complete renovation of the existing building. However, this plan was changed as the work progressed. For economic reasons it was decided to renovate the original buildings before constructing the new galleries—a decision that was to have a profound effect on gallery development.

Gene Kinoshita, who was appointed design architect, has put on record, in the summer 1982 issue of *Rotunda,* an interesting account of how the final design concept was arrived at. It developed in response to a number of well-defined requirements. The first of these was the need to design a building in which the staff and visitors would not feel lost or disoriented or the visitors be overcome by "museum fatigue". Another requirement was that the "new buildings should be harmonious with existing ones and yet should interpret and reflect their own times rather than times past". The concept also had to be one that would provide all the varied environments required for different purposes; that would recognize the need for natural light as an important design element; and that would solve the problems created by complex differences of floor level between the existing building and the new buildings.

The existing building with its high-ceilinged galleries had five levels, four above ground and one below. The lower ceilings sufficient for the purposes to which the new curatorial centre was to be put permitted the centre to have six levels above ground while still rising no higher than the original four. The problems caused by the discrepancies of level were ingeniously overcome by separating the curatorial centre from the existing building, which surrounded it on three sides, by "atria"—perimeter wells rising to the full height of the buildings—and by adjusting the difference in the levels of the floors on opposite sides of the atria by such means as bridges, ramps, and stairs.

The atria would serve other, equally important, purposes. Their skylighted roofs would permit natural light with its—in Kinoshita's words—"mystical, ever-changing quality" to penetrate deeply to areas that otherwise would have been enclosed, windowless spaces. The atria would also help to solve the problem of "museum fatigue" by providing "the space and environment for orientation and rest, and also a very important transition space for reorientation and a change of perspective". In these spaces the visitor would obtain "visual and psychological relief" and in moving through them from one gallery to another would experience "changes in space and light conditions, views, vistas, and even humidity and temperature".

The demolition in April of 1978 of the exhibition hall that stood on the site where the foundations of the curatorial centre were to be dug gave the signal for the start of the actual construction program. The closing of the Museum was put off as long as possible, but in January 1980 the west wing was closed to the public, followed by the east wing in January 1981. The great entrance doors to the main building were not to swing back to admit the public again until September 1982.

It had been hoped, for a time, that the expansion and renovation of the main building could be carried out without the complete closure of the building at any time. But this had proved impractical. Renovation involved gutting the building almost to its bare walls, not only to repair the main fabric but also to install the amenities and environmental controls essential both for the conservation of the collections and the comfort of the public. Moreover, the new conceptions of gallery design to be embodied in the new Museum called for long windowless spaces for exhibition areas, and the renovation offered a splendid opportunity to provide them. Both the logistical and the security problems of moving millions of dollars' worth of valuable collections from place to place within the building for temporary storage as different areas were worked on in turn, while the public still had access to the building, were horrendous; and even if a solution had been possible, it would have enormously lengthened the time required for the renovation of the building. The more drastic alternative of closing the building completely for a time, carrying out the renovations unhampered by the need to accommodate the public, and then reopening as soon as possible seemed greatly preferable.

~~~

The problems involved in clearing the galleries so that the main fabric of the building could be renovated were complex. The objects to be moved— sometimes to a temporary location from where they would have to be moved again—varied in size from the massive Ming tomb to the lightest of entomological specimens, of which there were more than a million. Keeping track of everything would have been impossible but for the computerized Location Record Project designed by the Registration Department of the Museum and the coordinator of Collections Management, working in cooperation with the National Inventory Programme of the National Museums of Canada (later renamed the Canadian Heritage Information Network). The man appointed coordinator of collections management, Toshio Yamamoto, known to everyone as Tosh, had been a curatorial assistant in the Department of Entomology. His air of resolute calm and unwearying optimism was able to soothe and pacify even the most excited curator desperately searching for some particular item from his or her collection.

Altogether more than six million objects had to be moved. Each had attached to it an identification number, and the system provided an "audit trail" that enabled its movements to be tracked to its final destination. Sonja Tanner-Kaplash, head of the Registration Department, contributed a chapter to *Museum Documentation Systems: Development and Applications* in which she described the various phases of the operation. The precision of the operation is reflected in a paragraph on Phase IV (January 1981– December 1983).

Gradually, the Museum was closed to the public, and objects from display and storage areas were carefully packed into numbered MSU's [Movable Storage Units]. This operation was also undertaken by the same recording teams, using the most recent generation of computer printouts as working copies upon which to manually note a second location for each item. Since these printouts were the *only* location record in existence at that stage, they were treated as high-security documents and signed in and out by all staff. When each volume was completed, second locations were input into the computer as soon as possible.

It proved fortunate for the Museum that a few years earlier it had reversed its 1972 decision to remain aloof from the National Museums of Canada and had accepted associate membership. Such membership brought countervailing responsibilities, of course, and there was still curatorial opposition to assuming these at a time when the Museum was facing such a gigantic task on its own behalf. Now, however, the Museum began to reap one of the rewards, access to the computerized National Inventory Programme in Ottawa, for it was the registration of every artifact and specimen in the Museum's collections that enabled each of the millions of items to be tracked at any given moment.

In some instances, the complexity of the task of moving the collections arose not so much from the quantities of the objects to be moved and the problem of keeping track of them, as from their sheer size. For the Ming tomb the double move that had to be made while the Museum was under renovation was but the latest stage in the peregrinations that had begun when it was discovered and purchased for the Museum by George Crofts between 1918 and 1921. Hundreds of Chinese workmen and twenty-tonne railway cars had been involved in transporting the pieces to Tientsin for shipment to Canada. The marble plaques of the gateways, the two stone camels, and the two stone guardian officials had arrived, with a great bronze Buddha, aboard the *Jane L. Stanford* in 1919. The panels of the tumulus came in 1921, and the two great stone lions, which weighed about seventeen tonnes each and were not actually part of the tomb group, in 1923.

The tomb's first home in Toronto had been the exhibition hall on the south side of the building. From there it had gone to the Chinese garden on the north side. Now once more it had to be moved, first to a temporary location, and finally to the spendid glass-enclosed gallery on the first level of the terrace galleries fronting on Bloor Street.

Another challenge was presented by the three famous Chinese paintings. The largest, a Buddhist work entitled *Maitreya Paradise,* from the Yuan dynasty, had been secured for the Museum by Bishop White in China in 1927. The wall on which it was painted had been hurriedly cut by monks, at the approach of a warlord, into sections about ten centimetres thick, and had arrived at the Museum in eighty pieces. In 1933 the painting was assembled to form the north wall of what became the Bishop White gallery. The other two were Taoist (Daoist) paintings entitled *Homage to the First Principle;* they had been purchased in 1936 from a dealer in New York and mounted to form the east and west walls of the gallery. Both Taoist paintings are more than ten metres long and three metres high, and both had to be taken down piece by piece to permit the installation of a vapour barrier in the outside wall and conservation treatment of the paintings. Now that they have been reassembled, the three great wall-paintings adorn one of the Museum's most beautiful galleries, filled with statues of Bodhisattvas—a place of compelling quietude and peacefulness.

The task of clearing the galleries for renovation was greatly facilitated in March 1981, two months after the complete closure of the main building, when occupancy of the new curatorial centre began. By June most of the centre had been handed over to the Museum. Built at a cost of $20.5 million, the curatorial centre had almost everything that the professional museum worker could hope for. It created a sense of unity in an institution that had begun its existence as five separate museums and in which, during the intervening years, curatorial offices and laboratories and storage areas had had to disperse to whatever corners of the building were available or else to move off site altogether. Now, for the first time, each department had its own self-contained offices, designed to its own needs and adjacent to its own laboratory and storage areas, in a filtered-air environment and with temperature controlled to suit individual collections. In addition, there were cold storage areas for those collections requiring it, "wet rooms" for those, like furniture, needing high humidity, and "dry rooms" for objects such as bronzes and iron artifacts that need a dry environment.

Now, too, for the first time, all the necessary conservation facilities were available in eight fully equipped on-site laboratories, and preparators had their own specialized workrooms for their delicate tasks of preparing or packing artifacts for display or shipping. A spacious modern library occupied most of the first level of the centre, replacing the dusty, crowded converted gallery space that had formerly had to serve. Even such a basic and utilitarian facility as a properly equipped mail-room was something that was now available to Museum staff for the very first time.

～～

While the fabric of the new buildings that were to house the Museum's collections was taking shape, an intense and sometimes acrimonious debate was going on as to how those collections were to be displayed in their new setting. Decisions in this field had become the responsibility of the Exhibits Communication Task Force, under the chairmanship of Assistant Director Joseph Di Profio. Members of the task force, either singly or in pairs, visited more than twenty other leading North American museums to learn from their experience in gallery design, and they met together at least once a fortnight to discuss and coordinate their findings.

The conclusions of their deliberations were set forth in a two-volume report, entitled *Mankind Discovering,* published in 1978/1979. These words expressed the theme that the Exhibits Communication Task Force had chosen to replace David Scott's "Meaningful Survival", and the report contained a detailed master-plan for the placement of galleries in the approximately twenty thousand square metres of gallery space that would eventually be available in the new Museum.

It had not been a simple task. All curatorial departments had received a gallery proposal form, forewarning that a lower limit of about ninety square metres had been established for individual galleries. Not surprisingly, the total gallery space requested was far greater than what the expanded and remodelled Museum could provide. The departments had also been asked to name other disciplines with which their own had some affinity, and to give their views on their possible association in interdisciplinary galleries. What emerged from the responses was that the galleries represented networks of interrelated concepts rather than isolated ideas; the Exhibits Communication Task Force consequently began to consider the possibility of using these interrelationships to group the galleries into "clusters".

In an article published in the 1982 summer issue of the Museum's quarterly, *Rotunda,* Robert Barnett of Exhibit Design Services explained some of the characteristics of clusters.

Each cluster has an introductory area where basic concepts, theories, historical sequences, and background ideas are discussed.... The sequence of galleries within a cluster is explained in a "user's panel" at the entrance to each cluster.... The user's panel explains by means of text and graphics the physical and conceptual layout of the cluster or gallery....

In some clusters there are overview areas that relate subjects from several galleries within the cluster to specific common themes, such as trade or town planning....

Clustering allows visitors to make the most of their time in the Museum by following up particular themes that are of special interest to them....

Upon entering the Mediterranean world cluster, for example, the visitor will encounter first the orientation/user's panel, which enables him to orient himself... within the historical periods and the geographical regions to which the cluster refers. The panel also suggests a path through the cluster and identifies the sequence of galleries, giving their titles and the concepts that they illustrate.... Whether the visitor chooses to view the Imperial Roman busts or the coins, or perhaps to trace the rise of the state, he will have available a general introduction to the subject, a more detailed survey of groups of artifacts, and a series of individual artifact labels.

The following spring Dr Louis Levine, one of the curatorial members of the Exhibits Communication Task Force, also in an article in *Rotunda*, described the evolution of the new Museum galleries: "What began to take shape was not a series of departmental galleries exhibiting in separate, unrelated spaces, but a number of 'clusters', each telling a story and each structured around common themes and concerns."

Beyond the cluster concept lay a view of the role of museums that was at variance with the time-hallowed, traditional one. In the plans of the designers and others charged with the task of devising the exhibits for the Museum, galleries were no longer regarded as places to muse, to wonder, to allow the imagination free range, or simply to learn about the past. Now the visitor was to be taken firmly by the hand and conducted through what has come to be called a "learning experience". "Story-line" became an increasingly common part of the terminology of gallery design. Though there were many who deplored the new didacticism as intellectual authoritarianism and as an attempt to channel rather than to expand the viewer's thinking, the new approach to museum exhibits was, in part at least, a response to public demand. The audiences served by museums were now huge compared with those of fifty years earlier. There was a hunger for knowledge that was more than mere curiosity. To the post-Darwin generation, evolution had become an accepted fact. They wanted to know how things had begun, how they had developed, where they would end. Museums could no longer afford to be oriented solely towards the past; perhaps they could even be guides into the future.

The Royal Ontario Museum's movement towards the new philosophy of display had already been under way for more than a decade. Harley Parker and his kind of display experts had been groping after a story-telling element to engage the attention of the viewer. Their attempts had been rather crude by today's standards and had offended the élite without being particularly enlightening to the commonalty. But exhibit design was a developing science. That the museum community had its attention fixed on the subject had been demonstrated at the conference of museum directors in New York in 1967, which Parker and Marshall McLuhan had addressed. They had spoken a good deal of nonsense, perhaps with the deliberate intention of arousing their audience, and had been tactfully but firmly put in their place by the chairman, Jacques Barzun. Barzun had deplored the invasion of the privacy of the viewer's mind by exhibits that told him what he should think, and his speech had been greeted with a standing ovation. Nevertheless, the trend was one that was bound to be taken up by a futurist like David Scott, so that now, only a decade later, the Royal Ontario Museum was planning its gallery clusters according to the master-plan in *Mankind Discovering* and an introductory "theme" gallery with that same name.

Following the publication of *Mankind Discovering,* nineteen gallery development teams were formed to implement its proposals. Their task, as defined by the director, was to see that "our exhibits and galleries communicate dynamically and effectively with our public". The process elicited strong differences of opinion. Curators tend to identify with their collections and to treat them as extensions of their own egos. The designers were sometimes impatient with this attitude. An article entitled "Romanticism in the Hallowed Halls", by Leslie Patten of the Museum's Exhibit Design Services, in the Canadian Museums Association's *Gazette,* traced existing conceptions of galleries to the romantic tradition of the 18th century, asserting that they were now out of date.

> To truly interpret objects and events, context should be not simply situational but sociological. Objects and events are broadly meaningful only if they reveal certain fundamental social or cultural patterns....
>
> We are in the 20th century and we have learned that the measurer affects the measurements, and that we are either part of the problem or part of the solution.

There was a strong case to be made against this didactic and dogmatically stated view, and some staff members did not hesitate to make it, eloquently and firmly. One commentator observed drily that the belief that an idea is right simply because it is new was "part of the problem". But, for the time being at least, nothing could stem the tide. Renovation was in the air, the audience had changed, and those who disliked the homogenization of culture implicit in the programming of gallery design were overborne.

Joseph Di Profio consequently replaced David Scott as the main target of the curators' disapprobation. There was a good deal of curatorial criticism of the amount of money being spent on the expansion program, particularly on the many programmers, designers, educationists, and other "communicators" intent on the preparation of "story-lines". The agitation culminated in a public hearing before the Accounts Committee of the Ontario government. The Museum's new chairman, Sydney Hermant, and the director, James Cruise, were commanded to appear and give evidence on a complaint of Opposition members of the committee that money was being wasted. A body of curators, constitutionally opposed to rapid change, went along, uninvited, to express their view. But nothing happened. The government committee had no interest in internal friction in the Museum, and the curators were dismissed without being asked to testify. Hermant disposed of the incident in his annual report as the Museum's being "caught in the political crossfire between Government and Opposition". The director offered the board his resignation, since he could not carry out his task if even a part of the curatorial body was against him, but it was refused. Di Profio did resign, perhaps as the victim chosen for the sacrifice, and from that point on opposition to the changes relaxed. Di Profio was replaced by R. McCartney Samples, a former consul general for the United Kingdom in Toronto, who was well known and very popular in the community, and as highly skilled in publicity as Di Profio.

The curatorial body was not, of course, unanimous in supporting any of the conflicting philosophies of gallery display. The differences of opinion—which were no more than one might expect in an intellectually healthy and vigorous community—cut across occupational lines. The Exhibits Communication Task Force had included six curatorial members—half the total number—and its *Mankind Discovering* report owed at least as much to them as to the other members. After the flurry of dissension that culminated in Di Profio's resignation and the board's reaffirmation of confidence in the director, overt opposition to the plans for the galleries appeared to die down. The gallery design teams went to work producing the detailed plans for Exhibit Design Services to execute. This department had replaced the old Design and Display Department in 1977, and Lorne Render, an experienced designer from the Glenbow Museum in Calgary, had been brought in to head it. By the time the Museum reopened in 1982, Exhibit Design Services had become the largest department in the Museum.

~~~

In keeping with the movement towards a new role for museums in a changing world is the Members' Volunteer Committee of the Museum. This had its origin during the first expansive years of Heinrich's directorship, in 1957, when a dozen women members, inspired by the director's aspiration to make Toronto one of the three great art centres of North America, volunteered their services in the pursuit of that goal. The aim of this enthusiastic service committee was to assist the staff of the Museum in any way required and to encourage public interest in the Museum. The members first requested individual placement in the understaffed curatorial departments, where they could undertake routine tasks like filing, typing, cataloguing, and sorting specimens and slides.

And there it might have ended, had the members of the committee been content with nothing more than token involvement in the life of the

Museum. But they had more serious aims and imposed upon themselves a discipline marked by earnestness and dedication. The membership of the committee was based on requirements within the Museum and projects undertaken, rising during the next twenty-nine years from the original 12 to 186.

To attract the public to the Museum and to help ensure that visitors found their visits both enjoyable and instructive, the committee's activities were widened to include the arrangement of special functions and the conducting of daily tours of the collections and of special exhibitions. In this latter activity the members took on the role of interpreters, a task for which they were intensively trained by a course of lectures, wide reading, and script preparation and public speaking under curatorial supervision. So heavy were the demands on this small group that in 1968 an auxiliary force of nearly two hundred men and women was formed. These "member volunteers", later to be called "ROM volunteers", took over the more routine tasks of tending the information and membership desks in the Museum.

By 1973 the undertakings of the Members' Volunteer Committee had become so extensive that the members were restructured into several subcommittees. Three years later the board of trustees asked the committee to organize tours of historical and art centres abroad under the guidance of curatorial experts, and soon afterwards the committee began to sponsor as well day-long bus tours to places of historical interest in Toronto and southern Ontario. In recognition of these efforts, the board of trustees, at its meeting of 4 May 1977, moved that the "position of the Members' Committee be more firmly established in the Museum's organization" and that it become "in effect a Department in the Education and Communication stream".

When the main Museum building was closed for twenty months in 1980/1982 for renovation and expansion, the Members' Volunteer Committee did much to maintain the public's awareness of the institution and of what it had to offer to its members; to existing programs were added luncheon tours in the Sigmund Samuel Canadiana Gallery, which had remained open, and walking tours of sites within the City of Toronto. Funds raised by means of these and other activities were effectively doubled by the matching grant offered by the Ontario government from its Wintario lottery funds.

After the "new" Museum reopened in September 1982, the gallery tours conducted by the Members' Volunteer Committee docents were more than ever necessary for accustoming visitors to the changed landscape and interpreting to them the new displays. The ROM volunteers were able to find an expanded role for their services—as classroom assistants for Education Services, in the Discovery gallery, in the routine tasks of servicing special exhibitions, and as guides for Museum tours on weekends and in the evenings.

The many fundraising projects of the Members' Volunteer Committee were so successful that the committee was able to honour its pledge, made in 1981/1982, of a contribution of $500 000 to the Museum's renovation and expansion fund. It was fitting recognition of the Members' Volunteer Committee's services that it was now granted permanent representation on the Museum's board of trustees.

19

Mankind Discovering

When the doors of the Royal Ontario Museum were reopened in September 1982, visitors familiar with the old building, flocking in to see what changes had been made during the twenty-month closure, were hardly prepared for what they found. The view inwards from the Rotunda had always been much admired. The entrance was on an axis with the broad gallery leading to the west wing, known as the Currelly gallery and also as the Armour Court, since it was here that the Museum's extensive collection of medieval and early Renaissance arms and armour had been displayed. The gallery had been well lit, and its highly polished handmade display cases of black walnut had provided a warm, soft glow, stimulating to the historical imagination and giving an impression of spaciousness and elegance appropriate to the entrance to a great museum.

This cherished view had now vanished, leaving an awkward sense of incompletely filled space. Where the Armour Court had provided a sweeping vista through to the west wing, a columnar structure of stainless steel and plexiglass now stood, identified by a glass panel pointing to its entrance as the Mankind Discovering gallery. This was the "theme" gallery, ordained in the *Statement of Intent* to be placed near the entrance to the Museum, to emphasize by its own displays the interdependence of "man and all things in nature". It was assumed that by its position at the entrance the gallery would invite visitors' attention, and that the display would give them an understanding of what goes on behind the galleries of a museum. This could not be counted on, of course, but curiosity is a compelling human quality, and most visitors yielded to it, to find themselves confronted by a striking demonstration of how a research project is conceived, planned, and carried out.

An information panel at the entrance to the gallery announces that

Museum researchers are earth scientists, life scientists, palaeontologists, ethnologists, archaeologists, and art historians. The display shows first how these specialists proceed from a preliminary hypothesis—an experimental or possible answer to a problem—to gather evidence through research. The procedure varies according to the discipline. It may consist of digging in the earth for fossil bones or the remains of ancient cultures; collecting specimens of animals, plants, or minerals; poring over ancient manuscripts; attending a sale of art objects; or a variety of other activities.

After evidence has been gathered, it is submitted to analysis. Analysis, again, involves a variety of activities—sorting, counting, measuring, comparing—in an attempt to make the evidence yield as much information as possible. During this process patterns may emerge suggesting experimental procedures that will test the hypothesis. The results of the testing may support the hypothesis and produce a satisfactory synthesis of the known facts, or they may not. But the invalidation of a hypothesis is not just a dead end. It may in itself suggest a different hypothesis leading to more far-reaching discoveries and a more comprehensive synthesis than any that was originally envisaged.

To convey without a mass of verbal explanation the essence of this subtle process, capable of assuming so many forms, is the contribution made in the Mankind Discovering gallery by the art of display. The depiction is a series of framed tableaux, not unlike shop windows or stage settings in a theatre in function and purpose. These provide the background against which the action is taking place, enabling the viewer to identify, without great difficulty, the different disciplines and the particular stages depicted in the research process. An archaeological site in the process of being excavated, an invertebrate palaeontologist standing on a mountain of shale, a vertebrate palaeontologist hacking at a piece of rock from which protrudes the bone of a dinosaur—all are shown in blown-up photographs. Tools, equipment, gear necessary for researchers diving to coral reefs, hip-boots and nets used for gathering specimens from marshes—all these, and much more, lend their supporting testimony. There are scenes of laboratories where microscopic specimens are being examined; an art historian is shown examining an art object to verify its authenticity; another is seen at an auction where he may bid for an object to fill a gap in a collection—in these and in the many other situations depicted, the emphasis throughout is on man and his world, and on the inseparable relationship between them.

What the gallery is illustrating is the search for knowledge, and some of the areas of study of the specialists who guide us in that search. The human species is a species like any other in nature. It has evolved through more primitive forms of life, and to understand it we must understand how other forms of life, other species, evolved. This is the province of the life sciences. But in studying a species we must study its habitat. The human habitat is Earth, and we must learn how that habitat was formed, how it has changed, and is still changing, how the environment came to be such that life—including human life—could arise in it and flourish. This is the province of the earth sciences. But the dividing lines are seldom hard and fast. Botany, certainly a life science, is essential for an understanding of the habitat; palaeontology, unquestionably concerned with the study of prehistoric life, leans heavily on the earth sciences and is often characterized as one.

Man stands rooted in nature, but he also transcends nature. He creates cultures, primitive at first, but of increasing complexity and sophistication. Here we enter the area of study of the archaeologist and the ethnologist. The main evidence we have for prehistoric man is in the flint sherds and debris of the sites he occupied, the cooking pots and other artifacts he came to fashion, and the weapons with which he defended himself and hunted for food. The evidence increases with the passing of time, and the archaeologists uncover at other levels the first signs of social and political organization and religion. Finally, from the more advanced cultures come those exquisite products of human art that are the supreme expression of the human spirit, and here we need the art historian's knowledge to guide us through the most recent chapters of the complex story of how man has reacted with his world to create the culture of today.

It was in 1955, when the original museums, by that time three in number, were integrated under a single director, Theodore Heinrich, that the word "art" was added to "archaeology" in the title of the division that replaced the Royal Ontario Museum of Archaeology. But the stamp that Currelly had put upon his museum was too strong to be radically altered by an art specialist who had never known the rigours of field archaeology and the intensity and excitement of collecting objects with a minuscule acquisition fund; and so the Art and Archaeology Division remained firmly archaeological in intent, with art objects valued primarily for their cultural rather than their artistic interest. Even the European and Canadiana departments with their large collections of art objects continued the tradition of treating these objects less as artistic works than as evidence of the nature of the cultures that produced them.

~~~

Visitors to the Mankind Discovering gallery can hardly fail to be impressed by the number and the diversity of the scholarly disciplines from which examples have been drawn to illustrate the processes of research. They may well wonder how or why so many different fields of research are still encompassed within a single institution. The trend in museums in the 20th century has been towards specialization and the compartmentalization of knowledge. In Ottawa there are several national museums, including the National Museum of Man, the National Museum of Natural Sciences, the National Museum of Science and Technology, and the National Gallery. A similar pattern prevails in many of the other great cities of the world. The Royal Ontario Museum, by contrast, has moved in the opposite direction, from five museums to one, priding itself on being one of the few remaining museums of world class with collections of art and archaeology and the sciences under one roof and one administration. The vision had been present from the beginning, for although the five founding museums had kept their separate identities in their titles, a committee of the five directors had met regularly from the beginning to make their joint recommendations to the board of trustees.

In this respect the Museum was following the traditions established in the collecting patterns of the Renaissance, where the juxtaposition of art and natural history in collections was characteristic of the desire for knowledge of all areas of thought. The five museums had coalesced to three through natural affinity, and from three to one through the conviction that all knowledge must be brought into a coherent and consistent unity. After analysis there must be synthesis. What is discovered in one field may have a bearing on what is accepted, or being sought, in another. Boundaries between disciplines should be matters of convenience, not impassable frontiers.

In the new Museum there is constant communication and exchange of knowledge between departments. When sherds of European pottery are found at sites being excavated by the Department of New World Archaeology, the European Department can be consulted for information about their age and origins. Such information is important for dating the levels of the site. Works of art that feature decoration in rocks, minerals, and gemstones may yield knowledge of their history when taken to the Department of Mineralogy and Geology for study. The Department of Botany can identify the woods from which furniture and certain types of tools are made; and so on. This is the kind of day-by-day consultation that is possible in a multi-discipline museum. Time is saved and assurance doubly confirmed in the process of analysis leading up to synthesis.

Interdisciplinary cooperation in research projects has increased noticeably since World War II. There have been two reasons for this. Commercial and industrial companies anxious to expand in the postwar boom economy, especially in the natural resource areas of mining, lumbering, and fishing, needed the data accumulated by the scientific departments. At the same time federal and provincial ministries, eager to encourage the exploitation of these resources, were conscious of their responsibilities for protecting the environment. Both needed the specialized knowledge, the statistics, and the vast data banks built up by the science departments in their close faunal and floral survey of Ontario and large parts of Canada during the years when lack of funds had confined their research to this country. Geologists and mineralogists, botanists and ornithologists, palaeontologists and New World archaeologists could sometimes find on joint field trips solutions that would have escaped their synthesis if their specialized knowledge had not been combined.

The chief constraining factor in research is generally lack of funds. In the early years after World War II only about thirty-five per cent of the cost of Museum research came from the operating budget. The remainder came from the system of cross-appointing curators to teaching posts in University faculties. The money earned by teaching was credited to the research fund of the curator's department in the Museum. It constituted a useful supplement to what was available from the operating budget, but even so, the totals available were nothing like enough for the purpose, and research in both archaeology and the natural sciences had remained limited.

A new era in Museum research began with the appointment of Dr A. D. Tushingham as head of the Art and Archaeology Division in 1955. Tushingham had accepted the appointment on the condition that he would be allowed to continue his own archaeological endeavours and to broaden the Museum's field program generally—in Canada and abroad. In 1956, with the financial backing of the Toronto *Globe and Mail,* which also provided syndicated coverage of the expedition, the Royal Ontario Museum became the first museum in Canada to undertake archaeological excavations overseas. It did so in collaboration with the British School of Archaeology in Jerusalem, under the overall direction of the famous British archaeologist Miss (later Dame) Kathleen Kenyon, carrying on Tushingham's involvement in the project dating back to 1952. The Jericho project led to a like collaboration with the British and French archaeological schools in the excavation of Jerusalem itself from 1961 to 1967. The Royal Ontario Museum contingent was augmented by staff and received financial support from a number of Canadian universities and colleges. That project continued even through the aftermath of the Arab-Israeli war of the summer of 1967 and constituted a breakthrough in the knowledge of the city's historical topography from its foundation as a walled town in about 1800 B.C. to the present. On the death of Dame Kathleen Kenyon in 1978, Tushingham, as associate director of the project, became chairman of an international committee charged with responsibility for the publication of the results. The Royal Ontario Museum has now published the first volume of the Jerusalem report.

Once this overseas involvement was begun, funds became available from Canadian and American foundations to support other expeditions. In 1966 the Near Eastern Department was reconstituted into two separate departments, the Egyptian and the West Asian. The Egyptian Department's area of study and research was to be the high civilizations of ancient Egypt, the West Asian's the rest of the Near and Middle East, including Old World prehistory, the high civilizations of Babylon, Assyria, and Syro-Palestine, and all of Islamic culture from Moorish Spain to Mughal India.

As a result of the research interests of Dr T. Cuyler Young, Jr, who became the first head of the West Asian Department, the Museum initiated a project in western Iran in 1965. Excavations at the ancient site of Godin Tepe unearthed important remains dating from 3000 to 500 B.C., including a fortified manor house of the 7th century and a trading post from the earliest date.

Two other curators, Dr L. D. Levine and Dr E. J. Keall, joined the department. Dr Levine became part of the Godin Tepe project, working at the neighbouring mounds of Seh Gabi, where excavations carried the scope of the project back to the fourth and fifth millennia B.C. During the last season in 1973 the project had grown to the point that it involved twenty-five archaeologists and supporting technicians from five institutions in three different countries. Meanwhile Dr Keall had developed a program at the site of Qaleh-i Yazdigird, close to the Iraqi border, where a mountain-top fortress was found to contain the remains of an elaborately decorated palace of the 2nd century A.D.

When it became apparent that the effects of the 1979 Iranian Revolution were to be long-lasting, the West Asian Department concentrated on its program of publication of the Iran project, including the results of postexcavation surveys in the Kangavar and Mahidasht valleys, but it also turned to new initiatives in other countries. Dr Young involved himself with excavations in Iraq on sites threatened by the construction of dams, while Dr Keall opted to explore Islamic culture in Yemen at the southern tip of the Arabian Peninsula.

New World archaeology had undergone a similar expansion. No longer confined to the excavation of Ontario forts and prehistoric land sites, it now included, under Dr Walter Kenyon, underwater archaeology

The renovated and expanded Royal Ontario Museum in June 1982, looking south from Bloor Street. In the foreground are the Queen Elizabeth II Terrace Galleries in the last stages of construction. The new curatorial centre can be seen rising in the southern courtyard and the dome of the McLaughlin Planetarium is visible to the south of the curatorial centre.

Above: Liao dynasty (A.D. 916–1125) Buddhist *Luohan* in the Far Eastern collections. The piece was purchased by the Royal Ontario Museum in 1914 from the dealer S. M. Franck, who had obtained it from George Crofts.

Opposite, top: The royal visit, 30 September 1984, for the official opening of the Queen Elizabeth II Terrace Galleries. *Foreground:* Her Majesty Queen Elizabeth II escorted by Edwin A. Goodman; behind them are (*left to right*) Mrs Edwin A. Goodman, Prince Philip, and James Cruise. (Photo: Paul J. Hoeffler.)

Opposite, bottom: The entrance display to the Mankind Discovering gallery. It represents the collections upon which the Museum's research is founded and contains specimens and artifacts ranging from a 350-million-year-old fossil of coral to a 19th-century tall clock from Quebec.

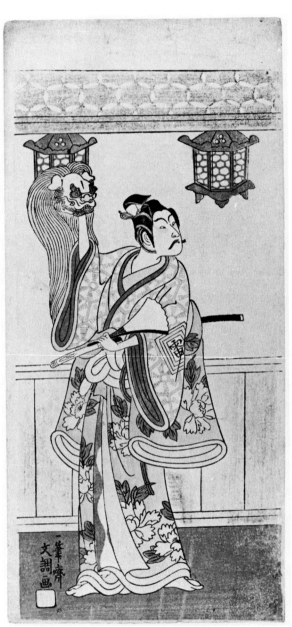

An 18th-century Japanese woodblock print of an actor, designed by Ippitsusai Bunchō. It is one of the prints from the Sir Edmund Walker Collection in the Far Eastern Department.

Above: An oracle bone from the James M. Menzies collection, which came to the Far Eastern Department after Dr Menzies' death.

Opposite, top: The new Bishop White gallery of monastery art from North China, opened in 1982. On the north wall is a monumental Buddhist wall-painting (*right*) acquired for the Museum by Bishop White.

Opposite, bottom: The Ming tomb, acquired by George Crofts between 1918 and 1921, in its new home in the Queen Elizabeth II Terrace Galleries.

Above: Allosaurus valens, a dinosaur that lived between 150 and 140 million years ago. This cast of a composite skeleton stands in the Jurassic display of the Museum's vertebrate palaeontology galleries.

Opposite, top left: Pseudogygites latimarginatus trilobites of Upper Ordovician age. This sample of 450-million-year-old fossils, ranging in length from 4 cm to 6 cm, is in the collections of the Department of Invertebrate Palaeontology.

Opposite, top right: Specimen of the great auk acquired for the Department of Ornithology in 1965 through the fund-raising efforts of James Baillie.

Opposite, bottom: Pride of lions in the African Savannah diorama in the new mammalogy gallery, which opened in 1983.

Above: A view through the arches of the reconstructed *suq,* or market, in the new Islamic gallery which opened in 1982. Displays are set up as shop windows and photo murals recreate street scenes.

Opposite, top: Limestone relief sculpture from the palace of Ashurnasirpal II, King of Assyria, at Nimrud, 9th century B.C., now in the West Asian Department's collections. Two kneeling human-headed genies flank a "sacred" tree. Acquired through the Reuben Wells Leonard bequest.

Opposite, bottom: A team, led by T. Cuyler Young, Jr, (then) of the West Asian Department, excavating at Godin Tepe, in the Zagros Mountains of Iran, in 1969. Five seasons of excavation took place between 1965 and 1973.

Right: Attic black-figure amphora of about 530 B.C., found at Tarquinia, Etruria, now in the collections of the Greek and Roman Department. The decoration depicts Herakles wrestling with a Triton, surrounded by sea creatures. Gift of Sigmund Samuel.

Below: The Sculpture Court in the new galleries "The Greeks and the Etruscans" which opened in July 1986.

Above: Roman wall-painting on plaster over mud brick of the early 4th century A.D., discovered by the Dakhleh Oasis Project in 1979 at Amheida.

Left: Decorated mummy case containing the body of Djema'estes'ankh, a Theban priestess of the 9th century B.C. Acquired by Charles Currelly for the Egyptian collections.

Allegorical figure of Winter, a bronze in the European collections, attributed to Alessandro Vittoria (1525–1608). The statuette has been designed to hold a supply of oil so that it may be used as a lamp. Gift of The W. Garfield Weston Charitable Foundation. (Photo: Eberhard Otto.)

Lady's sack dress of cream corded silk with red stripes and borders of brocaded floral meanders. French, 1775 to 1785. Gift of Mrs Harry Hopkirk to the Textile Department.

Indian chintz quilt from the northern region of the Coromandel coast, first half of the 18th century. The quilt is in the collections of the Textile Department.

Right: Detail of cotton and wool appliquéd quilt made near Caledonia, Ontario, in the late 1860s, depicting scenes from the life of Joseph. Gift of Mrs Ellen Emsley to the Textile Department.

Below: A display in the new Canadiana gallery, which opened in 1985 in the main building of the Museum. Craft products for domestic use from 1780 to 1900 are placed in a room setting.

Left: A diorama in the Ontario Prehistory gallery which opened in 1985. The scene depicts a Woodland man drying and husking rice in a harvesting camp in southern Ontario sixteen hundred to four hundred years ago.

Below: Watercolour by Selwyn Dewdney of an Indian rock painting at the Agawa site, Lake Superior Provincial Park, Ontario, one of the more than two hundred rock art sites that he recorded. The painting depicts Mishipizhiw (*top right*), the spirit of swift and troubled waters. Dewdney's records are in the Department of New World Archaeology.

Right: Zuni vessel decorated with an animal design characteristic of the Zuni Pueblo, made in New Mexico in the mid-19th century. The piece is in the collections of the Department of Ethnology.

Below: Structure B-4, the tallest ceremonial structure at the Maya site of Altun Ha, Belize, excavated by a team led by David Pendergast. One tomb contained in this structure yielded the spectacular full-round jade carving of the head of Kinich Ahau, the Maya Sun God.

as a means of tracing and dating early European trade routes in northern Ontario, and an important project on Indian rock paintings and carvings; this latter became the life's work of Selwyn Dewdney, who recorded more than three hundred sites in the Canadian Shield. Dr Peter Storck, meanwhile, with Canada Council support, pursued his search for traces of Early Man along the shorelines of Lake Algonquin which in the glacial period overspread the region now occupied by modern Lakes Michigan and Huron and Georgian Bay and their adjacent land areas.

Far to the south, in Belize (then British Honduras), there had been some initial probing of a pre-Columbian site as early as 1961. In 1963/1964 the Museum's Maya interest developed into what eventually became a seven-year program at Altun Ha under Dr David Pendergast. The first season's excavation revealed a number of stone pyramids and three tombs with rich contents. By 1968 the work was receiving broad coverage by newspapers, television, and radio, as the treasures of two thousand years of Maya civilization were revealed, including the tomb of the Sun God, Kinich Ahau, and a fine carved jade head of the Sun God himself. In 1974, following the completion of the work at Altun Ha, excavation was begun at Lamanai, a site occupied from about 1500 B.C. through the Postclassic era of Maya civilization and on into the early years of the Historic period.

Members of life sciences departments that had already extended their collections to include specimens from tropical regions often accompanied the archaeologists to these sites. The Museum's ornithological collection was now among the ten largest in North America, and in the British Commonwealth was second only to the British Museum's massive collection. The Department of Mammalogy had the largest collection of bats in the world. The Department of Ichthyology and Herpetology, with a very limited operating budget, almost all of which was needed for collection maintenance, had begun its long-range studies of the biology, ecology, and systematics of coral-reef fishes in the West Indies, which continue today. The archaeological presence of the Museum at Belize, so near to the sites where the field work of the scientific departments was being carried on, offered an opportunity for observation and collection too good to miss.

The Museum's reputation as a research-based museum of world standing was well established. To advance their research, the curators had frequently found their own means of promoting the projects which they wished to pursue. Without these individual initiatives, much of the research would never have got started—research that was later to attract support from American as well as Canadian foundations. The Canada Council, too, was able to provide support on an increased scale after it began to receive annual grants from the federal government to supplement the endowment income which was at first its only revenue. To a large extent the grants and subventions were a recognition and an acknowledgement of what the Royal Ontario Museum had now become.

It is perhaps true that all scientific discovery begins with inspired insight. The interval between the initial insight and scientific confirmation is often a long one. Darwin's brilliant theory was conceived in the Galápagos Islands; but it was three years after the *Beagle* had completed her voyage before he wrote it down, and not until 1859 was he ready to publish it in its entirety. The theory of continental drift had been advanced in the first decade of the 20th century, but not until after World War II was the evidence strong enough to win general acceptance. In comparison with the grand explanatory hypotheses like Darwin's theory of evolution by natural selection, or the theory of continental drift, the patient and painstaking enquiries of Museum researchers may seem modest and parochial. But it is on these modest, step-by-step researches that great comprehensive hypotheses may depend for confirmation (or invalidation).

~~~

The Mankind Discovering gallery provides not only an introduction to the new Royal Ontario Museum but also what is in many ways a symbol of it. In its form it exemplifies *par excellence* the arts of display, on which so much emphasis has been placed, and also, perhaps, the didacticism which some critics have found unwelcome. Here, at any rate, it is evident that the role of the viewer is not merely to see, to admire, and to wonder, but to *learn.*

In its content, the gallery has a single emphasis—research—and this fact, too, has provided ground for criticism. It would be impossible here— nor would it be appropriate—to survey all the fields of research in which the Royal Ontario Museum is active, but a brief account of three may give some idea of their range and variety.

At the end of World War II a number of scientists at the Carnegie Institution in Washington, who had worked on the Manhattan Project, redirected their research on radioactive isotopes towards the development of geochronology, a new field of geological research. Geochronology is based on the fact that certain naturally occurring isotopes of uranium, rubidium, and potassium undergo radioactive decay and are converted into other elements at specific rates. They can thus be used as "time-clocks"; by taking a sample of a rock and measuring precisely the amount it contains of a particular radioactive parent isotope like uranium, and of its radiogenic daughter, lead, and by knowing the rate of decay through laboratory experiments, it is possible to determine the age even of a rock that is several billion years old.

In 1966 a young Canadian, Dr Thomas Krogh, joined this group as a postdoctoral fellow to continue his research on rubidium-strontium dating, a method of dating Precambrian rocks. During this time he developed a technique to make uranium-lead dating much easier to apply; it is even more accurate than rubidium-strontium. Dr Krogh found an alternative method of dissolving zircon, a crystal, which holds minute amounts of uranium incorporated when the crystal was formed, as well as lead, formed from some of the uranium by radioactive decay. The virtue of Dr Krogh's method was that the amount of lead contamination was reduced by a factor of one thousand. It now became possible to resolve the complex sequence of geological events that led to the formation of the Archaean crust, which formed for the most part between 2750 and 2700 million years ago, with errors of as little as 2 million years in the ages of the rocks.

As a result of these developments the Museum's Department of Mineralogy and Geology was able to negotiate a grant of $300 000 from the Ontario Ministry of Natural Resources with which to build an advanced geochronology laboratory. Krogh returned from the United States in 1975 to head this new laboratory and to install the accurate system of dating he had perfected.

The equipment required consists of an advanced mass spectrometer and ancillary facilities for rock crushing, mineral separation, and chemical and petrographic analysis. Fifty kilograms of rock has to be crushed, from which is extracted the tiny pinch of dust, 0.1 milligrams in weight, that reveals the secret of age. One of Krogh's early studies was of the famous Sudbury nickel irruptive, which contains some of the world's richest nickel deposits. Earlier dating techniques had yielded ages for the rocks differing by more than 200 million years; other tests had errors ranging from 50 to 125 million years. Krogh's method dated the rocks to within 1 million years.

In dealing with events that may have occurred over a period of a few tens of millions of years, an error of a few million years may be critical in unravelling geological history. The unprecedented degree of accuracy provided by Krogh's technique is invaluable to the Canadian mining industry. Nearly two-thirds of the exposed rock in Ontario is Precambrian, the type of rock that contains a major portion of the earth's mineral resources. Most of the Precambrian mineral deposits in Canada exposed at the surface have now been located, and many of the accessible deposits have been developed. Over a period of years the laboratory will provide the data necessary for deciphering the complex geological evolution of the Precambrian Shield and its rich mineral resources, and delineate more precisely the locations where additional mineral resources are likely to be found.

Since his arrival at the Royal Ontario Museum, Dr Krogh has made further technical refinements to the uranium-lead dating method and has expanded its application to Canadian geological research. Research sponsored by the Museum, the Natural Sciences and Engineering Research Council of Canada, and the Ontario Geological Survey continues to expand the application of Dr Krogh's method, as do recent cooperative research projects of the Museum's geochronology laboratory with the Geological Survey of Nova Scotia, of Newfoundland, of Manitoba, and of Canada.

The study of reptiles, which in all their diversity dominated life on earth for about 160 million years in the Mesozoic era, provides a chapter of vital importance in the story of evolution. The most prominent and most numerous of these reptiles were, of course, the dinosaurs, which were to be found everywhere in a world in which the land areas had not yet been separated to the same extent as today by continental drift. One of the areas richest in their remains is the Badlands of southern Alberta, where the Red Deer River cuts through the laminated sandstone. The Museum's collection, begun by Dr Arthur Parks in the years immediately following World War I, was greatly extended by Dr Loris Russell, who became chief biologist of the Museum and added greatly to our knowledge of these early reptiles.

Since the discovery in southern Germany in 1862 of the skeleton of an archaic bird, *Archaeopteryx lithographica*, that bore a close resemblance to the dinosaurs, it had been generally believed that birds, which appeared late in the Mesozoic era, were descendants of the dinosaurs. Modern research on this subject centres on the question of flight. Flying birds, which have a keeled sternum rather than a flat breastbone, are called carinates. There are also flightless birds with a keeled sternum and fairly well developed wings—flightless ducks, parrots, grebes, cormorants, and rails, among others—and these are obviously descended from flying ancestors.

There are, however, other species of flightless birds, such as the ostrich, the emu, the rhea, the kiwi, and the extinct moa, with very small wings or no wings at all; these are known as ratites. Traditionally it has been held that the ratites evolved from carinates by losing the power of flight, but anatomical and other evidence supports the view that they may be primitive among birds and that they did not evolve from a carinate ancestor.

This matter of flightlessness in birds has been the subject of an interdisciplinary research project conducted by Dr Christopher McGowan, a palaeontologist, and Dr Allan Baker, an ornithologist. Together they have made field trips to the Galápagos, New Zealand, Tierra del Fuego, and other parts of the world to observe and to collect specimens of flightless birds. Their joint study has included a group of strange South American birds called tinamous, which previous study and observation had suggested were primitive carinates. They have a flight range of only about thirty metres and are awkward in flight. A successful culture of tinamou chromosomes in a Museum laboratory has shown that the chromosomes are intermediate in form between those of ratites and those of carinates. Further studies remain to be made, but the work done thus far is likely to prove of the first importance in clarifying the evolution of birds.

It was an Egyptian Egyptologist visiting Toronto in 1974 who urged Geoffrey Freeman, the president of the Society for the Study of Egyptian Antiquities, to consider the Dakhleh Oasis as an area that would repay investigation. It had been visited in 1819 by Sir Archibald Edmonstone, a noted British traveller and author, who had observed its monuments, and in 1908 by a curator from the Metropolitan Museum of Art. But nothing had come of these visits.

The region, about six hundred kilometres southwest of Cairo, is the largest of the Egyptian oases in the western desert. Sausage-shaped, it measures about eighty by twenty-five kilometres, roughly three times the area of Metropolitan Toronto. It had been visited by Old Stone Age hunters one hundred thousand years ago, and Neolithic man had left evidence of his presence in the form of sherds. Since the dawn of Pharaonic Egypt in 3100 B.C., the oasis had been in constant communication with the Nile valley.

In 1976 Geoffrey Freeman, having finished work a few years earlier on a project at Luxor, made application to the director-general of Egyptian antiquities for a concession licence to mount an archaeological investigation of the Dakhleh Oasis. The licence was granted and in 1977, with the backing of the Social Sciences and Humanities Research Council of Canada, Geoffrey Freeman and Anthony Mills, an associate curator in the Egyptian Department, made a trip to inspect the area. The reconnaissance was so reassuring that a joint venture, known as the Dakhleh Oasis

Project, was initiated by the Egyptian Department and the Society for the Study of Egyptian Antiquities. Anthony Mills was appointed project director and application was made immediately to the Social Sciences and Humanities Research Council of Canada for funds for an intensive survey. With contributions from the Royal Ontario Museum and the Society for the Study of Egyptian Antiquities, and grants from the Research Council, the Dakhleh Oasis Project continues today.

The program drawn up by the Dakhleh Oasis Project envisaged a study of the whole area since the beginning of human habitation in 100 000 B.C. The project was specifically designed for a study of the environmental composition and the evolution of the oasis, and of its archaeological history. The environmental researches were to be conducted by a geomorphologist (geomorphology is the study of the characteristics, origin, and development of landforms), a palaeobotanist, and a palaeontologist; the archaeological studies by specialists in Egyptology, ceramics, prehistory, classics, and epigraphy. The team included postgraduate doctoral students who acted as assistants in both branches. The project, a truly interdisciplinary venture on a very broad scale, was largely staffed and financed by Canadians. The archaeological studies ranging over a long period from the Palaeolithic and Neolithic eras to the 4th century A.D., combined with environmental study of an area settled for so long a stretch of time, made this an undertaking of the greatest importance, indicative of what modern museum scholarship can contribute to the edifice of knowledge.

The survey has involved going over the ground looking for natural features and the evidence of their changes, and at the same time recording all the archaeological remains in an area still populated by thirty-five thousand souls. The area is fed by underground water which comes to the surface by an artesian process. After annexation to the Roman Empire in 30 B.C., Egypt became known as the "bread basket of Rome" and the Dakhleh Oasis, a valuable contributor to the "bread basket", was in communication with the Nile valley, ten days' camel-ride away. Dakhleh was noted particularly for its wines and the extensive array of its agricultural products, including dates, olives, grain, and grapes, which are pictured in some of the tomb paintings that the survey has revealed. At the height of its prosperity, a large Roman bureaucracy must have been established there, evidence of which is to be found at Amheida, a large town within the oasis, in the more elaborate houses and the more than two thousand tombs, some of them ornate and richly decorated, in the Roman cemetery. In Amheida the walls of some structures still rise above the ground, the remains of the second storeys of buildings now buried under sand dunes piled up by almost two thousand years of desert winds.

With the preliminary work almost completed after seven seasons, and with some 425 archaeological sites marked, the general plan of excavation has been drawn up. It is estimated that the work will take another five or six seasons—a period to which the Royal Ontario Museum and the Society for the Study of Egyptian Antiquities have committed themselves. The final result should be an environmental and archaeological study, in which nearly all disciplines have cooperated, of an unbroken period of cultural evolution from the Old Stone Age hunters, through Neolithic man, to the beauty and splendour created in Dakhleh by the sophisticated culture of the 4th century A.D. in the final years of the Roman occupation. The survey has found some evidence that suggests that an environmental change may have occurred at the end of this period, which caused the farming community and the bureaucracy to diminish. The discoveries to come will tell us more.

~~~

From the ancient rocks of Canada's Precambrian Shield to the woods of New Zealand, to the desert sands of Egypt, and in a score of other places around the globe, the work of the Royal Ontario Museum goes on—the work of observing, collecting, measuring, recording, of assembling the data for the patient, methodical process of analysis and testing. Eventually, sometimes only after years of study, perhaps not even in the researcher's lifetime, occasionally in a sudden exhilarating flash of insight, the reward may come in one of those reconciling syntheses that mark yet another tentative step forward in the unending journey of Mankind Discovering.

20

Epilogue

Seventy years after the Duke of Connaught, great grand-uncle of Queen Elizabeth II, had opened the Royal Ontario Museum, the Queen herself officially opened the new terrace galleries of the renovated and enlarged Museum in 1984. The year was the occasion of a double celebration in Toronto. It was the bicentenary of the Province of Ontario, as well as the sesquicentenary of the City of Toronto, and the Queen and Prince Philip had arrived to participate in the celebration. In the early autumn the royal yacht *Britannia* sailed through the St Lawrence Seaway into the heart of the continent and tied up at dockside in Toronto's inner harbour. The yacht was to be the royal residence for the duration of the Queen's visit.

Both the times and the city were different from those that the Duke of Connaught had known during his governor generalship of Canada. The ceremony at the Museum too was different in style, reflecting the changes that had affected the pace of life during the intervening decades. The duke's visit had been a leisurely one. He had arrived at the Museum an hour before lunch for a private viewing of the collections, had then gone on to a splendid luncheon with the Museum's patrons and donors at the York Club, and had returned to the Museum at three o'clock to perform the opening ceremony. At the end of his visit that evening he had invited Sir Edmund and Lady Walker to spend the weekend with him at Rideau Hall in Ottawa.

The royal visit of 30 September 1984 was blessed by a day of gloriously bright sunshine. After a swift tour of the new Museum and of the exhibition *Georgian Canada: Conflict and Culture 1745–1820,* with which the Museum was marking the year's celebrations, there was a little ceremonial speech-making, the unveiling of a plaque, and the presentation of members of the board of trustees and some of the staff, before the royal couple departed to other celebrations and ceremonies elsewhere.

It had been an exciting and colourful occasion. But amid the celebrations of the "new" Museum, a curator with a philosophical turn of mind, brooding on the changes, reflected morosely that every time a museum becomes involved in updating its image, or refurbishing and enlarging itself, it destroys some of its own past. Change, however, is inescapable, and it is difficult to see what change can mean if it does not mean discarding, for better or worse, at least something of the past.

And it was more than the Museum that had changed. In the first decade of the 20th century, eighty-seven per cent of Toronto's population had been of British extraction, and the connection with the Old Country had been a matter of special pride. By 1984 the population of the metropolitan area had grown to nearly three million. A large part of this growth had taken place in the years after World War II, with the great influx of people from the war-devastated countries of Europe and from a Third World in the toils of political, social, and economic revolution. Though the ties to homelands remained strong (eventually receiving recognition in something called "multiculturalism"), the British connection was inevitably attenuated and diminished, becoming merely one strand among many of the bonds connecting Toronto to the Old World. Gone forever was the milieu in which the Royal Ontario Museum could be viewed almost as an overseas version of the museum complex that had grown up in South Kensington during the 19th century.

In the changed milieu the whole purpose and function of museums were coming to be seen in a new light. No longer were museums thought of simply as places where the remains of past cultures could be exhibited to delight the eye and exalt the spirit, and where, perhaps, craftsmen and artists could look for edification and instruction. That attitude belonged to a more secure and settled era. People who had had to learn to live with the threat of mass extermination had other preoccupations; to them the maintenance of life posed problems of more moment and greater immediacy than artistic improvement. This shift of interest was clearly observable at the Royal Ontario Museum. The schoolchildren who descended every day in their hundreds from the yellow school buses, and the other visitors who came in their hundreds of thousands year after year, were more interested in the Museum's study of life—its beginnings, its development, and its historical continuity—than in aesthetic pleasure alone. The board of trustees had caught this mood in its *Statement of Intent* of 1975 when it declared that the goal of the museum was to "open to all people a deeper understanding of man and the universe in which he lives". Germain Bazin wrote in *The Museum Age:* "Only when men sense the waning of a civilization do they suddenly become interested in its history. . . . Man consoles himself for what he is by what he was."

The rapid increase in attendance at museums after World War II has certainly been remarkable. A survey made in the United States in 1938 had revealed that there had been fifty million visitors to American museums in the previous year. Thirty years later the annual figure was three hundred million. The number of museum visitors was increasing much faster than the population itself—so fast, in fact, that museums were becoming unable to supply all the services requested of them. The same phenomenon, on a reduced scale, could be observed in Canada, and in particular at the Royal Ontario Museum. In the postwar period two out of three immigrants to Canada settled in Ontario. Under these circumstances, there was a demand for educational and cultural services which museums were uniquely equipped to provide.

In some respects museums may be said to have supplanted churches as the emblematic focal points of the North American city. The churches of old Toronto had grown old along with the city's Victorian façades. The chasm between the prewar and postwar eras, symbolized in its most dramatic form by the horror of Hiroshima, left nothing unaffected. In the architecture of the new building opened by Queen Elizabeth II in 1984, and in the new way of looking at things which it was designed to induce in visitors, a new world was reflected. The curator who had commented morosely on the process of change—an art historian—observed that a museum says as much about itself in the appearance it presents to the world as in its exhibits—the museum itself becomes an exhibit. The new terrace galleries opened by the Queen, reaching skywards from Bloor Street in a series of giant steps, with the Ming tomb clearly visible to passers-by at street level, flowed backwards in a way that suggested a climb from the past to the unknown future of man in space. Inside the Museum, the gallery clusters, when completed, will portray the whole story of biological life from its beginnings on this planet, itself not yet fully explored.

~~

In June 1985 Dr James E. Cruise retired and was succeeded by Dr T. Cuyler Young, Jr. It had fallen to Dr Cruise to launch and to guide the program of renovation and expansion which had already been under discussion for some years before his arrival, and it was largely through his organizational talents that the process was coordinated and pressed forward despite the discord that not infrequently interrupted its progress. By the time of his retirement, more than $60 million had been spent on new construction and renovation, and the equally formidable and certainly no less costly task of mounting the new galleries and exhibits was under way. Not until the final decade of the century will the work be completed, but it is beyond doubt that when it is, one of the finest and best-equipped museums in the world will stand as a monument to the vision that Charles Currelly had when he first moved his collection into the original Museum building in 1911.

Notes and References

Among the principal sources on which I have drawn in writing this book are the Archives of the Royal Ontario Museum and those of the University of Toronto, the latter for correspondence to and from boards of governors and presidents of the University (see excerpts pp. 79, 100, 104, 116–117, 127, 133, 140, 142, 149). The letters and journals of Sir Edmund Walker in the Thomas Fisher Rare Book Library of the University were an invaluable source, particularly for the early chapters. They include the extensive exchange of correspondence between Sir Edmund Walker and Charles Trick Currelly during the first decade of this century, when the Museum was still in the planning stage and Currelly was building his hopes on becoming its curator. I have also drawn on the Archives of the United Church of Canada, held in Victoria College, for the papers of Chancellor Nathanael Burwash and Professor James Mavor, Currelly's confidants in his early years of struggle as a collector and archaeologist in Egypt (see excerpts pp. 22, 24, 28).

I am deeply grateful to Currelly's son and daughter, Judge John Currelly and Mrs Suzanne Hamilton, and to Sir Edmund Walker's descendants, for family memories recounted and for access to letters and papers that are not in public collections.

1   The Beginnings

Sir Basil Willey's *The Eighteenth Century Background: Studies on the Idea of Nature in the Thought of the Period* (London: Chatto and Windus, 1940); Germain Bazin's *The Museum Age,* translated from the French by Jane van Nuis Cahill (New York: Universe Books, 1967); and *The Letters of Erasmus Darwin,* edited by Desmond King-Hele (Cambridge: Cambridge University Press, 1981) have been most helpful in bringing the long museum story into focus.

Mr Peale's Museum: Charles Willson Peale and the First Popular Museum of Natural Science and Art, by Charles Coleman Sellers (New York: Norton, 1980), provided details of the first museum of natural sciences in North America (see excerpt p. 4).

For information on Charles Fothergill, I am indebted to the exhibition catalogue *Some Canadian Ornithologists* (Toronto: Thomas Fisher Rare Book Library, 1981) and to James L. Baillie's *Charles Fothergill 1782–1840,* Royal Ontario

Museum of Zoology Contribution no. 26 (Toronto: Royal Ontario Museum, 1944). The life and career of David Boyle are well documented in Gerald Killan's *David Boyle: From Artisan to Archaeologist* (Toronto: University of Toronto Press, 1983). Carl Berger's *Science, God, and Nature in Victorian Canada,* The 1982 Joanne Goodman Lectures (Toronto: University of Toronto Press, 1983) and *The Royal Canadian Institute: Centennial Volume 1849–1949,* edited by W. Stewart Wallace (Toronto: Royal Canadian Institute, 1949), along with the Institute's *Transactions* and *Proceedings,* were excellent sources for tracing the increasing interest in the natural sciences. Short excerpts from the Berger work and *The Royal Canadian Institute* appear on page 7.

2   The Founders

G. P. de T. Glazebrook's *Sir Edmund Walker* (Oxford: Oxford University Press, 1933) and Michael Bliss's *A Canadian Millionaire: The Life and Business Times of Sir Joseph Flavelle, Bart. 1858–1939* (Toronto: Macmillan of Canada, 1978) give revealing insights into the life and times of some of the Museum's earliest supporters. A short excerpt from the Glazebrook biography appears on page 10. *The Report of the Royal Commission on the University of Toronto* (Toronto: Printer to the King's Most Excellent Majesty, 1906) and "An Act Respecting the University of Toronto and University College", Chapter 55 of the Statutes of Ontario, 1906, which became known as the University Act, 1906, document the progression in the organization of a federated university and early provision for a museum.

Flinders Petrie's autobiography, *Seventy Years in Archaeology* (London: Greenwood Press, 1932) and the *Dictionary of National Biography* (Oxford: Oxford University Press, 1961/1970) were excellent sources of information on many of the people with whom Charles Currelly was associated during the time he spent with the Egypt Exploration Fund. Currelly's contributions to the reports of excavations are to be found in the following: E. R. Ayrton, C. T. Currelly, and A. E. P. Weigall, *Abydos, Part 3, 1904,* Special Extra Publication of the Egypt Exploration Fund (London: Egypt Exploration Fund, 1904); W. M. Flinders Petrie, *Ehnasya, 1904,* 26th Memoir of the Egypt Exploration Fund (London: Egypt Exploration Fund, 1905); W. M. Flinders Petrie, *Researches in Sinai* (London, John Murray, 1906).

Charles Trick Currelly's memoirs, *I Brought the Ages Home* (Toronto: Ryerson Press, 1956) give a very personal account not only of his own life but of the continuing story of the Museum from its beginnings through the years that he was director of the Royal Ontario Museum of Archaeology.

3   Laying the Foundations

The Egypt Exploration Society, London, very kindly provided copies of letters pertinent to Currelly's work with the Egypt Exploration Fund and granted permission to quote excerpts from them (see excerpts pp. 21, 21–22).

The Han dynasty ceramic piece in the collections of the Victoria and Albert Museum discussed on pages 23 to 24 (of which Currelly obtained almost an exact duplicate in Egypt) is illustrated in Stephen W. Bushell's *Chinese Art, Volume 2,* figure 2 (London: Board of Education, South Kensington, Victoria and Albert Museum, 1909).

4   The Opening

Charles Currelly's article "The New Museum" appeared in the *University of Toronto Monthly* (vol. 11, March 1911, pp. 159–165). The privileges and responsibilities of the board of governors of the University of Toronto and the makeup and mandate of the board of trustees of the Royal Ontario Museum are clearly defined in Bill 138 of the Ontario Legislature—"An Act to Provide for the Establishment of a Provincial Museum"—which gained assent on 16 April 1912 and became known as the Royal Ontario Museum Act, 1912.

In an article entitled "The Mohawks Arrive at the Royal Ontario Museum: The Vicissitudes of the Museum's First Ethnological Habitat Group" in the *Canadian Collector* (vol. 17, no. 4, July/August 1982, pp. 51–54), Dr E. S. Rogers of the Department of Ethnology of the Royal Ontario Museum tells a delightful story of the first North American habitat group in the Museum.

Three prominent Americans spoke at the opening of the Royal Ontario Museum: G. P. Merrill, director, United States National Museum, Washington, D.C.; John M. Clarke, state geologist of New York, Albany; and F. A. Lucas, director, American Museum of Natural History, New York. "Addresses Given at the Opening of the Royal Ontario Museum, March 19th, 1914" appeared in the *University of Toronto Monthly* (vol. 15, December 1914, pp. 73–84).

5   The Age of Innocence

Madeleine A. Fritz's *Outline of the History and Development of the Royal Ontario Museum of Palaeontology,* Contributions of the Royal Ontario Museum of Palaeontology, no. 1 (Toronto: Royal Ontario Museum, 1939) gives an account of the development of the Museum and its collections. Her *William Arthur Parks 1868–1936,* Life Sciences Miscellaneous Publications (Toronto: Royal Ontario Museum, 1971) is a short biography of the man, with a very long list of his publications from 1894 until the year of his death. Loris S. Russell's article "Charles Mortram Sternberg 1885–1981" in *Proceedings of the Royal Society of Canada* (series 4, vol. 20, pp. 133–135) gives an account of Sternberg's life. The story of the development and collections of the Royal Ontario Museum of Zoology begins to unfold in B. A. Bensley's *The Royal Ontario Museum of Zoology: What It Offers and How You Can Help* (Toronto: University of Toronto, Director of University Extension, 1923) and is told more fully in J. R. Dymond's *History of the Royal Ontario Museum of Zoology,* Contributions of the Royal Ontario Museum of Zoology, no. 18 (Toronto: Royal Ontario Museum, 1940).

The few letters written by George Crofts to Charles Currelly and to Margaret MacLean that are to be found in the Archives of the Royal Ontario Museum reveal very clearly his great devotion to the institution and to Currelly as well.

Terry Shortt's *Not As the Crow Flies* (Toronto: McClelland and Stewart, 1975) is a charming anecdotal account of his many field expeditions that ranged from the Arctic to the tropics (see short excerpts pp. 51, 97). In "Stones and Bones and Skeletons: The Origins and Development of the Peter Redpath Museum" (*McGill Journal of Education*, 17, Winter 1982, pp. 45–64), Susan Sheets- Pyenson traces the history of the Peter Redpath Museum. As coordinator of science and human affairs at Concordia University, Montreal, she has analysed the approach to scientific research over the years, notably in a paper entitled "Civilizing by Nature's Example: The Development of Colonial Natural History Museums", which is to be published in *Scientific Colonialism: A Cross-Cultural Comparison,* Papers from a Conference at Melbourne, edited by Nathan Reingold and Marc Rotenberg (Washington: Smithsonian Institution Press, 1986).

6   The End of the Beginning

From G. P. de T. Glazebrook's *Sir Edmund Walker* (Oxford: Oxford University Press, 1933), I gained some insight into Walker's very active support of many cultural institutions, both of the arts and of the sciences. The work also records Walker's many trips abroad—to England, to continental Europe, to South America, and to the Orient.

Dr Katharine Lochnan, curator of prints and drawings at the Art Gallery of Ontario, very kindly reminisced with me about her talks and correspondence with Henry P. Rossiter while she was preparing the exhibition catalogue *Sir Edmund Walker, Print Collector* (Toronto: Art Gallery of Ontario, 1974). Henry Rossiter, who spent more than forty years as curator of prints at the Museum of Fine Arts, Boston, was a friend of Walker's. A mutual interest in prints had brought Walker and the much younger Rossiter together in the early decades of the century and from Rossiter we get still another impression of Walker.

7   Education in the Museum

In *Education in the Royal Ontario Museum 1913–1975* (Toronto: Royal Ontario Museum, 1976), Norma E. Heakes, who was head of Education Services from 1952 to 1975, documents the history of education in the Museum.

8   Gaining Ground

Loren A. Oxley's article "Retrospect—The First 75 Years: Expansion Is Nothing New to the ROM" (*Rotunda*, vol. 15, no. 2, Summer 1982, pp. 6–13) gives a vivid picture of the building of the east wing of the Museum in 1931/1933. Loren Oxley is the son of the late J. Morrow Oxley, one of the architects of the 1931/1933 addition.

A. L. Parsons, the second director of the Royal Ontario Museum of Mineralogy, recounts the early history of the mineralogical museum in *The Royal Ontario Museum of Mineralogy,* University of Toronto Studies, Geological Series, no. 42 (Toronto: University of Toronto, 1939). In *History of the Royal Ontario Museum of Geology,* Contributions of the Royal Ontario Museum of Geology, no. 1 (Toronto: Royal Ontario Museum, 1939), E. S. Moore, who succeeded A. P. Coleman, the first director of the Royal Ontario Museum of Geology, traces the early history of the geological museum.

The thorough study of Canadian museums made by Sir Henry A. Miers and S. F. Markham is recorded in *A Report on the Museums of Canada* published in 1932. Both the study and the report were funded by the Carnegie Corporation of New York.

9 Bishop as Archaeologist

Two searching studies of William C. White were the main sources for this chapter: Lewis C. Walmsley's *Bishop in Honan: Mission and Museum in the Life of William C. White* (Toronto: University of Toronto Press, 1974; see excerpts pp. 77, 81) and the section entitled "Bishop William White" in Charles Taylor's *Six Journeys: A Canadian Pattern* (Toronto: Anansi, 1977, pp. 41–72). The letters exchanged between Bishop White and Currelly and Bishop White and Dr H. J. Cody are also very revealing.

Sigmund Samuel's *In Return: The Autobiography of Sigmund Samuel* (Toronto: University of Toronto Press, 1963) documents F. St George Spendlove's contribution to the expansion of the Canadiana collection.

In an article entitled "China: New Perspectives on the Past" (*Rotunda,* vol. 6, no. 4, Fall 1973, pp. 4–17), Barbara Stephen, then associate curator in the Far Eastern Department, gives a very interesting account of Chinese archaeological excavation in recent decades.

10 In Search of an Identity

A. L. Parson's *The Royal Ontario Museum of Mineralogy,* University of Toronto Studies, Geological Series, no. 42 (Toronto: University of Toronto, 1939) and E. S. Moore's *History of the Royal Ontario Museum of Geology,* Contributions of the Royal Ontario Museum of Geology, no. 1 (Toronto: Royal Ontario Museum, 1939) document the growth of the staff in the two museums, as well as the growth of the collections, as does J. R. Dymond's *History of the Royal Ontario Museum of Zoology,* Contributions of the Royal Ontario Museum of Zoology, no. 18 (Toronto: Royal Ontario Museum, 1940) for the zoological museum. In *Reading the Rocks: The Story of the Geological Survey of Canada 1842–1972* (Toronto: Macmillan in association with the Department of Energy, Mines and Resources and Information Canada, 1975), Morris Zaslow traces the long history of the Geological Survey (see excerpt p. 90).

The article on the Smithsonian Institution in the *Columbia-Viking Desk Encyclopedia* (New York: Columbia University Press, 1968) gives details of the founding of the institution. Michael Olmert's article "At the Ashmolean and the Fitzwilliam a Special *Frisson*" (*Smithsonian,* vol. 14, no. 6, September 1983, pp. 114–125) provided the insight into Sir Sydney Cockerell's directorship of the Fitzwilliam (see excerpts pp. 92–93).

A. D. Tushingham's *The Beardmore Relics: Hoax or History?* (Toronto: Royal Ontario Museum/University of Toronto, 1966) and Charles Currelly's article

"Viking Weapons Found Near Beardmore, Ontario" (*Canadian Historical Review*, vol. 20, no. 1, March 1939, pp. 4–7) give thorough documentation for the alleged finds at Port Arthur.

Bill No. 156 of the Ontario Legislature, Royal Ontario Museum Act, 1947 (Toronto: Printer to the King's Most Excellent Majesty, 1947), documents the makeup and mandate of the board of trustees of the Museum.

11   A Time of Transition
The Report of the Royal Commission on National Development in the Arts, Letters and Sciences (Ottawa: The King's Printer, 1951), which came to be known as the Massey Report after its chairman, Vincent Massey, ran to more than five hundred pages. It covered all aspects of the arts and sciences in Canada and had far-reaching effects. One of its recommendations—"that a body be formed to foster and promote the study and enjoyment of works in the arts"—led to the establishment of the Canada Council in 1957.

12   Taking Stock
Report on Survey of Royal Ontario Museum 1953–1954 (Toronto: Clarkson, Gordon & Co., 1954), which became known as the Glassco Report, documents the history of the Royal Ontario Museum and recommends sweeping changes. The recommendation that received immediate attention was that the component museums should become divisions and one overall director should be appointed.

13   A New Era
Theodore Heinrich's annual reports for the years 1956/1957, 1957/1958, 1958/1959, 1959/1960, 1960/1961, and 1961/1962 provide a lively account of the initiatives undertaken by the first overall director.

14   Calmer Waters
Report of the Special Committee of the Board of Governors on the Affairs of the Royal Ontario Museum (Toronto: University of Toronto, 1963), which became known as the Bissell Report, documents the relations between the University and the Museum and makes recommendations regarding the administration of the Museum and the contributions of the Museum to the community, the province, and the nation.

William E. Swinton's annual reports for the years 1963/1964, 1964/1965, and 1965/1966 trace events and accomplishments during his directorship.

15   Stormy Petrel
Bill No. 152 of the Ontario Legislature entitled "An Act Respecting the Royal Ontario Museum" was passed in 1968. It established the Museum as an independent corporation and completely changed the character of the board of trustees. Henceforth, University of Toronto representation on the Museum's board of

trustees would consist only of the president and the chairman of the board of governors, as *ex officio* members.

Peter Swann's "A New Era" (*Rotunda,* vol. 1, no. 3, Summer 1968, pp. 2–9) recapitulates the history of the Royal Ontario Museum and enthusiastically discusses initiatives for the future. His annual reports for the years 1966/1967, 1967/1968, 1968/1969, 1969/1970, and 1970/1971 tell an exciting story of the years of his directorship.

The in-depth study by Price Waterhouse Associates "of the operations of the Museum, extending to all areas of administration and accounting" reached the Museum in seven volumes: *Review of Operations, Phase I—Preliminary Report,* January 1971; *Report on Study of Director's Compensation,* February 1971; *Analysis of Trust Accounts,* April 1971; *Report on Guidelines—Introduction,* June 1971; *Report on Guidelines, Section I—Organization,* June 1971; *Report on Guidelines, Section II—Policy,* July 1971; *Report on Guidelines, Section III—Reporting,* August 1971.

16 Projecting the Future
Marshall McLuhan, Harley Parker, and Jacques Barzun were principal speakers at a seminar held in New York in 1967. The proceedings were published two years later (see excerpt p. 152): *Exploration of the Ways, Means, and Values of...Museum Communication with the Viewing Public* (New York: The Museum of the City of New York, 1969).

An Expansion Feasibility Study (Toronto: Moffat Moffat & Kinoshita, 1970) explored all avenues of renovation and new building for the Museum. David H. Scott's *Guidelines for Planning* (Guelph: David H. Scott Consultants Limited, 1975) was intended "to provide an overview and a synthesis of a wide range of matters related to the planning of the future of the ROM". David Scott requested a *Statement of Intent* from the Museum, which was duly promulgated by the board of trustees (Toronto: Royal Ontario Museum, 1975). Scott, who was now project director for the ROM expansion, then prepared the *Interim Planning Report* (Toronto: Royal Ontario Museum, 1976), in which he stated, "The purpose of this report is twofold: to inform the Board of the status of all of the main elements of the ROM planning process as of this date; and to provide a key reference work in the future, should circumstances require a delay in that planning."

17 Planning the Future
The Communications Design Team's *Communicating with the Museum Visitor* (Toronto: Royal Ontario Museum, 1976) was intended to "integrate and synthesize all of the foregoing [research and accumulated knowledge] into a Guidelines document adequate to serve as a basic reference work and common denominator for all those involved in the conceptualization, design, preparation, operating, maintenance and evaluation of exhibits".

There followed two reports from the Royal Ontario Museum Project Office: *Interim Planning Report* (Toronto: Royal Ontario Museum, 1976) and *Final Planning Report* (Toronto: Royal Ontario Museum, 1977). These with *Opportuni-*

ties and Constraints (Toronto: Royal Ontario Museum, 1977), prepared by the Exhibits Communication Task Force, fully documented all the planning to date.

18   Expansion and Renovation

Gene Kinoshita's article "Museums Are for People: The Evolution of a Design Concept" (*Rotunda,* vol. 15, no. 2, Summer 1982, pp. 18–23) is a delightful account of the evolution of the design for the new museum. Sonja Tanner-Kaplash's chapter "The Royal Ontario Museum, Toronto" in *Museum Documentation Systems: Developments and Applications,* edited by Richard B. Light, D. Andrew Roberts, and Jennifer Stewart (London: Butterworth, 1986, Chapter 4, pp. 25–34), documents the very detailed planning and recording of the movement of the millions of Museum artifacts during the renovation and expansion. *Mankind Discovering, Volume 1: A Plan for the New Galleries at the Royal Ontario Museum* (Toronto: Royal Ontario Museum, 1978) and *Mankind Discovering, Volume 2: Evaluations—The Basis for Planning* (Toronto: Royal Ontario Museum, 1979) were the result of twenty-two months of research and activities on the part of the Exhibits Communication Task Force. A statement in the foreword of Volume 1 clearly defines the vast extent of the project: "*Mankind Discovering* provides a plan for the development of the Royal Ontario Museum's galleries over the next twenty years."

Several people involved in the planning and design of galleries later wrote articles about the process: Robert Barnett, "The Cluster Concept" (*Rotunda,* vol. 15, no. 2, Summer 1982, pp. 24–25); L. D. Levine, "Mankind Discovering: Finding the Theme" (*Rotunda,* vol. 16, no. 1, Spring 1983, pp. 10–13); Leslie H. Patten, "Romanticism in the 'Hallowed Halls'" (*Canadian Museums Association Gazette,* vol. 13, no. 3–4, Summer/Fall 1980, pp. 26–31).

19   Mankind Discovering

A. D. Tushingham's *Excavations in Jerusalem 1961–1967, Volume 1* (Toronto: Royal Ontario Museum, 1985) documents the excavations and archaeological finds of the Jerusalem Project. The first two volumes of David Pendergast's report on Altun Ha have been published: *Excavations at Altun Ha, Belize, 1964–1970, Volumes 1 and 2* (Toronto: Royal Ontario Museum, 1979 and 1982); the third volume is in production, and there are two volumes yet to come. In "Lively Paintings: Roman Frescoes in the Dakhleh Oasis (*Rotunda,* vol. 13, no. 2, Summer 1980, pp. 18–25), A. J. Mills gives a lively account of the Dakhleh Project.

20   Epilogue

The elegant foreword to Germain Bazin's *The Museum Age,* translated from the French by Jane van Nuis Cahill (New York: Universe Books, 1967), is a concise and very pleasing account of the development of museums (see excerpt pp. 191–192).

Index

entific collections, 90–1; takes control of Museum, 99–100; financial problems and strained relations with Museum, 111–12; and Glassco Report, 115–17; relationship with Museum, 119; and McLaughlin Planetarium, 136; separation of Museum from, 141–3; takes over museology program, 158; and Lillian Massey Building, 162
University of Western Ontario, 100
Urban Design Consultants, 164
Urquhart, F. A., 109–10, 132
Users' Committee, 141, 144

Varley, Frederick, 97
Vassar College, 96
Vaughan, Mrs O. D., 118, 119
Vertebrate Palaeontology, Department of, 44
Victoria and Albert Museum, 34, 92, 103, 104, 111
Victoria College (Toronto), 8, 13, 14, 18, 28
Vikings, 94

Walker, (Sir) Byron Edmund, 7, 8; childhood and education, 9; joins Canadian Bank of Commerce, 9; posted to New York, 10; general manager in Toronto, 10; marriage, 10; university trustee, 8, 10; member of senate, 10; member of Royal Commission on the University of Toronto, 11–12; correspondence with Currelly, 13, 18; meets Currelly, 19; further correspondence with Currelly, 19, 24–5; president of Canadian Bank of Commerce, 26; prevails on Ontario government to build Museum, 27–8; visit to England (1909), 28–9; with

Currelly in London, 29; returns to Toronto, 29; knighted, 32; stores Museum material, 33; member of "committee of five", 35; as mediator, 34, 36; arranges opening of Museum, 37; called to Ottawa, 39; as Museum benefactor, 40; urges expansion, 55, 66; visit to Orient, 55–6; collector of Japanese prints, 56; friendship with H. P. Rossiter, 56–7; visit to South America, 57; death of wife, 57; chancellor of U. of T., 57; death, 58; summing up, 58–9; authority over Museum directors, 61; see also 105, 113, 128–9, 190
Walker (later Webb, q.v.), Dorothy, 55
Walker, Edmund (Jr), 13, 17
Walker (née Alexander), Mary, 10, 29, 55, 57, 190
Walker, Thomas Leonard, 35, 89
Wall-painting, Buddhist, 77, 169
Walmsley, Lewis C., 74, 77, 85, 86
Warren, H. D., 20
Warren, Mrs H. D., 20, 30, 31, 40, 41, 45, 105, 109, 121
Watt, James, 3
Wearne, Harry, 105
Webb, Sir Aston, 34, 38
Webb (née Walker, q.v.), Dorothy, 59
Wedgwood, Josiah, 3
Welch, Robert, 160
Wellington County Board of Education, 5
West Asian Department, 182
White, Gilbert, 97
White, (Bishop) William Charles, early missionary work in China, 73; marriage, 73; posted to Foochow, 73; surveys Honan, 73–4; bishop at Kaifeng, 74; missionary accomplishments, 74; develops interest in archaeology, 74–5; meets Dr John Ferguson and Dr James Menzies, 75; visits Toronto and meets Currelly,